Mobile and Social Media Journalism

Sara Miller McCune founded SAGE Publishing in 1965 to support the dissemination of usable knowledge and educate a global community. SAGE publishes more than 1000 journals and over 800 new books each year, spanning a wide range of subject areas. Our growing selection of library products includes archives, data, case studies and video. SAGE remains majority owned by our founder and after her lifetime will become owned by a charitable trust that secures the company's continued independence.

Los Angeles | London | New Delhi | Singapore | Washington DC | Melbourne

Mobile and Social Media Journalism

A Practical Guide

Anthony Adornato

Ithaca College

FOR INFORMATION:

CQ Press
An Imprint of SAGE Publications, Inc.
2455 Teller Road
Thousand Oaks, California 91320
E-mail: order@sagepub.com

SAGE Publications Ltd.
1 Oliver's Yard
55 City Road
London EC1Y 1SP
United Kingdom

SAGE Publications India Pvt. Ltd.
B 1/I 1 Mohan Cooperative Industrial Area
Mathura Road, New Delhi 110 044
India

SAGE Publications Asia-Pacific Pte. Ltd.
3 Church Street
#10-04 Samsung Hub
Singapore 049483

Acquisitions Editor: Terri Accomazzo
Editorial Assistant: Erik Helton
eLearning Editor: Jennifer Jovin
Production Editor: Kelly DeRosa
Copy Editor: Cate Huisman
Typesetter: C&M Digitals (P) Ltd.
Proofreader: Lawrence W. Baker
Indexer: Molly Hall
Cover Designer: Gail Buschman
Marketing Manager: Jillian Oelsen

Printed in the United States of America

Library of Congress Cataloging-in-Publication Data

Names: Adornato, Anthony author.

Title: Mobile and social media journalism : a practical guide / Anthony Adornato, Ithaca College.

Description: Thousand Oaks, California : CQ Press/SAGE, [2017] | Includes bibliographical references and index.

Identifiers: LCCN 2017004407 | ISBN 9781506357140 (pbk. : alk. paper)

Subjects: LCSH: Online journalism—Study and teaching (Higher)—United States. | Journalism—Study and teaching (Higher)—United States. | Social media—United States. | Mobile communication systems—United States.

Classification: LCC PN4784.O62 A36 2017 | DDC 071/.3—dc23
LC record available at https://lccn.loc.gov/2017004407

This book is printed on acid-free paper.

17 18 19 20 21 10 9 8 7 6 5 4 3 2 1

Brief Contents

Detailed Contents

Preface

Isn't journalism dying?

It's a question I'm often asked when people learn I teach journalism. As a journalism instructor or student, you've probably confronted the same question. My answer? Journalism is alive and well. In fact, this is one of the most exciting times to teach, study, and practice journalism. I consider myself fortunate to be part of journalism's evolution. I hope you feel the same way.

Never before, in such a short amount of time, have new technologies allowed journalists to connect with the audiences and tell stories in such innovative ways. At the same time, professional journalists are needed now more than ever to make sense of, and provide context for, the onslaught of information on social media.

Twitter. Facebook. Instagram. Snapchat. These are just a few of the social media platforms and applications altering how journalists do their jobs and how people consume news. You can't discuss journalism today without focusing on the monumental impact of mobile devices and social media. The two are dramatically transforming journalists' responsibilities and how news organizations produce and deliver content.

ABOUT THE BOOK

That's where this book comes in. *Mobile and Social Media Journalism* prepares budding journalists to use mobile devices and social media as professional journalists in three main ways: newsgathering, distributing content, and engaging with the audience. They will learn the fundamental skills that news organizations are expecting from today's journalists.

The book addresses the topics of mobile and social media together. You can't discuss one without the other. The audience is increasingly accessing news on mobile devices and through social media, which directly impacts how and where journalists publish news. A digital-first approach means journalists nowadays are using mobile devices to share information on social media platforms while reporting in the field. Mobile devices are needed in the field to streamline the process of gathering, producing, and publishing content to multiple platforms. You see, then, mobile and social go hand-in-hand.

Before digging into reporting with mobile devices and social media, the book begins by taking a look at big-picture concepts and strategies related to technology's impact on journalism. It's important to understand where we've been in order to fully grasp the changes taking place today—and envision where journalism may be headed. My hope is you will walk away with a better understanding of the changing journalism landscape.

An important element of *Mobile and Social Media Journalism* is its emphasis on applying the core values of journalism—such as verification and objectivity—to emerging media platforms and strategies. Evolving with technology while maintaining high journalistic standards is key. Traditional journalistic values must not fall by the wayside. They're more important than ever with so much information, and misinformation, spreading in an instant on social media platforms.

Among the most important concepts in this book are the following:

- The audience's active role in the news production process, and the resulting impact on journalism

- Mobile and social media strategies and policies in news organizations

- Building a professional journalistic brand on social media platforms

- Digital-first story pitch: creating a plan to use mobile devices and social media while covering stories

- The use of mobile devices and social media to gather, produce, and distribute news content

- Locating credible user-generated content from social media to enhance reporting, and at the same time, identify misleading and unbalanced content

- Identifying sources and story ideas on social media platforms

- Writing for social media and mobile news consumption

- The increasing role of social media optimization in journalism

- The use of analytics platforms to monitor and analyze the effectiveness of journalists' and news organizations' social media activity

One of the benefits of *Mobile and Social Media Journalism* is that it provides a structure for a course dedicated to the topic, as instructors navigate how to teach social media and mobile reporting skills. The book could also serve as a guide in other multimedia journalism courses. I've written the book so that each chapter builds on the previous one, but you can also read chapters in any order you choose in order to learn about specific skills at any time.

You can't master journalism without doing. Any journalist will tell you that honing reporting skills comes from years of practice. I have structured the book with that in mind. Each chapter includes checklists—guides for students to gain hands-on experience by immediately practicing what they learn. I have my students use the checklists to build their own professional social media brands and to produce portfolios of stories using social media and mobile devices.

You'll also hear from professional journalists throughout the book. Each chapter has a "From the Newsroom" feature in which journalists share their perspectives.

THE BACK STORY

I was compelled to write this book after launching the mobile and social media journalism course at Ithaca College in 2014. While developing the course, I was unable to find an appropriate textbook. The book's structure, concepts, and checklists have already proven effective, as they have been tested in my classroom. Students walked away with a keen understanding of today's journalism industry and skills that easily landed them jobs. In fact, later in the book (Chapter 8), you'll meet several of these students as we explore the importance of social media in your job hunt and career.

Writing this book had me thinking about my own career in newsrooms and the changes that I saw firsthand. I've been working in newsrooms since I was in middle school, more than 25 years ago. Experimenting with new technologies to tell stories was critical. No matter the technology though, I always considered myself to be working in the interest of the public. As you will see in this book, social media and mobile devices can strengthen the connection between journalists and the audience. I believe this will ultimately lead journalists to better serve the public.

That's not to say sometimes the future seems a bit uncertain. Your future in the industry will require you to evolve and experiment with new ways of gathering news and telling stories on platforms on which audiences become active. Evolve. Experiment. That is very much at the heart of this book.

LET'S CONNECT!

There are a number of ways we can connect beyond the book! Social media pages and a companion website provide up-to-date content related to mobile and social media journalism.

Social Media. A Twitter feed (@MobileJourn) and Facebook page (*fb.com/ MobileandSocialMediaJournalism*) allow us to carry on a conversation about the topic of this book and journalism in general. I provide news on the latest industry trends and updates related to my own teaching. I also want to hear from you! I'm particularly interested in learning about how students are using what they learn in this book.

Website. A companion website (*MobileandSocialMediaJournalism.com*) provides resources, including examples from professional journalists, video tutorials, industry related news, and sample assignments.

Course Materials. Because the book is based on a course I developed, the companion website provides a sample syllabus and PowerPoint slides.

I'd love to know how you answer the question: Isn't journalism dying? Feel free to tweet me at @MobileJourn or @AnthonyAdornato. You can also drop me a line the old-fashioned way: E-mail me at *anthonyadornato@gmail.com*.

I look forward to hearing from you!

Acknowledgments

Writing a book is no easy endeavor. It requires passion for the topic at hand as well as steadfast guidance from others. From the time the seed was planted to write this book, many people offered their advice and encouragement. Journalists, faculty members, current and former students, and the editorial team at SAGE Publications provided valuable feedback that led to what you're about to read.

I especially want to thank my former student Kyle Stewart and the following professors who reviewed the manuscript and offered thoughtful suggestions:

Gina Baleria, San Francisco State University

Jake Batsell, Southern Methodist University

G. DeBlasio, Northern Kentucky University

Melissa Dodd, University of Central Florida

Myles Ethan Lascity, Chestnut Hill College

Dante Mozie, South Carolina State University

Sara Baker Netzley, Bradley University

Leslie-Jean Thornton, Arizona State University

Mercedes Vigon, Florida International University

Insight from those in the industry is one of the key features of *Mobile and Social Media Journalism*. I'm grateful for the perspectives shared in these pages by

David Muir, ABC News

Hallie Jackson, NBC News

Trish LaMonte, Syracuse Media Group

Neal Augenstein, WTOP-FM

Justin Auciello, Jersey Shore Hurricane News

Blair Hickman, formerly of ProPublica

Brian Foster, KMBC-TV

Karen Magnuson, Rochester *Democrat & Chronicle*

Amber Smith, Gray Television

Many thanks also to the team at SAGE Publications who fostered this project along: Terri Accomazzo, Erik Helton, Kelly DeRosa, Cate Huisman, Lawrence Baker, and Molly Hall.

Finally, I'm indebted to my partner, Andrew Horsfall, a source of constant support, who read (and reread) this manuscript.

Forces at the Gate: An Active Audience

When NBC News correspondent Hallie Jackson covered the 2016 US presidential election, the frenetic pace of reporting on the race for the White House went far beyond producing stories for the network's newscasts.

Armed with a mobile device, Jackson brought her social media followers along for the ride as she spent the better part of a year reporting from the campaign trail.

Between live shots, writing packages, and chasing down politicians, she tweeted (@HallieJackson), created stories on Snapchat (hallienbc), and shared photos on Instagram (hallie_gram). Her social media posts provided the latest campaign news while also giving followers a behind-the-scenes look at her reporting process and some of the more lighthearted moments.

"Mobile and social media are ways to open the reporting process and bring more people into it. It's a natural part of how I report, because in this day in age I can't wait for my next live shot to get info out there," said Jackson.

"The interactions we have with the audience now are so different from when I began in the business in 2006. You're always continuing the conversation online."

At one point, Jackson's producer used a selfie stick, iPhone, duct tape, and a live-streaming app to produce one of her live reports—something that was unheard of just years prior. And yes, that moment was shared on Twitter and Snapchat.

Jackson even did many live shots from inside a moving car as she followed campaign busses from event to event. Those roving live reports that viewers saw on television were also made possible by simply using a mobile phone. No fancy equipment or traditional video cameras involved.

In this chapter you will

- Identify how mobile devices and social media are fundamentally different from past technologies such as television and the printing press.

- Discover how mobile devices and social media allow two-way conversations between the audience and journalists versus the old one-way model of mass communications.

- Learn how social media has led to the public's active role in the news production process and changed how audiences consume information.

- Understand that while journalists retain discretion on what makes the "news," an "active" audience plays an influential role.

- Explore the three areas in which mobile devices and social media are impacting journalists' work: newsgathering, distribution of news, and audience engagement.

Frank Thorp V @
@frankthorp

Follow

Selfie stick + tripod + tape + iPhone +
livestream app = @HallieJackson #MacGyver
liveshot

Sometimes you improvise

With her mobile device in hand, NBC News correspondent Hallie Jackson is constantly connected to the audience while reporting in the field. While covering the 2016 US presidential race, her producer even used an iPhone and selfie stick for a live shot.

Welcome to journalism today. The tools of the trade are now in the palms of our hands. With a single mobile device, journalists produce and share content across different platforms—social media, mobile, websites, and TV.

But it's not simply about journalists "pushing out" content on multiple platforms.

Journalists are expected to interact with audiences—meet the public in spaces where they're now spending an increasing amount of time consuming *and* producing information. Audiences are actively engaged with news on social media platforms and mobile devices, whether by posting photos from the scene of breaking news, tweeting with reporters about their stories, or sharing a news outlet's story with their circle of social media followers.

These interactions, fueled by new technologies, are reshaping journalists' relationships with news consumers and how news is produced.

Flashback: What's the Internet, Anyway?

The year was 1994. NBC News *Today* show anchors Katie Couric, Bryant Gumbel, and Elizabeth Vargas discuss, with some confusion, this new "thing" called "the Internet."

Gumbel asks, "What's Internet anyway?" His coanchors chime in: It's "that massive computer network that is becoming really big now."

The anchors are also puzzled over the @ symbol in an e-mail address displayed on the screen. "I wasn't prepared to translate that . . . that little mark with the *a* and then the ring around it," says Gumbel.

"At," says Vargas.

"See that's what I said," responds Gumbel. "Katie said she thought it was 'about.'"

Years after this entertaining exchange took place, it was posted online and, you guessed it, went viral. I show this video on the first day of class because the clip demonstrates how in a such a short time span the online medium has gone from uncharted territory for journalists to a space where we produce nearly all of our work. Of course, the Internet was the launching point for what came next: the birth of social media.

View the video: *bitly.com/InternetFlashback*

TECHNOLOGY AND JOURNALISM

Before diving into specific mobile and social media skills, strategies, and tools, it's critical to understand how journalism reached this crossroads. Reflecting on the past provides an important perspective on where the industry stands now and where it may be headed.

From the printing press to computers, technology has always shaped how journalists perform their craft and where the public turns for news. The printing press, which gave rise to newspapers, allowed for mass distribution of news in the written form. At first, the process of transmitting news from the field to print was slow and cumbersome. By the time news reached people, it was days—sometimes weeks—old. The telegraph sped up the process, allowing reporters to transmit stories so people could learn of news the day it happened.

Radio and television brought more immediacy to journalism, a new way of telling stories. Journalists were now able to bring audiences to the scene of news through the use of audio, video, and live reports.

The Internet opened up an entirely uncharted world for journalism and audiences. In the late 1990s, most news outlets' websites were simply a single static page. Print reporters were still focused on the newspaper and broadcast reporters on their stories for TV or radio newscasts. As the audience increasingly turned online for information, news outlets' websites became more robust, and with that came new tasks for journalists.

Journalists' responsibilities went far beyond stories for print or TV—producing multimedia web stories with a mix of photos, video, and audio became the norm. You can see that each new technology has affected how and where people get their news as well as how journalists do their jobs.

Fast-forward to the present day. Social media and mobile devices are the latest technologies shaping the field, and they have reached this position in a relatively short amount of time, considering the first iPhone was released in 2007 and Twitter was launched in 2006. Never before in such a short amount of time has a new technology had such a dramatic impact on so many facets of communications.

Before Social Media: One-Way Communication

The reason behind this has to do with fundamental differences between today's technologies and those in use prior to the introduction of social media, such as the printing press and television. Traditional print and broadcast journalism are based on the mass communications model of one-way communication.

The characteristics of traditional mass communications are these:

- From one entity, person, or group to a large audience
- One-way communication
- Passive audience

Producers of information, such as journalists, told the public what they needed to know with little or no interaction with the audience, in a one-way flow of information. It's the equivalent of someone talking at you, albeit with interesting and important information, but you're not allowed or able to respond. A single voice speaks to many. That's not much of a conversation.

There's a concentration of power in this model. News consumers were considered passive, because previous technologies didn't foster immediate engagement with content and journalists. Consumers received the news but had little interaction with it. Writing a letter to the editor or calling a newsroom tips line were the extent of the feedback.

This model—what I call the "voice of God"—has been turned upside down with the emergence of mobile devices and social media now that nearly anyone can produce and share content. The audience has shifted from a passive one to an active one.

After Social Media: Journalism as a Conversation

The audience is at the center of social media. They're in the driver's seat. Jay Rosen (@jayrosen_nyu), author and journalism professor at New York University, describes the current audience as passengers on your ship who have a boat of their own.[1] They can connect with each other and with journalists, and they have the means to speak to the world.

Therefore, mobile devices and social media are characterized by

- Accessibility: Nearly anyone has access to these tools.
- Active audience: The audience can create and publish content.
- Interactivity: Messages and feedback happen simultaneously.

These characteristics challenge the traditional notion of mass communications. Because of broad access to mobile devices and social media, creating and publishing content has been opened up to the masses. This is in direct contrast to the closed model of traditional media.

The audience can turn to Twitter to complain about a product. They can snap images of a protest and instantly share them on Instagram. They can use Facebook to generate buzz about an event. The list of things this now-active audience can do is endless.

In addition, interactivity fosters a two-way conversation. When someone tweets at a company or journalist, for example, there's the expectation that the person on the other end will respond almost instantaneously. Just like a conversation.

What does this mean for journalism? Journalism has shifted from a one-way to a two-way conversation that is redefining how journalists report and interact with the audience. Think of journalism as a conversation, rather than a lecture. News outlets can't ignore audiences active on mobile devices and social media. Journalism as a conversation is a shared action with shifting journalist–audience relationships.

Journalism as a conversation fosters interactivity between the audience and journalists, an informal tone, and an openness on the part of the journalist to audience feedback. As we'll discuss later in the chapter, this engagement can build trust with the audience. Mobile devices and social media allow journalists to strengthen their connections with the public and ultimately better serve them.

As was the case with NBC News correspondent Hallie Jackson, journalists are expected to not simply wait to share information on the traditional newscasts, in a newspaper, or in an online story. That's an old way of thinking. As the story unfolds in the field, journalists must turn to social media to share the latest, track online conversations about the story, and respond to people who reach out to them.

Those are just a few of the evolving responsibilities addressed in this book. The skills you will need in today's newsrooms go well beyond one, or even two, platforms.

Let's take a deeper look at how mobile devices and social media are impacting the audience and journalists. We start with the audience, because their changing role and habits directly affect how journalists do their jobs.

CHANGING ROLE OF THE AUDIENCE

January 2009. A US Airways plane makes an emergency landing in New York City's Hudson River. Janis Krums, commuting home on a nearby ferry, snaps a photo of passengers huddled on a wing of the plane.

Krums (@jkrums) tweets out one of the first images of what became known as the Miracle on the Hudson. "There's a plane in the Hudson. I'm on the ferry going to pick up the people. Crazy," wrote Krums in a tweet heard around the world.

Krums had shared his dramatic photo before any journalist could get to the breaking news scene. Within a half hour, the tweet spread like wildfire well beyond his 170 Twitter followers. News outlets around the world were showing the image, and Krums was being interviewed live on TV news networks.

"This may be among the most striking instances yet of instant citizen reporting," wrote the *Los Angeles Times* the day of the emergency landing.[2]

Indeed, the Miracle on the Hudson was a turning point, an eye-opening moment that showed the impact of social media on journalism. It was one of the first instances in which journalists realized the power of the audience in a mobile and social media world.

@jkrums
Janis Krums

http://twitpic.com/135xa - There's a plane in the Hudson. I'm on the ferry going to pick up the people. Crazy.

Janis Krums. Twitter Post. January 15, 2009.

Miracle on the Hudson: Janis Krums tweeted out this photo in 2009 after a US Airways plane made an emergency landing in the Hudson River. Within minutes of Krums sharing this image, news outlets around the world were using it as part of their coverage.

Twitter, Facebook, and other social networking sites are more than just ways for people to keep in touch with friends and family. They're platforms for news. Platforms where everyday citizens can share newsworthy content alongside professional journalists.

This was never more evident than during the Boston Marathon bombings and their aftermath, major news events that underscored the changing role of the audience. From the initial explosions at the finish line to the manhunt for the two suspects, the chaos unfolded live—on social media. Immediately after the explosions, many peoples' first reaction was to reach for their mobile phones and share via social media platforms.

Andrew Kitzenberg @AKitz · 19 Apr 2013
Bullet hole through our wall and the chair #mitshooting #mit #boston

↩   ⇄ 7.1K   ♥ 999   •••

Andrew Kitzenberg captured the shoot-out between one of the Boston Marathon bombing suspects and police outside of his home in Watertown, Massachusetts. Bullets came flying into his apartment, and the world was watching it unfold in real time on his Twitter feed.

Hours later, Andrew Kitzenberg (@Akitz) gave the world a front-row seat to a shootout between authorities and the suspects. Kitzenberg heard pops outside of his home in Watertown, Massachusetts, darted to look out a window, and saw gunfire.

He too grabbed his iPhone and began posting to Twitter: "Shoot out outside my room in Watertown. 62 Laurel st. #mit #boston #shooting." A round of gunshots entered his home and became lodged in his office chair, another image he shared on Twitter.

Social media users and journalists were living the frantic events in real time through his words and photos. Kitzenberg, interviewed on the CNBC documentary #TwitterRevolution, said he never even thought about calling a TV station or newspaper.

"They didn't even cross my mind. It was Twitter."[3]

The tables were now turned, as journalists and others learned about news events via social media.

Who Are the Gatekeepers Now?

The term *gatekeeping* is used as a metaphor to explain the process of selecting content that will make it through the "gates" and into a news product, such as a news website, newspaper, or newscast. Gatekeepers hold the keys to the gates. They determine which content is most relevant, who it's intended for, and how it will be delivered.

Prior to social media, editors, news directors, producers, and reporters were gatekeepers in journalism. They were the guarders of the gates, controlling what information got through to the audience.

In editorial meetings, without much input from the audience, they would decide which stories to cover and how much space or time to dedicate to them, among other considerations. Traditionally, this meant journalists relied on predictable newsgathering channels dominated by official sources, press conferences, news releases, and government proceedings.[4]

The Boston Marathon bombings and the Miracle on the Hudson raise the question: Who are the gatekeepers now?

There are new forces at the gate: the active audience. The concept of traditional gatekeeping has been turned upside down. Editors, news directors, producers, and journalists no longer have sole control over content that makes it through the gates. While they make the ultimate decisions about what news is included on a website, in a broadcast, or in a newspaper, the audience influence on the process is unquestionable.

Mobile devices and social media are now at the heart of today's editorial discussions. Audience members have become a source of news items, as they create their own content. The audience is also able to communicate stories or topics that interest them, which in turn influences news outlets' judgments about an event's newsworthiness and which stories ultimately are considered "news."

My nationwide survey of news directors, those who manage broadcast television newsrooms, explored the impact of the active audience on the gatekeeping process in newsrooms.[5] Nearly all of the 126 news directors who took part in the study indicated their newsrooms regularly find story ideas or content from social media users that ends up in newscasts. It should come as no surprise that this practice is the norm and is indicative of the practices in all types of news organizations.

The results of the study also show that what is being talked about or "trending" on social media is a significant factor in choosing stories to cover. Would newsrooms cover these stories if they were not popular on social media? Eighty percent of TV news directors said there would be only some chance or little chance that they'd even think about covering these stories if it weren't for their popularity on social media.

As one reporter who I spoke with about the changes put it, "It used to be that we told them [the audience] what was happening. Now, because of social media, they are trying to tell us. . . . Who online 10 years ago was telling us what our top story was going to be?"[6]

Once-passive audience members, then, are not only consumers of news, but also influential producers of content. Consumers *and* producers—habits at the heart of the changes in the field.

Content Producers: The Power of an Active Audience

The power of the audience as producers is reflected in the term "user-generated content." User-generated content refers to photos, videos, and other information captured by people who are not professional journalists and shared to social media platforms.

CNN iReport is one of the earliest examples of user-generated content. Citizens turned into roving reporters, snapping up videos and photos of newsworthy events, and then sending them to CNN for distribution online and on air.

When iReport launched in 2006, the term *social media* wasn't even part of our everyday vocabulary. Many of us were just hearing about a new "website" called Facebook. The first generation iPhone hadn't even hit store shelves.

The dominance of mobile devices and social media platforms in the years following has created a flood of user-generated content. Nearly 70 percent of smartphone owners use their phone to take and share pictures, videos, or commentary about events happening in their community, with 35 percent doing so "frequently," according to the Pew Research Center.[7]

The audience now has the tools (mobile devices) in their hands to easily create content and new platforms (social media) to instantly share content with anyone. This has shifted their habits from those early days of iReport. Many nowadays don't even consider contacting a news outlet with content. Instead, Twitter, Facebook, Instagram, and Snapchat are just a swipe and tap away.

"When people are uploading content, they're not sending it to a newsroom, they're sharing it with their friends," says Claire Wardle (@cward1e), former research director at Columbia Journalism School's Tow Center for Digital Journalism.[8]

People sharing this content may not have intended for it to be used by journalists. But, by chance, it may happen that the content is the story or becomes a key part of a story. We saw this in the Boston Marathon bombings and Miracle on the Hudson coverage.

Journalists are relying on social media content, particularly in breaking news situations, to provide audience members with information from a location prior to a reporter's arrival. User-generated content is also helpful when a news event is taking place in a remote area.

For instance, when a Carnival cruise ship was stranded in the Gulf of Mexico, news outlets turned to Twitter, Instagram, and Facebook for photos, video, and other information posted by the ship's passengers.

Searches of the keywords and hashtags "Carnival" and "Triumph" revealed first-hand accounts from aboard the ship—images of sewage backed up and people sleeping on outdoor pool decks because of the unsanitary condition aboard the ship. Because news outlets could not get their own crews to this news event taking place in the middle of the gulf, they relied on the passengers' social media posts to paint a picture of what was unfolding.

Sometimes, the audience unknowingly shares news, as was the case for Sohaib Athar. Athar didn't realize he was tweeting about one of the most historic news event of our times—the raid that killed Osama bin Laden. Athar noticed helicopters circling near his home in Abbottabad, Pakistan. He then heard a blast and ended up live-tweeting the raid by US Navy SEALs on bin Laden's compound.[9]

It wasn't until later that he learned what he was tweeting about. Seven hours after Athar's first tweet, US President Barack Obama officially announced bin Laden's death. Athar tweeted, "Uh oh, now I'm the guy who liveblogged the Osama raid without knowing it."

Journalists scrambling for information about the raid came across Athar's Twitter feed. He received over 200 interview requests.

Sohaib Athar live tweeted the 2011 raid in Pakistan that killed Osama bin Laden. Athar, who lived near bin Laden's compound, later learned that all the activity in his neighborhood was part of the raid.

Sohaib Athar. Twitter Post. May 2, 2011

While this type of user-generated content can be captivating and enhance reporting, there are pitfalls. Below are some of the important considerations journalists must be mindful of. These points will be addressed in future chapters.

- Journalists must first determine if the content has news value. Note the use of *content* and not *news* in the term *user-generated content*. This is an important distinction, because not all user-generated content is news. In the sea of social media content, some is newsworthy. Plenty is not.

- Before deciding to use newsworthy social media content in their reporting, journalists must be skeptical about information. The speed at which content travels over social media, the sheer volume of user-generated content, and the rise of fake news make fact checking even more important now. Social media information should be held to traditional journalistic standards. Journalists must verify the accuracy and authenticity of the information. The reliance on social media content has increased the chances that newsrooms will spread misinformation. In my nationwide study of news directors, a third of respondents indicated their stations had reported information from social media users that was later found to be false or inaccurate.[10]

- Another question to consider is whether journalists, before using the content, need to obtain permission from someone who's posted material on social media. Since the content is on a public platform, is it fair game to use without securing permission?

- News outlets must not become overly dependent on social media as a source for stories. Focusing on topics from social media can lead the public to perceive those issues as more important than stories uncovered through traditional means. Social media is not a replacement for journalists attending school board meetings, walking the halls of City Hall, or poring through the county budget, for example. Putting down the iPhone and pounding the pavement in search of stories is still critical.

Social media is like the wild west—exciting but chaotic, and often lacking order. It's the responsibility of trained journalists to make sense of all the noise, of the fire hose of information from the active audience.

This burden falls on everyone in a newsroom. Since social media content is such an integral part of news today, many newsrooms are hiring journalists whose sole responsibility is to manage audience engagement and user-generated content.

Fergus Bell (@fergb) was the first international social media editor and user-generated content editor at the Associated Press. Bell helped develop standards for verifying user-generated content and collaborating with social media users.

"Users know that they can contribute to news stories, so we need to find a way to work with them by giving them the credit they deserve," says Bell. "[They] should not be people we should be battling against. We need to get into a position where we're working together."[11]

News Consumption: Mobile and Social

The audience as producers is one piece of the evolving news landscape. How they're getting news today—and what they're doing with it—is also having a monumental impact on journalism.

The public's news consumption habits are undergoing a fundamental shift: mobile and social.

With the swipe of a finger, mobile devices are the go-to place to access news. Mobile phones and tablets are becoming the dominant platforms for news consumption.[12] They're portable and on-demand, giving people access anytime and nearly anywhere.

Think about your own habits. How do you typically get word of a major news story? It may be a local story, such as a car accident that shuts down a highway in your hometown; or, a story of national and international significance, such as the 2016 deadly shooting in an Orlando nightclub.

There's probably a good chance you first hear about these types of news stories through a breaking news alert on your mobile device or a social media post. Then, that may lead you to a news outlet's website for more details, all while using your mobile device. You may also interact with the news by sharing it on social media or commenting on it.

Not only are people increasingly reading and watching news on mobile devices, they're learning about news while on social media sites and engaging with it—in real time as news happens. That brings us to the idea of news as something "social."

These trends show no signs of slowing down. A survey conducted by the Knight Foundation showed that nearly 90 percent of mobile device owners in the United States access news and information via their smartphones.[13]

And hitting home the point of the active audience, their encounters with news are hardly passive. The audience participates with the news and therefore becomes part of the conversation about a topic or story. At least half of social network site

---

Key Points about News Consumption

- **News is mobile.** Mobile devices are becoming the dominant platform for news consumption. More and more people are visiting news websites on a mobile device. This "mobile majority" has news outlets rethinking how websites are designed and how news stories are packaged for mobile users. "We have more people reaching our content through mobile than desktop," said Karen Magnuson (@kmagnuson), editor and vice president of news at the *Democrat & Chronicle* in Rochester, New York. "A top priority is testing how our content looks on mobile devices, because that's likely how people are going to consume it."

- **News is social.** Rather than directly typing in the web address, people are being led to news websites by social media. Social referrals—links that are shared on social networks such as Facebook and Twitter—are a crucial source of website traffic. In addition, the trend is for people to first hear about news via social media, and then engage with the content by sharing or commenting.

users share stories, images, or videos from news outlets. Nearly as many discuss a news issue or event on social media.[14]

Taking a look at how people reach news websites is also eye opening. "You can no longer assume people are coming to you. You have to go out and get them," says Lisa Tozzi (@lisatozzi), news director at BuzzFeed.[15]

People are less frequently opening up a web browser and typing the address of a news website. Rather, more and more people end up at news websites by clicking a link in a social media post that catches their attention.[16]

The active audience on social media is a key driver of traffic to news websites. This means journalists must provide engaging content on social media platforms. Much of this book, particularly Chapter 6, focuses on this important skill.

Today's flow of news from a journalist to the audience is a far cry from the days of waiting for the morning paper or the evening news to tell you the top stories. The idea of news as mobile and social has significant implications for journalists. They must adapt to where the audience is spending a considerable amount of time and how they are interacting with news—on mobile devices and with social media. This means a shift in how and where journalism is produced and delivered.

"As journalism becomes ever more dependent on these new distribution platforms to find audiences, news publishers are forced to examine their business models and strategies for the future," says Emily Bell (@emilybell), director of the Tow Center for Digital Journalism and former director of digital content for Britain's *Guardian News*.[17]

Part of a successful strategy must be centered on where a news outlet's target audiences are spending their time. For younger generations, it's predominately mobile and social spaces. For older generations, it tends to be a mix of traditional and digital spaces.

All we have to do is take a look at where people got news about the 2016 US presidential election. For 18- to 29-year-olds, social media was the most helpful source for learning about the election, according to the Pew Research Center.[18]

Social media drops off for older Americans. Those 50 years and older named cable TV news as the most helpful. That's not to say mobile and social don't play an important role for them. While TV (78%) was the most common place for US adults to learn about the election, digital spaces (65%) including news websites, apps, and social networking sites weren't far behind. Radio (44%) and print newspapers (36%) trailed.

Even though this is only one snapshot in time, these findings are consistent with research on news consumption. It speaks volumes about the future of where journalism must be delivered. What will we see in 10, 20, 30 years as the younger generations age? It's unlikely that digital natives (students, that's you), those born with new technologies in their hands, will change their habits.

Older generations grew up accustomed to traditional print and broadcast, so they still rely on them for news more than their younger counterparts. But as the younger generations age, odds are they'll continue to rely on what they're familiar with, mobile and social spaces. This is key to the story of journalism's future.

It hits home the point of news organizations' need to evolve with the audience, because all signs indicate that news consumption on mobile and social will only increase and eventually outpace news consumption on traditional spaces—television, radio, and print—for all demographics. This isn't to say that these traditional spaces won't still be a source of information, but rather those outlets have to make mobile and social a top priority for delivering news and engaging with audiences.

The good news is that many newsrooms are already taking a mobile-first mindset (see Chapter 2). For example, fueled by the "mobile majority," making websites user-friendly for mobile device users has become a top priority.

It's a necessity when you consider that the majority of traffic to news websites comes from people using mobile devices, not desktop computers. As Table 1.1

TABLE 1.1

The portion of Americans who ever get news on a mobile device is increasing rapidly.

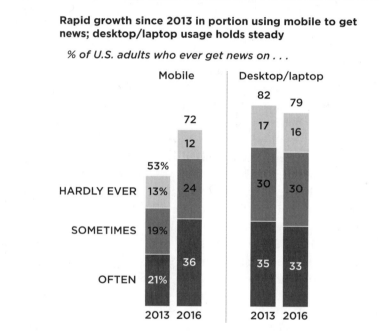

Rapid growth since 2013 in portion using mobile to get news; desktop/laptop usage holds steady

% of U.S. adults who ever get news on . . .

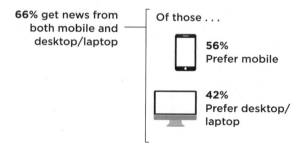

Among people who get news on both, more prefer mobile

66% get news from both mobile and desktop/laptop

Of those . . .

56% Prefer mobile

42% Prefer desktop/ laptop

Source: Survey conducted Jan. 12–Feb. 8, 2016.

"The Modern News Consumer." Pew Research Center, Washington, DC (July, 2016). http://www .journalism.org/2016/07/07/pathways-to-news/

shows, mobile traffic continues to gain prominence over desktop traffic in all sectors of journalism.[19]

The BBC News, for instance, said that two-thirds of traffic to its website is now generated by smartphones and tablets. In fact, most Google searches are now done by people on a mobile device.

In response to the "mobile majority," news outlets are developing new strategies to better serve the audience. For example, launching responsive websites is part of the approach. A responsive website is the industry standard. A website that is responsive gives visitors the best experience based on their device—mobile, tablet, or desktop.

Responsive websites adapt to which device a visitor is using in order to give the user optimal viewing and interaction with content. Google even boosts the search rankings of sites that are mobile friendly if the search was made from a mobile device.[20]

Stories also need to be mobile friendly. (We'll chat more about this in Chapter 6.) Journalists have to be mindful of the layout of stories and how they're written, so the stories can be easily viewed on mobile devices. You have to make the content digestible on a small screen while maintaining the attention span of the "mobile majority."

Or else, they might just swipe away.

IMPACT ON JOURNALISTS

Journalists must take an audience-centric approach to their work. It's essential in order to thrive in today's newsrooms.

The audience as producers and active consumers of news across many platforms clearly impacts the skills journalists need today. Making news stories user friendly for people viewing them on small screens is just one example.

Budding journalists entering the field, or those trying to stay relevant in their current jobs, will have to be able to assume a range of job responsibilities to serve the audience in spaces where they get information.

All you have to do is look at job openings for reporters. Mobile and social media skills are required of both new graduates and more seasoned journalists, in addition to reporting skills for traditional platforms.

When the MLive Media Group was hiring a reporter in Kalamazoo, Michigan, "understanding the imperatives of multiple platforms—print, mobile, Internet" was listed as a priority. The outlet, owned by Advance Publications, wanted someone experienced with using social media to source and promote content. The person was expected to have a "mastery of social media and digital interaction" and would be required to post frequently and incrementally throughout the day.

A job description for a general assignment reporter at WMUR-TV in Manchester, New Hampshire also highlights the importance of being able to report across multiple platforms. The person in this role "will contribute pictures, video and text updates to digital platforms, including social media, consistently throughout the day," the job post explained.

There are also newsroom positions, which we'll address in Chapter 8, dedicated to mobile and social media: Facebook editor at *The Boston Globe*, mobile newsroom

From the Newsroom

DAVID MUIR (@DAVIDMUIR)

Anchor and
Managing Editor

ABC World News Tonight
with David Muir

YOU STARTED IN TELEVISION NEWS MORE THAN 20 YEARS AGO. THE MEDIA LANDSCAPE LOOKED QUITE DIFFERENT THEN. HOW HAS NEW MEDIA IMPACTED JOURNALISM SINCE YOUR EARLY DAYS IN NEWSROOMS?

I vividly remember working in local news when the primary purpose for a station's website was to simply post pieces from a newscast that already aired. Reporters or anchors would often say, "For more on this, go to our website."

In today's environment, social media allows us to engage in a living, breathing conversation with the viewer all day long. I think the bar is much higher for what viewers will be interested in online. They don't want to watch a report they've already seen on television. There is an expectation we will deliver something they didn't see or something with added value, and rightly so. It provides us with an opportunity to take the audience along on the journey, and we've used it during reporting trips to the Syrian border on child refugees and during our historic conversation with Pope Francis.

YOU'RE CONSTANTLY CONNECTING WITH THE AUDIENCE THROUGH SOCIAL MEDIA, ESPECIALLY TWITTER. HOW HAVE THESE PLATFORMS CHANGED YOUR RELATIONSHIP WITH THE AUDIENCE?

Viewers have been given a voice in a way that wasn't even possible a few years ago. We learn immediately on Twitter or on Facebook about a question viewers want asked during a presidential primary debate or of factories that want us to profile them for our *Made in America* series. I love that. Viewers are helping to drive the conversation.

I grew up watching Peter Jennings, and I have long said he was masterful at having a conversation every night with America, but that conversation now truly goes both ways. Viewers can communicate with me before, after, and during the newscast, and they do.

DESCRIBE HOW YOU USE SOCIAL MEDIA ON A DAILY BASIS. (THAT'S YOU TWEETING FROM @DAVIDMUIR DURING COMMERCIAL BREAKS, RIGHT?)

I tweet during commercial breaks, but I'm not necessarily tweeting or posting on Instagram to drive people to their TV. I'm on social media, because America is on social media. And I believe our broadcast should reflect how people are living their lives. People are documenting their own lives in ways we never could have imagined. It's helped to build an army of citizen journalists who capture moments with their own phones that, when combined with the proper context, can give us a window into something we never would have seen.

developer at *The New York Times*, and social media producer at CBS News. In the not so distant future, these are some of the jobs you may find yourself working in.

So how do you make sense of what's expected of you as a reporter? It can seem a bit overwhelming at first. You use mobile devices and social media, but likely not in journalistic ways—at least not yet. You may be wondering, as a journalist, what do I tweet? How do I use social media to find credible sources? I should use Snapchat for . . . journalism?

This book will answer those questions and many more. Future chapters show you detailed ways to use these tools as a journalist. First, in this section, I want to help you better understand, in broader terms, how mobile devices and social media are impacting journalists' day-to-day routines.

There are three areas to consider: newsgathering, distribution of news, and audience engagement.

In my experience, approaching reporting responsibilities through these three areas provides students and journalists with a clearer sense of what's expected on mobile and social media platforms. It's a way to guide you through what may seem a bit chaotic, to wrap your head around how audience habits are directly shaping how journalists do their work. Remember, worrying only about what you're going to do for a web story or newscast is a thing of the past.

The bottom line in journalism is employers want reporters to use mobile devices and social media for newsgathering, distribution of news, and audience engagement (all while maintaining the fundamentals of journalistic standards, of course).

This book helps you gain hands-on experience in these three areas. Chapter 5, for example, provides you with a toolkit for a digital-first story pitch. A digital-first story pitch must include a plan for using mobile devices and social media for newsgathering, distribution, and audience engagement. For each story you cover, you'll come up with your own checklist, a game plan, to follow while reporting.

Now, here's a brief overview of the three key areas that you'll learn more about in future chapters.

Newsgathering

Journalists use mobile and social media in a number of ways during the newsgathering process:

- Tips line: To find story ideas
- Sources: To find sources for a story they're working
- Content: To find information for a story. This often includes user-generated content or crowdsourced information

Before journalists head into editorial meetings, it's common for them to scan social media platforms for what's happening in their city. For example, they might do a Twitter search of "Dallas." The daily routine as a reporter is quite different from years prior, when journalists started the day by making beat calls to police agencies, checking in by phone with other official sources, and sifting through news releases.

Social media is a modern-day tips line. It has become a powerful tool to find stories in your community. Monitoring social media platforms is a way to listen to the public, to put your finger on the pulse of what people are talking about.

Journalists now have immediate access to a wealth of new material and voices during the newsgathering process. Let me share one of my favorite examples of how scouring social media platforms, often referred to as "social listening," can turn up impactful stories.

I'm in and out of newsrooms frequently. One day I was visiting a newsroom in Syracuse, New York, when a reporter noticed a complaint on Twitter about paint dripping along a street after city workers painted new traffic lines. During a public meeting a few days prior, the mayor discussed how the city planned to save money by purchasing a different type of paint than it had previously used. The complaint on social media led the reporter to uncover a noteworthy story. She investigated whether the new paint was actually as cost effective as the city had presumed.

In addition to finding story ideas, journalists are also turning to social media to locate sources for stories they're already working on. Let's say you're assigned a story about the cost of school supplies. Speaking with parents is key to telling a compelling story. How can you use social media to track down someone to interview?

Tammy Palmer (@TammyNC9), a reporter covering this story for WSYR-TV in Syracuse, New York, logged onto Facebook.

"So I posted on our Facebook page, 'Hey, any moms about to go shopping?' That is how I connected with a mom," Palmer said. "Before you just had to kind of stumble upon people like this, and now you can look for them online. And it gave me options, because I had a number of moms respond. I had three moms who had different scenarios. That is where it created flexibility for me."[21]

Photo by Katie Hawkins-Gaar.

Tapping into the crowd: *The New York Times* turned to social media users for images of a blizzard. Some of these photos were published on the front page of the paper.

Tapping into content created by the audience has also become commonplace. Earlier we discussed how journalists are incorporating user-generated content into their reporting. Another way to gather audience content is through crowdsourcing.

Crowdsourcing is an open call by news outlets to gather a range of content including photos, data, and comments about an issue. In crowdsourcing, journalists make a specific request, usually through social media, for content from the audience. Crowdsourcing is different from searching for user-generated content that has already been created. It's a call to action, inviting people to take part in the reporting process.

The New York Times used crowdsourcing during a blizzard that paralyzed the northeast. *The Times* asked people to share their snow storm photos on Instagram and tag them with #NYTsnow. *The Times* published nine of the photos on the front page of its print edition. (By the way, the paper never notified users that their photos would actually be published, nor was it mentioned as a possibility in its crowdsource request. What do you think about this? Chapter 7 will address best practices related to user-generated content.)

How journalists receive content from and interact with traditional sources in the newsgathering process is also evolving, thanks to mobile devices and social media.

When traditional sources, such as police departments, release information, they often bypass journalists.

They're increasingly sharing information on social media pages prior to or in place of contacting news outlets. Journalists must routinely monitor the social media pages of these sources, particularly during breaking news.

When fire engulfed a 160-year-old church in New York City, journalists relied on the New York City Fire Department Twitter page for the latest details. As the fire raged, @FDNY shared video of firefighters battling the blaze and details such as the number of firefighters on the scene.

The Boston Police Department also turned to Twitter, instead of news outlets, to share urgent information during the Boston Marathon bombings. This is yet another instance in which the idea of journalists as the sole gatekeepers of news is turned upside down.

"In the past the police were at the mercy of the general media—to journalists—to tell their story. Now we can tell our own story. We can put out the information directly on Twitter," said Cheryl Fiandaca (@cherylfiandaca), spokesperson for the Boston Police Department at the time of the bombings.[22] Fiandaca, a veteran journalist, has since returned to investigative reporting.

The Boston Police Department even released on Twitter the first photos of the suspects. Within seconds of the tweets from @bostonpolice, journalists were holding up their phones live on-air, referencing the tweets.

Distribution of News

It should come as no surprise that reporting the news is a constant, never-ending process. Distribution of news in our mobile and social media world requires journalist to

- Share on multiple platforms as they report from the field.
- Provide real-time updates on stories.
- Use mobile devices to capture, produce, and publish content.

Journalists can't wait for a news broadcast, a morning newspaper, or even a web story to deliver the latest information about a story. Because the audience expects information in real time and across multiple platforms, journalists must share tidbits of information as they report from the field.

FDNY @FDNY 27m
170 #FDNY members on scene of 4-alarm fire at 25th & Broadway #Manhattan

0:23

311   121

FDNY @FDNY 32m
#FDNY members operating at 4-alarm fire at 25th & Broadway #Manhattan

@FDNY. Twitter post.

Traditional news sources are increasingly bypassing news outlets to get information to the public. Using social media, they can now share updates directly with the public. That was the case in 2016 when the New York City Fire Department battled a massive fire at a historic church.

"We operate almost like the AP [Associated Press] alerts that newsrooms use for breaking news. Well, now the everyday person is expecting those types of alerts for stories, especially for breaking news," one reporter told me. "The end user has already established the fact that they don't want to wait for news. They're going to consume news on their own time. Getting it out quicker serves the audience."[23]

This means embracing a digital-first approach to reporting, thinking about what needs to be distributed on social media platforms while in the field and ensuring all content can be easily viewed by people using mobile devices. Reporters have to juggle feeding information to audiences active in many spaces—Twitter, Facebook, website, and mobile applications, among others. Depending on where you work, you'll also be turning stories for TV, radio, or print. Stories live on mobile, social, and more traditional platforms.

At this point, the process may seem a bit messy. (It's also fun, believe me!) Gathering information in the field while almost simultaneously sharing the latest updates to a story will become second nature.

Any journalist will tell you that honing these skills comes from practice—repetition, repetition, repetition. This book is intended to get you in the field as soon as possible so you can put the strategies and skills into practice. The checklists in each chapter help you plan and prioritize the many tasks.

A smartphone or tablet will be your go-to tool. With a single mobile device, journalists can broadcast live from a scene. They can snap photos and record video and audio that can be instantly shared to social media platforms. They can live-tweet from the scene of breaking news. Mobile devices and apps allow journalists to easily distribute content in real time across platforms.

Taking a photo on a traditional camera, for example, and then sharing to social media would be a cumbersome process. You would have to get the image onto a computer or mobile device in order to share. That's a time-consuming workflow in today's news environment.

From small daily papers to major news outlets, it would be nearly impossible for journalists to do their jobs today without mobile devices. The Gannett Company, which owns dozens of daily newspapers across the country, including *USA Today*, was one of the first outlets to hand out devices to reporters. In 2011, Gannett purchased thousands of iPhones, iPads, and portable wireless hotspots for reporters to use in the field.

And journalists are grabbing their devices to produce content for more than just new mobile and social media platforms. Gannett and many other newspapers have their reporters use mobile devices to capture photos and video that accompany traditional website and print stories. In other words, all the multimedia elements distributed across all platforms can be produced with a single device.

At TV stations, the process may look slightly different. Most news packages that air on television newscasts are still shot with traditional video cameras. The main reason is that the quality of video recorded on mobile devices may not always be the best for high-definition television, although I would argue it's pretty close.

Some of my students and I experienced this firsthand while covering the 2016 South Carolina Republican primary for NBC News. Armed with iPhones, iPads, and traditional cameras, we crisscrossed the state to report from the campaign trail. The students shot video for two correspondents' packages that aired on *NBC Nightly News*. While that footage was recorded with traditional cameras, we used mobile devices to gather, edit, and distribute videos and photos for the TV news network's social media platforms and website. From my iPhone, we even took over NBC News's Snapchat account on primary day. More about this collaboration later in the book.

Distributing news across multiple platforms as quickly as possible presents challenges. Among the most notable concern is maintaining traditional journalistic values while sharing information at the speed that is now expected of journalists. You can't be first *and* accurate all the time. Those are two competing values. Fact-checking takes time. When in doubt, accuracy trumps speed. Unfortunately, there are far too many cases in which news outlets did not follow this basic journalistic principle.

Then, there's writing across all these platforms. Clear, concise, and accurate writing has always been a hallmark of good journalism. But reporters need to be mindful of their writing now more than ever. What you write in a tweet likely won't work for the headline of a web article. The tone of a post on Snapchat will be (a lot) different than the tone of one on Facebook. Being able to adapt your style and tone of writing based on where you're posting is an important skill.

The brevity of social media posts also requires a new way of thinking about what information to share, how often, and how to frame it. For example, tweets, with a maximum of 140 characters, do not allow for a detailed explanation. You have to be careful delivering news piecemeal, because you don't want it to be misinterpreted by your audience. Providing context and a consistent stream of information is key. Don't leave your audience hanging.

Audience Engagement

We've talked about newsgathering and distribution of news. Now, let's throw audience engagement into the reporting mix. Newsgathering, distribution of news, and audience engagement often happen all at the same time. Don't think of them as three neatly separated buckets. They occur in concert with each other.

Just take a look at a day in the life of NBC News correspondent Hallie Jackson, who you met earlier. Jackson traveled weeks at a time, covering the GOP side of the 2016 US presidential race.

As Jackson gathered news in the field, from candidates' rallies to polling centers, she kept tabs on what was being said about the campaigns on social media. Jackson almost simultaneously shared nuggets of campaign news with her Twitter followers.

On Snapchat, she took a laid back approach. Her Snapchat stories gave a behind-the-scenes, and sometimes comical, look at life on the road as she lived out of a suitcase. Lots of coffee! (She sometimes had to type in gas station bathrooms.)

Jackson also invited the public to "hang out" with her and fellow correspondents covering the election. They were dubbed "The Road Warriors." During live chats on MSNBC's Facebook page and on Twitter, The Road Warriors frequently answered questions from followers.

"As part of my Road Warrior travels, I think about what I can provide on social media that is going to be different than what other reporters covering the campaign are providing," said Jackson. "It's about finding those interesting elements and moments from my travels and bringing them to my audience."

And don't forget about her TV reports. Along with everything else on her plate, Jackson juggled the demands of reporting live for MSNBC and preparing packages for *NBC Nightly News.*

Technology brings people closer not only to the news she covers, but also to her as a journalist. They get to know her as a "real" person. They can connect with her at almost any time. Jackson says she thrives on this audience engagement.

So what does the term *audience engagement* mean? The collaborative nature—the idea of bringing an audience into the reporting process—is at the heart of audience engagement.

Effective engagement with the audience includes

- Consistent and authentic interactions.
- An informal yet professional tone.
- Openness and responsiveness to audience feedback.

It's about news as a conversation, rather than a lecture. It's about meeting people on platforms where they already are. It's about responding to social media followers' questions. It's about listening, not simply spewing out information or promoting your stories. All of these approaches will go a long way to make the audience feel invested in your work as a journalist.

This two-way conversation can help create a better understanding of issues people care about and lead to better journalism. Ongoing interactions can also build trust and credibility with the audience. Journalists who interact with their followers are seen as more credible and are rated more positively than journalists who use social media solely to distribute news.[24]

Using social media to lift the veil on the reporting process is one way journalists are doing this. Giving followers an insider's look at what it takes to get a story, as Jackson does, gives them a stronger connection with journalists. It's a more authentic approach than simply tweeting out headlines and links to stories.

Hallie Jackson. Twitter post. May 6, 2017.

Hallie Jackson. Twitter Post. September 22, 2016.

NBC News correspondent Hallie Jackson connects directly with audience members, offering them opportunities to "hang out" with her.

Through this type of engagement, journalists are also demystifying the reporting process, helping the audience understand that journalism is about much more than simply pushing out information.

You may have heard it yourself: Everyone is a journalist. That's simply incorrect. Yes, nearly anyone can "publish" content, but that doesn't make them journalists. Journalists have the skills to put information in context, verify, and fact-check.

Journalists' skills are needed now more than ever to help the audience navigate through the "noise"—to make sense of the flood of (mis)information. Social media is an avenue to let people in on what that journalistic process entails.

The hope is that through authentic engagement the active audience recognizes the value of journalists, and that keeps the audience coming back for more on the platforms they find most convenient.

Checklist

Welcome to your first checklist! Each chapter has at least one. They're a way for you to put into practice what we've discussed. This first checklist connects you with additional resources to keep tabs on the latest mobile and social media journalism news.

✓ **Beyond the Book.** Let's extend the conversation beyond the pages of this book and your classroom. Connect with me on Facebook (*fb.com/MobileandSocialMediaJournalism*) and Twitter (@MobileJourn). I'll share updates on the industry and my own teaching. I also want to hear from you. Have a question about something you read here? Come across a neat example of how a journalist is using mobile and social media? Doing something cool with what you've learned in the book? Drop me a line! We can learn from each other.

> Start by tweeting me one item you found interesting from this chapter, and tell me why. (Of course, I hope you find everything in this book to be interesting!)

✓ **Class Hashtag.** As a class, create a Twitter hashtag that can be used throughout the semester. I have one for my mobile and social media journalism course at Ithaca College's Park School of Communications (#ICParkSM). A class hashtag serves as a channel for discussions about course topics. Use it to share insights from guest speakers to your class. It's also a great way to share with your classmates interesting items you come across related to mobile and social media journalism. Simply include your class hashtag when you share on Twitter. In future checklists, we'll chat more about using your class hashtag.

✓ **Stay Informed.** There are a number of trade organizations that distribute e-newsletters with related content and research. You can also follow them on Twitter. Subscribing to their e-newsletters and following them on Twitter will provide you with ideas for the Teaching Moment assignment that is part of Chapter 5's checklist. The following

(Continued)

(Continued)

are my go-to sources. I've provided Twitter handles and links for you to subscribe to e-newsletters:

> MediaShift's Daily Must Reads: @MediaShiftOrg and *bitly.com/MediaShiftNewsletter*

> Poynter: @Poynter and *bitly.com/PoynterNewsletter*

> Pew Research Center: @pewjournalism and *bitly.com/PewResearchNewsletter*

> Nieman Lab: @NiemanLab and *bitly.com/NiemanNewsletter*

> Knight Digital Media Center: @KDMC and *bitly.com/KnightNewsletter*

✓ **Discussion.** Consider the following as a class:

> What are the positives and negatives of an age that allows nearly anyone to create and publish content?

> What is meant by an "active" audience? How have news consumers' habits changed?

> Describe the relationship between journalists and the audience today.

> What are the skills journalists need in our mobile and social media world?

Managing Change:
The Mobile-First Newsroom

"Imagine, if you will, sitting down with your morning coffee, turning on your home computer to read the day's newspaper."[1] Flashback to 1981. That's how a San Francisco television anchor introduced a report about two of the city's newspapers experimenting with the Internet. At that time, it took two hours to download a paper.

This story about the infancy of online news surfaced decades later on, where else, social media sites. It's a must-watch video—fascinating and comical considering what we now know about the monumental changes in the way we consume and deliver news.

There's also a bit of irony in the story. The report goes on to say, "We're not in it to make money. We're probably not going to lose a lot, but we aren't going to make much either" and "the new tele-paper won't be much competition for the 20-cent street edition."

Today, we're witnessing what was once thought to be far-fetched. The online medium provides countless channels for people to consume information, and the impact on the newspaper and broadcast industries has been seismic. Print newspaper readership has plummeted and television news viewership has steadily decreased as people increasingly turn to online resources.

And, out of a need to survive, advertisers followed the audience. Companies have shifted much of their marketing effort from traditional platforms to online spaces where people are spending time. This has spelled trouble for media outlets relying on traditional revenue from print and broadcast advertising.

The recession of the late 2000s only exacerbated this situation by adding to the erosion of advertising dollars on traditional platforms. People were spending less, and

In this chapter you will

- Gain a deeper understanding of the evolving business models in journalism.

- Learn what mobile-first means, and explore how it's transforming business models and editorial strategies.

- Discover three factors at the heart of mobile-first: the audience experience, newsrooms serving as multiplatform hubs of content, and evolving business models.

- Develop a mobile-first mindset that will equip you to plan news coverage that best serves today's audiences.

that hurt many businesses' bottom lines. Companies, including big advertisers such as car dealers and furniture stores, slashed their advertising budgets.

The loss in advertising dollars hit news outlets, especially print, hard. For example, between 2007 and 2010 alone, print newspaper advertising revenue was cut nearly in half, plunging from $42 billion to $22 billion.[2] This downward trend has continued. Meantime, digital advertising revenue has steadily moved in the opposite direction, but not at a fast enough pace to make up for the drastic losses on the print side.

It was a perfect storm: people going online for news coupled with a loss in the stream of traditional advertising revenue.

Journalists felt the impact. During and immediately following the economic downturn that started in 2007, the journalism industry experienced layoffs of newsroom staff and the closure of some media outlets, particularly in the newspaper industry.

As a result, news outlets have had to change their business models in order to remain competitive in today's marketplace. Businesses can collapse if their "theory of business"—assumptions a business is based on, including customers, competitors, values and behavior, and technology—is not revised to keep up with the changing marketplace.[3]

In an attempt to remain competitive, newsrooms are reaching audiences in new ways. First it was through traditional websites, and now it's increasingly about mobile devices and social media. From the audience's perspective, newsrooms today must meet the needs of news consumers who are flocking to mobile devices and social media.

A mobile-first culture is taking shape in newsrooms across the country.

> "It has become a cliché: The only constant in the media industry today is change. The cliché however is reality."[4]

This chapter gives you an overview of how mobile-first is transforming newsrooms' business models and cultures. You'll walk away with a better understanding of the business of journalism today and its relationship with newsroom editorial strategies. After all, regardless of your role in a newsroom, your responsibilities will be directly tied to these changes.

Sure, there's uncertainty about what lies ahead. But that's part of the excitement of teaching, studying, and practicing journalism today. I strongly believe we're witnessing a rebirth of journalism. And you have a front-row seat. You're part of it.

"There's a sense of energy that hasn't existed inside the industry for quite some time," said Amy Mitchell (@asmitch), Pew Research Center's director of journalism research.[5]

The industry has rebounded in many ways since the Internet disrupted journalism more than a decade ago. There are exciting ways to tell stories and connect with the public that weren't possible before.

The hemorrhaging of jobs, particularly in print, has slowed down tremendously overall. As traditional print and broadcast newsrooms make mobile and social media a priority, they're hiring staff members to specifically manage these platforms. In addition, digital-only outlets are setting up shop, all part of a new business model.

This has also led to the creation of new jobs within the industry, though not enough to offset the layoffs of years prior.

Thousands of journalists, including many veterans, are now working at these digital-only news outlets—from smaller start-ups such as Philadelphia's Billy Penn to bigger sites such as The Huffington Post. The digital news world has created roughly 5,000 full-time jobs, according to the Pew Research Center. Nearly 3,000 of these jobs were created by 30 large digital-only news outlets.[6]

Journalists have to be willing to embrace this change in order to survive—and thrive. What is most striking to me about the San Francisco TV report about "tele-papers" is how two newspapers were willing to experiment with the Internet at least a decade prior to most newsrooms.

This foresight and innovate spirit in newsrooms is critical at this juncture, as mobile devices and social media now disrupt "business as usual."

It's not good enough to say, "We have been around for 50, 75, 100 years, so come to us." The active audience has plenty of other options to get news on platforms that are convenient for them.

The traditional way of doing business will leave news outlets in the dark.

MOBILE-FIRST MINDSET

Just as the infancy of the Internet was a wake-up call for newsrooms, so too are mobile devices and social media. Newsrooms are using lessons learned a decade ago to try to stay ahead of the curve this time around. Some are moving quicker than others.

Digital-first is a term that is often used in newsrooms. After the rise of the Internet, digital-first meant publishing news on websites first—where people were flocking to keep up to date.

Then mobile devices and social media came knocking. Today, digital-first means mobile-first. Again, following the audience's lead.

Mobile-first is about making it a priority to deliver quality content that can be easily accessed by audiences on mobile devices and in social media spaces. As we discussed in Chapter 1, this mindset requires journalists to share information to mobile and social media platforms first in many cases, prior to a web story or broadcast report.

News websites and other traditional platforms are increasingly becoming the secondary places to publish information. That's because Facebook, Twitter, and the like are the audience's portals into the world of news. They're the avenues where people are exposed to journalists' work and news outlets' brands.

We also have to think about the user experience more than ever before. The content must be optimized and packaged in a user-friendly way for viewing (we'll explore this in Chapters 5 and 6). The key to mobile-first, National Public Radio's Brian Boyer said, is thinking: "Who are your users and what are their needs?"[7]

Key Points about a Mobile-First Mindset

- **Audience experience.** Journalists must reimagine how news is reported and in what spaces in order to make it accessible to audiences who move among devices and platforms. A positive user experience with quality content in all of these spaces is key. Engagement, a two-way conversation with your audience, is also part of this experience.

- **Multiplatform hubs of content.** A news outlet can no longer plant its flag as a newspaper, television station, or radio station. The same goes for reporters. Newspaper reporters are doing more than just print. TV reporters are doing more than just TV. Radio reporters are doing more than just radio. Think of each newsroom as a hub of content. They have many different platforms to reach audiences, and each story must be told across these platforms. Often that means taking different approaches for each space, as we'll discuss later in this chapter and in future ones.

- **Evolving business models.** Different business models are emerging that tap into new revenue streams from the mobile audience and digital advertising. Solid journalism still needs to be funded. That's always been the case. What has changed is how it's funded.

"We don't do journalism for our own satisfaction," Boyer (@brianboyer) added, "so if folks can't use your stuff because they're on the bus, you're doing it wrong."

This mindset is directly tied to the business side of journalism. A seamless user experience with content is one important factor to keep the audience coming back for more.

Mobile-first has given rise to evolving business models. News outlets are tapping into new revenue streams on these platforms. They're experimenting with how they can monetize the news products they offer people on their small screens and how to capitalize on the digital advertising market.

Here are a few examples of how a mobile-first approach is taking shape at news outlets. Note how **audience experience**, the idea of newsrooms as **multiplatform hubs of content**, and **evolving business models** come into play in each of these case studies.

The New York Times.   Today's story pitch meetings inside the *New York Times* are radically different from those of years prior. In 2015, Dean Baquet, the *Times* executive editor, announced the newsroom was retiring the system of pitching for page 1, the front page of the print edition. The process of selecting page 1 stories will play a less prominent role, Baquet wrote in a staff memo. Under the new system, editors now pitch stories to be considered for a list of stories that get "the very best play on all our digital platforms"—web, mobile and social.[8]

Baquet noted the system would give more flexibility for the paper to target people using mobile devices and social media. "These changes are intended to ensure that our digital platforms are much less tethered to print deadlines."

This is a significant shift in strategy for an outlet whose culture has been tied to page 1. For many reporters, getting a story on page 1 of the *Times* has been the holy grail, a career-defining goal. Revamping of editorial meetings was one step toward the mobile-first strategy outlined in an internal *New York Times* innovation report.

"Our home page has been our main tool for getting our journalism to readers, but its impact is waning. Only a third of our readers ever visit it," acknowledged the report.[9] "Readers are finding and engaging with our journalism in vastly different ways. More readers expect us to find them on Twitter and Facebook, and through email and phone alerts."

Syracuse Media Group.   At regional outlets, old-school ways of doing business are also being kicked to the curb. In Syracuse, New York, the *Post-Standard* and its website Syracuse.com were run out of two different newsrooms. In fact, the newsrooms weren't even in the same building. The print and digital operations were located across town from each other.

This silo approach changed in 2013. Advance Publications, which owned the print and digital divisions, implemented a new, digitally focused strategy. The news operation and business model were overhauled.

The wall between the print and digital came down. The *Post-Standard* and Syracuse. com were combined into one integrated operation called the Syracuse Media Group. News staff now work out of new headquarters, a collaborative workspace with no assigned desks. All reporters here are mobile journalists. They're given backpacks with mobile devices and laptops they need to report and distribute news directly from the field. It's now every reporter's job to think about how his or her stories can live across mobile, social, web, and print platforms.

These changes also came with layoffs. The shift to mobile-first eliminated some long-standing newsroom positions while creating new digitally focused jobs. The newspaper laid off 115 full- and part-time employees, nearly a third of its staff. Syracuse Media Group then hired about 60 people focused on creating digital news content.[10]

While ramping up the digital side, the news outlet reduced home delivery of its print edition from seven days to three days per week.

Advance Publications was one of the first media companies to implement such a top-to-bottom mobile-first culture, making an attempt to leap ahead of the changes. This cultural shift wasn't limited to Syracuse. The company owns newspapers and associated news websites across the United States. It has implemented a similar strategy at its other media outlets, including the *Times-Picayune* in New Orleans, Louisiana, and the *Plain Dealer* in Cleveland, Ohio.

Cable News Network (CNN).   The cable network is focused on much more than just TV these days. "We're no longer a TV news network," said Samantha Barry (@samanthabarry), CNN's head of social media. "We're a 24-hour global multi-platform network."[11]

This is quite an evolution from when CNN launched in 1980 as the first channel to provide 24-hour television news coverage. The network has pumped $20 million into a digital expansion dedicated to mobile. In 2016, CNN announced it planned on hiring more than 200 new staffers, including a mix of reporters, mobile and social media video producers, analytics and audience development experts, and mobile product developers.[12]

National Public Radio launched the NPR One app as a way to provide content to a new generation of listeners—those on mobile devices. The app offers a customizable experience for users.

About 50 CNN staffers lost their jobs in the overhaul. The laid-off staff members included people who worked on CNN's traditional desktop website. (They were invited to apply for the new positions.)

As part of the mobile-first strategy, CNN has built a team solely focused on creating and distributing content on platforms such as Facebook and Snapchat.

National Public Radio (NPR).   The graying of NPR's traditional audience has the media outlet rethinking its journey with listeners in a new age. As its core demographic of listeners ages, NPR is strategizing how to attract a younger audience to its brand. It's an audience NPR needs to capture in order to survive.

The public radio broadcaster launched the NPR One app, a way for public radio to reach listeners who might not be tuning to terrestrial radio. The app gives users a personalized stream of mobile content. It pulls in stories from national shows, local newscasts, and podcasts outside the NPR world. NPR One users are significantly younger than NPR's traditional broadcast audience: 40 percent are under 35 years old.[13]

The app also opens up new revenue opportunities for NPR member stations. For instance, NPR One promoted a podcast from a member station in San Francisco to a national audience rather than the local one. Because the local station got a big enough audience, it could begin selling sponsorships.[14]

ADAPTING TO A MOBILE AUDIENCE: EVOLVING BUSINESS MODELS

Let's take a brief look at the evolving business models in four main sectors of journalism: newspaper, television, radio, and digital-only. I'm not a fan of thinking in silos; nonetheless, I segment them out here because each type of outlet is taking a different approach.

From the Newsroom

**TRISH LAMONTE
(@TRISHLAMONTE)**

Director of Digital
Operations, Syracuse
Media Group

Syracuse, New York

The teams Trish LaMonte manages include web and mobile producers, community engagement specialists, graphic designers, social media specialists, videographers, writers, and a search engine optimization specialist for the Syracuse Media Group (Syracuse.com and the *Post-Standard*), an affiliate of Advance Local.

WHAT DOES DIGITAL-FIRST LOOK LIKE IN YOUR NEWSROOM?

Digital-first means reporters no longer factor in the print product when they're writing a story. Nobody is concerned with how big the news hole is that needs to be filled or how many column inches their story should be. The reporter's goal is to get content up online as quickly as possible while being factually correct. We break news in real time, posting a bulletin to start, that can be as simple as headline and a sentence, and filling in more details as we get information—that never would have been done in the old newspaper days. Can you imagine a reporter filing a story before they had every single detail nailed down?

We started really focusing on digital-first in 2013 and now it's so ingrained that we've moved on to thinking even more about mobile-first. With an ever-increasing percentage of our traffic coming from phones and other devices, we now believe if it doesn't work on mobile, it doesn't work period. You can create the coolest graphic but if it won't load in our app or is unreadable on the phone then it's not worth doing.

HOW HAS THE BUSINESS MODEL EVOLVED AT THE SYRACUSE MEDIA GROUP?

The business model is continually evolving to accommodate the inevitable decline of the print business. The Syracuse Media Group is positioning itself now for the day when the newspaper no longer exists, so that means focusing on finding new customers and selling a wide variety of digital products, not just ads. It's a team effort, so I think it's important for everyone to understand how the other side works, whether you're in sales and marketing or content. We have monthly town hall meetings where we look at how we're doing as a company. Employees tell interesting stories, often successes, that help everyone gain a better understanding of what's happening around them, and because of that there's a lot more collaboration.

BASED ON THIS NEW MINDSET, WHAT SKILLS DO YOU EXPECT REPORTERS YOU HIRE TO HAVE?

Of course, being a good writer is still the most fundamental skill a reporter needs to have, along with innate curiosity. But that's just the beginning; it's not enough anymore. The reality of most newsrooms today is that there are fewer copy editors, so reporters need to be able to look critically at their own work and make corrections and adjustments on the fly. They have to be able to work quickly and accurately. The deadline is no longer hours from now. It's now, or even five minutes ago. Reporters also have to be willing to engage readers in the comments and on social media, and they need to have some technical skills. They can't be clueless about how to add a photo, video or audio clip to their stories anymore because nobody is going to do it for them. The most successful

(Continued)

reporters now also take their own photos and videos. They're multimedia journalists, not just writers.

YOU MENTIONED ENGAGING THE AUDIENCE. HOW DO YOU INVOLVE THE AUDIENCE IN THE REPORTING PROCESS?

I know there's a lot of angst out there about online comments, but honestly we get a lot of great information from our commenters. On crime stories in particular, our reporters find new angles and people to talk to because of the comments people leave. When a friend or a loved one comments, we can often track them down for information and interviews. Some of our best stories have come from the comments, and when we have written about people in need, we've been able to match them up with people in the community who want to help because of the comments section. We also use social media a lot to reach out to our readers—to ask their opinions, encourage them to share content and to solicit story ideas and find interesting people to write about.

WHAT NEW POSITIONS HAVE BEEN CREATED IN YOUR NEWSROOM THAT FOCUS SOLELY ON MOBILE AND SOCIAL MEDIA?

We have producers who focus the majority of their time on social, including a social media lead. They're tasked with analyzing and optimizing our best content for a variety of platforms including Facebook, Twitter, Instagram, Snapchat, and anything new that comes along. They help train the newsroom staff and develop practices around what works best with our audience. They're constantly experimenting with new kinds of social posts and tools, such as Facebook Live video, figuring out what the social audience wants and how it's different from our website users. The producers who manage the homepage and the rest of the site are responsible for constantly checking our mobile site and app to make sure all content is appearing optimally.

Newspaper

I start with the newspaper industry because it has undeniably been the journalism sector most impacted by new technologies. In response to the sharp drop in print readers and advertising dollars, the industry is experimenting with a host of modern approaches to generate revenue, most notably paywalls, subscriptions, and digital advertising.

Nearly 80 percent of the 98 US newspapers with circulations over 50,000 charge for their coverage online, according to an American Press Institute study.[15] The majority do so through metered paywalls. And for the most part this approach has been positive, although longer-term success remains to be seen.

A news website with a paywall charges readers to access content online. Metered paywalls allow readers to view a certain number of articles for free. Beyond that, they must purchase a subscription to view more.

The *Dallas Morning News*, for instance, has a metered paywall that limits non-subscribers to 10 articles a month. Readers can then buy a monthly digital subscription. Otherwise, they have to wait a month to read another 10 free articles. The newspaper tried several other approaches that weren't successful, including a model in which some articles were free for all readers while others, such as investigations, were available only to subscribers.

Bundling is also common. Newspapers with paywalls typically give online access to their print subscribers. In certain areas, that print edition is showing up in mailboxes fewer days of the week. Some newspapers, such as those owned by Advance Publications, have reduced the number of days they publish a print edition. A drastic decline in print subscribers is a major factor. This strategy saves on costs while shifting attention to digital spaces.

Digital strategies include not only a mobile-friendly website, often behind a paywall, but also a mobile app. Some newspapers charge readers to access content via mobile apps as well. Access to apps is often tied to a digital subscription. For example, in order to get full access to an app from a newspaper owned by the Gannett Company, which operates outlets in nearly every state, you have to purchase a subscription.

A small number of newspapers are testing out other approaches, such as a micropayments paywall. Micropayment plans let people pay per article. One goal of this, like other strategies, is to convert these people to purchase digital subscriptions.

The question remains, though: How can you compel people to pay for news online when they've been accustomed to getting it free for so long? Very few news outlets charged to read online articles when they first launched websites in the late 1990s. Asking readers to start paying years later is a challenge. As we'll discuss shortly, audience members' willingness to open up their wallets is tied to the value news outlets provide them: consistent quality journalism combined with a positive experience and authentic engagement across all platforms.

Keeping the audience coming back for more is also important for attracting advertisers. Armed with data about website traffic, mobile app downloads, and subscriber demographics (among many other metrics), sales teams at all types of media outlets are approaching companies focused on digital advertising. Considering newspaper ad revenue is now less than half of what it was a decade ago, newspapers are trying to make inroads with marketers advertising on digital platforms.[16]

That has been a struggle. Digital advertising is growing, but each sector of journalism is getting a small piece of the pie. Technology companies, such as Facebook and Google, are reaping most the benefits, taking in at least half of all money spent on digital ads.[17]

Businesses are now easily able to target potential customers on platforms beyond news outlets' mobile apps and websites. This is one reason gains in newspapers' digital advertising revenue are failing to make up for the drop on the print side.

Television

Changes are playing out a bit differently at television outlets. TV news continues to maintain healthy viewership levels, despite drops from years prior. But the enormous disruption that print saw may be just around the corner for TV.

Nearly half of Americans say they still watch local TV news on a regular basis. However, taking a look at the younger demographic tells a different story. From 2006 to 2012 alone, according to the Pew Research Center, the number of adults under 30 who regularly watched local TV news dropped from 42 percent to 28 percent.[18] That number continues on a downward trend.

The younger generation is accustomed to getting news via mobile devices and social media, a habit that is unlikely to change as they get older. That could spell trouble for traditional TV news.

This hits home an earlier point about newsrooms serving as multiplatform hubs of content—focusing on one platform, or even two, is not enough. Newsrooms have to reach this younger audience on platforms beyond TV in order to attract them as loyal and, hopefully, lifelong customers. News outlets' financial health will depend in part on this approach.

TV newsrooms have stepped up their mobile and social media game. One way has been to make their on-air newscasts more "social." A majority of stations integrate social media into traditional newscasts, with most including a recurring social media segment.[19] For example, they have asked Facebook followers to comment about a story, and then news anchors have read the feedback on-air. This also works in the other direction. Anchors ask newscast viewers to weigh in on a story by posting a comment to Facebook or tweeting at the station.

Some stations have even experimented with social media–only newscasts. KOMU-TV in Columbia, Missouri, tested out a first-of-its-kind interactive newscast. The show's social media–driven structure and content were a departure from the traditional mold of local television news. As the newscast name, U_News, suggests, audience members played an active role. As many as 10 people joined the anchor on a "cyber couch" via Google Plus Hangouts and other social media platforms, while tweets and Facebook comments flashed on the screen and were read on-air.

So you may be wondering how a television station, or any outlet, makes money from all of this social media activity? The hope is this engagement enhances the connection with the audience and ultimately pays off by driving them to watch a station's newscast, visit its website, and download its app. The more eyeballs on those platforms, the better chance an outlet has at attracting advertisers.

Televisions stations have also launched mobile apps and mobile-friendly websites. How TV outlets monetize these platforms is different from how the newspaper industry does it. They sell advertising on these digital spaces, but it's highly uncommon for TV outlets to charge for access to their app or website. Only four TV stations have website paywalls, according to a study by the Radio Television Digital News Association and Hofstra University.[20] The study also found that the majority of local TV news apps are free of charge.

The vast majority of TV outlets haven't yet felt the pressure to put up paywalls because revenue from TV commercials is strong. TV news still generates most of its revenue from commercials.

There are also new streams of advertising on websites and mobile platforms. Mobile, in particular, is a growing area of ad dollars.

In fact, at WCMH-TV in Columbus, Ohio, mobile ad sales are outpacing sales for other digital formats. "Local businesses seem more interested in mobile campaigns than any other forms. With the emerging mobile trend and interest, we foresee much more demand on the horizon," said Gary Vogel, that station's digital sales manager.[21]

TV stations have always used data about their newscast audiences to attract advertisers. Now, that's just one piece of the puzzle. Just as they are used at other types of media outlets, metrics about the station's digital audience, even the number and demographic of followers on platforms such as Facebook and Twitter, are used to attract advertisers. With this data, stations' sales departments are able to sell customized advertising packages that include ads on the web, mobile devices, social media, and TV.

Stations may have to come up with more creative ways to bring in money, though, as all signs point to a continued decline in TV news viewing. With the TV news business still profitable, now is the time to experiment with new business models before the other shoe drops.

Interestingly enough, some media companies have split their television and newspaper operations into two separate companies, a strategy to protect their stable broadcast business from the newspaper industry's financial troubles.

Radio

Even though habits of the listening audience are changing drastically, local radio stations have been slower to adapt. I don't have to tell you that tuning into an AM/FM radio is becoming a thing of the past. A website or app is becoming the go-to place for radio listeners to stream radio.

The number of Americans 12 years and older who have listened to online radio in the past month has more than doubled since 2010.[22] And the majority of this group listens via smartphones rather than desktops.

Local radio stations have beefed up their online websites to provide streaming of local news and other programming. However, when it comes to mobile apps, radio stations lag behind their newspaper and television counterparts. Despite the audience's shifting habits, only half of local radio stations had mobile apps in 2015.[23] Two-thirds of radio news directors and general managers said they did nothing new in mobile that year.

"Spot" advertising—ads aired during radio broadcasts—continues to be the main revenue stream for radio stations. As it is in other journalism sectors, though, this traditional way of making money is on the decline. Meantime, revenue from digital advertising and "off-air" efforts saw gains.

Off-air is the one radio revenue category that is showing the most serious growth. Off-air includes sponsorships of community events hosted by stations. Newspapers, television stations, and digital-only outlets have also been experimenting with these nontraditional ways to generate new revenue. For example, the *New York Times* hosts an annual travel show in New York City. The digital-only outlet Billy Penn generates 80 percent of its revenue from events. In addition to the financial benefits, these events are a way to connect the community to an outlet's brand.

Podcasting is an area that could hold revenue potential for local radio stations and breathe new life into audio journalism. Podcasting is gaining momentum. The number of people who listened to podcasts has more than doubled in the past decade. NPR reports that downloads of its podcasts were up 41 percent in 2014 alone.[24]

The challenge facing many local radio stations is the lack of resources. It's one reason they haven't moved more aggressively on mobile platforms, and the same problem prevents local stations from building podcast offerings.

To build a bridge to the mobile audience, some radio outlets have their stations hosted on streaming services such as the TuneIn app. Users of TuneIn can listen to radio stations and podcasts from around the world. The one downfall: In most cases, radio stations don't receive any of the money these services generate from advertising and subscription fees.

Digital-Only

New players have entered the journalism field: digital-only news outlets.

Digital-only news organizations present a unique opportunity for journalists to tell stories and engage with audiences on mobile devices and social media. Unlike newspaper, television, and radio, they rely solely on new media to distribute content. Most of the digital-only players are start-ups testing out different ways of being funded.

Digital-only includes large outlets such as Vice and The Huffington Post as well as hyperlocal ones such as the Charlottesville Tomorrow and The Village Green.

As I mentioned earlier, they've created thousands of journalism jobs. Even high-profile journalists from major news outlets are now working at these newer ventures. These newsrooms are also ripe with opportunities for younger journalists who have the mobile and social media skills that are so critical to the outlets' digital-only strategy.

The outlets are filling gaps left in reporting by newsrooms that have trimmed their staffs. And they're producing award-winning journalism. Take, for example, the Pulitzer Prize–winning ProPublica.

It takes money to fund this type of quality journalism, and digital-only outlets are trying to figure out a consistent formula. One positive, for the most part, is these outlets don't have the same overhead costs of traditional news outlets. Inexpensive digital tools are all they need to produce and share digital-only content. A challenge though is that they must build news consumers' awareness about the value of their work. Even though hiring at these outlets has skyrocketed, a maintainable business model is critical to keeping these journalists employed.

Where the money comes from is varied. Tech giants have invested in digital-only operations. eBay founder Pierre Omidyar invested $250 million into First Look Media, a start-up by a group of noted investigative journalists. (This followed Amazon founder Jeff Bezos's purchase of the *Washington Post*.) Vice, Vox Media, BuzzFeed, and Business Insider are other digital-only newsrooms that have received significant investments from players with deep pockets.

Unfortunately, this type of funding alone isn't enough to keep the hundreds of digital-only news operations afloat. Smaller outlets, some of them nonprofits, have limited resources, even relying on part-time staff and volunteers to produce content.[25]

Digital-only outlets are tapping into digital advertising, sponsorships, events, and user-supported models (paywalls and subscriptions).

The Frontier, an investigative journalism start-up in Tulsa, Oklahoma, is betting on subscribers to keep it financially sound. The Frontier has a team of veteran journalists. A handful of reporters and editors from the *Tulsa World* newspaper joined the new venture, including two Pulitzer Prize finalists.

The Frontier, a digital-only news outlet, represents a new model of journalism. Instead of relying on traditional advertising to remain financially viable, The Frontier offers a monthly membership and welcomes financial support from individual and corporate sponsors.

Most of The Frontier's content is behind a paywall. Readers can pay a $30 monthly membership or per article. The outlet has also partnered with a local TV station to share some of its investigative stories in an effort to promote The Frontier's work and draw more traffic to its digital content. The Frontier has corporate sponsors but is ad-free—for right now anyway.

"What we're trying to sell is the value of having someone in your community be a watchdog," Robert Lorton, its founder, told the *Columbia Journalism Review*.[26]

The Village Green, a hyperlocal outlet in New Jersey, also hopes the community appreciates the value of its journalism—and is willing to pay for it. The Village Green's reporting digs into issues in neighborhoods that are often not covered by traditional news outlets.

After a period of providing stories free of charge, the outlet eventually had to put up a paywall. In a letter to its readers, The Village Green's founders explained the move:

> Gathering news costs money. The kind of content we feature every day on The Village Green—local stories brought to you by journalists who ask questions, attend meetings, know the issues and the community, and follow up on readers' suggestions and comments—takes time, skill and a willingness to tackle sometimes thorny issues with humanity and fairness. We don't just aggregate what other media have written; nor do we "drop in" for the big stories then disappear. We cover the towns day in, day out. We're here for the long haul.

> The revenue the paywall generates will help to ensure the continuation of The Village Green for years to come and enable us to expand our coverage to give readers even more local news, with bylines from more diverse writers and photographers.[27]

Rebooting the Newsroom: The Rochester *Democrat & Chronicle*

In May 2016, the *Democrat & Chronicle* in Rochester, New York, moved from an old cavernous building (some parts couldn't get Wi-Fi) to a state-of-the-art facility with a street-facing digital studio.

"What a far cry from the D&C of the past. When I joined as managing editor in 1999, I was greeted by an overwhelmingly print-centric culture with a workflow that served a morning newspaper in a building that was built for the needs of 1928," said Karen Magnuson (@kmagnuson), now the outlet's editor and vice president of news. "While leaving that beautiful old building was bittersweet, having a different kind of environment was absolutely essential for our transformation to a newsroom of the future."

Magnuson is leading the outlet's efforts to "reboot the newsroom." The new building, she said, was one of a number of "huge" changes at the D&C.

"We launched new products, including mobile and tablet offerings, and fundamentally changed our business model," added Magnuson. "We rewrote virtually every job description. We issued new tools such as iPhones to our reporters and photographers. We reformatted planning and communication processes. We introduced reprogramming of content distribution based on reader and user behaviors. And the list goes on."

As a veteran in the industry, Magnuson said she also underwent her own transformation. "I needed some additional tools in my editor's toolbox." So she pursued a master's degree in innovation management.

"The program helped me think more critically and creatively. It gave me an opportunity to lead the transformation to mobile and social while studying the bigger picture about the evolution of consumers and media consumption in general."

To read more about the D&C's digital transformation and hear from other key players in the newsroom, visit *bitly.com/DemocratandChronicle*.

Photo by Scott Norris.

Photo by Tina MacIntyre-Yee.

The *Democrat & Chronicle*'s new building includes an innovation lab on the first floor.

NEWSROOM MOBILE AND SOCIAL MEDIA EDITORIAL STRATEGIES

By now, it should start becoming clear that the business side of journalism is tied to the editorial side of journalism. The bottom line is that newsrooms must draw an audience to their work in order to entice readers to pay for content or for a sales department to bring in advertising dollars. In turn, this money allows reporters to keep chasing down stories. You see the cycle here.

That's where newsrooms' editorial strategies come into play.

Now that we've discussed evolving business models of mobile-first, the remainder of this chapter explores key components of successful newsroom mobile and social media editorial strategies.

No matter your position in a newsroom, you play a part in carrying out—and even shaping—the strategy. And your role in that process starts with being knowledgeable about the business and editorial sides of mobile-first.

You'll be able to ask important questions and make informed decisions, whether it's in a newsroom where you're already working or during a job interview.

Shouldn't we structure stories differently so people can more easily navigate them on mobile devices? What's the newsroom's policy for verifying user-generated content? Which mobile app does the newsroom use to produce videos? What type of content works better on Snapchat versus Facebook?

These are just a few of the important items for journalists to consider. Future chapters dig into these nitty gritty details and skills. Now, though, a look at the bigger picture. An understanding of editorial strategies will equip you to plan news coverage that best serves the audience.

Keep Them Coming Back for More

So how do newsrooms and journalists keep audiences coming back for more? Trust is key.

"News organizations that earn trust have an advantage in earning money and growing audiences," according to research conducted by the Media Insight Project.[28] People who trust news outlets are more likely to pay for news, download news apps, and share news with their friends.

How do journalists become worthy of the audiences' trust? Trust can be earned by providing value to the public through **quality content** across platforms, a **positive audience experience**, and **authentic engagement**. This underscores my previous point about mobile-first: Newsrooms, to be successful, must act as multiplatform hubs of content that focus on serving the audience.

If audience members are to keep craving more, they need to walk away feeling satisfied. People aren't going to invest their time and money in a news product unless they find consistent value in it, which ultimately builds their trust with journalists and new outlets.

It's all about a relationship with the audience, and trust is the foundation of a meaningful one.

Quality Content. Journalists must remain vigilant about the quality of news they produce, or else they risk breaking the trust of the audience. That's because people value quality content. The Media Insight Project found that accuracy of information and receiving the most up-to-date details about a news event are important trust factors for news consumers, no matter the platform.

Eighty-five percent of Americans rate it extremely or very important that news organizations get the facts correct; this is higher than they rate any other principle. The second most valued trust factor has to do with timeliness. In this digital age, a majority of people say it's critical that news reports have the very latest details.

BBC News has a rule that readers should be able to get the key points of a story within the first four paragraphs. Readers who can't find the information within the first few paragraphs can get frustrated and swipe away. Many of BBC's stories begin with bullet points that highlight key details.

They've become accustomed to getting the most up-to-date details at their fingertips. The trick for journalists then is to find the proper balance between sharing the latest information quickly and taking the time to make sure it's accurate.

Unfortunately, some outlets have lost sight of providing consistent quality content for those accessing content on mobile devices and social media platforms. The use of clickbait, for instance, has compromised quality. Clickbait, which we explore in Chapter 6, is sensational content shared on social media that is intended to drive traffic to a website and increase the number of social media shares and likes. The content is often gimmicky and lacks journalistic value. The audience is smart. They know when they're being fed bait. It's a sure way to break trust. Maintaining journalistic integrity is imperative, or else the public may respond with distrust, ultimately undermining the profession and making it more difficult to attract an audience.

Knowing your audience is key to providing valuable content and building trust. News outlets have mounds of data about audience habits and demographics that help guide editorial strategies. For example, NPR uses this data to build audience affinity for content on its NPR One app. The app emphasizes quality local content because that's what listeners are telling NPR they want.

"One of the biggest indicators of people coming back to NPR more often is the presence of a local newscast. If you hear a local newscast, you come back more often," said Sara Sarasohn (@SaraKeiko), NPR One managing director. "It's not just us saying local is important—we follow our audience, their behaviors, and our audience is *telling* us that local is important: When people don't hear local stuff, they say, 'Where's my local station?!'"[29]

Of course, the hope is that listeners value this content enough to open up their wallets and support their local NPR station.

Positive Audience Experience. Quality content alone isn't enough to keep the audience coming back for more. The content is only as good as the audiences' experience with it on different platforms. In order to have a positive experience, the audience needs to be able to easily access content across devices and platforms.

With so many people getting news via mobile and social media, they're now evaluating news sources' competency on these platforms. As Table 2.1 shows, a majority of digital news consumers cite factors related to news presentation and delivery as

TABLE 2.1

The Media Insight Project shows that news consumers value content that provides a seamless experience and can be easily accessed.

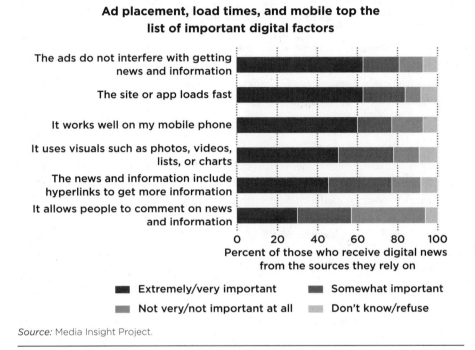

Ad placement, load times, and mobile top the list of important digital factors

Percent of those who receive digital news from the sources they rely on

- ■ Extremely/very important
- ■ Somewhat important
- ■ Not very/not important at all
- ■ Don't know/refuse

Source: Media Insight Project.

critical to whether they trust a news source. The audience can be left frustrated by ads that interfere with viewing news, websites or apps that load slowly, and sites that don't work well on mobile devices.

These stumbling blocks make people question the value of a news outlet. And you risk losing them for good.

"If a news source or a website doesn't have a mobile version, I don't know why but I just feel like I don't even want to read it," said Tanushree, who took part in the study by the Media Insight Project.[30] "It makes me feel like if you don't have a mobile version, you're not keeping up with the times. It just makes me not want to go to the website. It makes me question it."

The layout of stories is also important to perfecting the audience experience and preventing people from swiping away from your work. Including visuals, such as lists and photos, in stories can enhance the experience. These elements help to break up the story text, making the content easily digestible and visually appealing for people viewing on small screens. Chapter 6 includes tips on optimizing your writing and story layout for mobile devices users.

Personalization is another way outlets are trying to create a positive experience in which people feel like they can't live without their content. Many news apps allow users to customize their experience by selecting which types of stories they're interested in and the types of news alerts they wish to receive. In addition, some outlets are using technology that monitors what people read to automatically personalize which stories show up for them on a website or app.

Selling an "experience" across platforms is an important part of an outlet's strategy. Just take a look at how the *Chicago Tribune* pitches its digital subscription. The *Tribune* highlights the value—through experiences—it offers customers:

> Subscription includes the eNewspaper, a copy of the daily *Chicago Tribune* delivered to you digitally every morning, and the *Chicago Tribune* App, an enhanced mobile experience for your smartphone and tablet. Plus subscribers receive exclusive benefits such as access to subscriber-only experiences and special discounts.[31]

Authentic Engagement. The other important piece of a mobile and social media strategy is authentic engagement. Authentic engagement with the audience builds trust. Journalists can act as a trusted source by listening and responding to the audience. That's why social media sites are such a critical platform for journalists. They are the places where you can have genuine interactions with the public.

Social media offers something that traditional platforms and newsrooms previously lacked—the more informal two-way conversation we discussed in Chapter 1. News can no longer "lecture." People expect to be part of a conversation. They value being heard. Think about a trusted relationship. It's as much about listening as it's about talking.

Authentic engagement includes what is called "social listening." Social listening is the idea that journalists not only promote their work and share information, but also listen and respond to what people have to say on social media. Responding to feedback, asking questions, crowdsourcing stories, and holding live online Q&As are just a few ways to make your audience feel like you care about them.

These interactions, this partnership, presents an opportunity to strengthen journalism. Journalists can better understand the wants and needs of the audience. In turn, bringing the audience into the journalistic process shows that you value their input and can leave them feeling more invested in your work.

But it's about delivering more than just a tangible "product." In a study I conducted about social media use in TV newsrooms, one manager stressed this point: "Social media allows people to have a personal and emotional connection to our newscasts and station."[32]

This connection can help set you apart from the competition, which is more important now than ever. Remember, people have plenty of options for news.

Audience engagement is so important that newsrooms now have full-time staff dedicated to this role. Among many responsibilities, they strategize the best type of content for different social media platforms and monitor analytics that measure how users respond to the content. But the responsibility doesn't fall just on their shoulders. Social media engagement requires all hands on deck in newsrooms.

Fostering and managing these conversations is a routine part of journalists' tasks. In fact, as the next chapter addresses, social media sites have created an opportunity for individual journalists to develop their own brands based on the value they bring to these online networks.

The trust you build with your online community can make you the go-to source for information. That's because with the overload of information—and misinformation—on social media, people still rely on trusted news sources. The Media Insight Project found that news consumers on social media look for cues to overcome skepticism about content they see there and to decide what to click. People judge the validity of news on social media based on the original source of the information and the credibility of the person who shared it.

"As such, their decisions to trust any piece of news in the moment actually has roots in a longer relationship with the person or brand who shared and originated it," says journalist Josh Stearns (@jcstearns).[33] That bodes well for journalists who put time and effort into ongoing interactions with the audience.

A final note about authentic engagement: It can foster a community. Newsrooms are tapping into social media's potential for creating communities around shared interests and passions. Take for example the Central New York Nostalgia site launched by Syracuse.com and the *Post-Standard*. (By the way, a former student in my mobile and social media journalism course leads this project.) Central New York Nostalgia digs into the newspaper's archives to engage modern-day audiences. The site highlights vintage images and memories, such as "the day Babe Ruth stopped traffic in Syracuse."

Central New York Nostalgia creates an emotional experience and connection with the audience. The site has people feeling, well, nostalgic. They're contributing their own photos, stories, and sentimental thoughts to the comments section of the site and on social media. The Central New York Nostalgia team reaches out to social media circles that would be interested in the content, including the Facebook group Nostalgic Syracuse. This helps keep the conversation going and encourages people to share the content among their circle of friends. Community can be powerful.

In the end, this **authentic engagement**, a **positive audience experience**, and **quality content** are the key pillars of an editorial strategy that can keep the audience coming back for more and ultimately sustain journalism.

The Power of Social Media Providers

"I get my news from social media."

You've undoubtedly heard someone say this. But there's more to this statement than might initially meet the eye. Who is providing the news—I'm not talking about photos from your friend's birthday bash—that people come across on social media? Journalists. The positive aspect of this trend is that audiences worldwide continue to consume and value news from journalists.

What has changed is how information flows from the journalists and newsrooms to the audience. The social media giants, from Facebook to Snapchat, play a key role in connecting audiences to journalists' content. These platform providers have significant power—they have access to the audiences that news outlets need to survive and to some extent what content users see.

Because of this, news organizations are rethinking their relationships with social media companies. It's the topic of much discussion right now in the industry, and one you should pay close attention to. More and more editorial strategies include collaboration with social media providers.

For instance, Facebook Instant Articles allow newsrooms to publish full stories directly to Facebook. Users can view the articles without having to click on a link or leave the Facebook app. The articles are optimized for mobile viewing and load as much as 10 times faster than a standard web article. Newsrooms report that Instant Articles has resulted in three to four times the traffic they would expect to get from stories.[34] Views of Instant Articles are counted as regular website traffic, which is key for attracting advertisers. Facebook is also paying newsrooms, including NPR, to experiment with its Facebook Live streaming feature. Journalists can use Facebook Live as an informal way to engage followers through in-the-moment videos that show up in their news feeds.

In addition, Snapchat has created opportunities for bigger media outlets to produce stories specifically for its platform. Snapchat Discover is the "newsier" side of the app that's so popular among millennials. Open up Snapchat, swipe over to the Discover section, and you'll find crisply edited videos customized for the small screen. CNN, the *Wall Street Journal*, and Vice are a few of the news outlets that provide Snapchat Discover stories. Snapchat has a team, including staffers with the titles of news producer and story editor, dedicated to its news content. Some newsrooms have also created positions focused on strategizing and creating Snapchat stories.

A downside to social media providers' role in the news distribution process is the filtering of content. Some social media companies control which news shows up in users' feeds. Facebook, for example, uses an algorithm, a mathematical formula that predicts what will appeal to individuals. Even though journalists and newsrooms can post their own content directly to Facebook, it doesn't always make it through "the gates." Let's say someone "likes" your newsroom's Facebook page. You might expect every time an item is posted to that page, it will show up in the feeds of people who've "liked" your station's page. That's not the case. The Facebook algorithm places only certain stories in followers' feeds.

The idea of journalists' work being filtered in this way makes some in the industry uneasy. Newsrooms no longer have sole control of how news is distributed, and it demonstrates how powerful social media companies are. This power shift beckons the reimagining of outlets' relationships with the audience and social

Fake News

"Real" journalism is now competing with "fake news." An entire industry of fake news websites popped up during the 2016 US presidential campaign. Some social media users were duped into sharing this information because they thought it was real. Others knowingly shared the bogus information because it affirmed how they felt about a candidate even though the content was inaccurate. Fake news has become part of a broader discussion about media literacy, the value society places on facts, and the role of social media providers in filtering this type of content. At the time of this writing, Facebook and Google had just released plans to crack down on phony news stories. The content is not only being shared on Facebook and other social media platforms, but has also turned up high in Google search results.

media providers—that includes letting go of the traditional notion of news media as gatekeepers of information.

What's so interesting is that social media platforms were never intended for news. Take Snapchat—this certainly was not launched as a place to get news. Yet, since these are the places where so many people are living out their lives, they've become the go-to platforms for news distribution and engagement. We need to meet the audience where they're hanging out.

Different Platforms, Different Approaches

In order to be successful at engaging people on social media, you must know more about these digital water coolers and who's hanging out at them. Each social media site is like a different water cooler. What you share with coworkers is going to be different from your chat over dinner with good friends. The same can be said for social media.

Each platform requires a different approach. What works on Twitter won't work on Facebook, and what works on Facebook won't work for Snapchat.

NBC News correspondent Hallie Jackson (@Hallie Jackson) follows a platform-specific approach. "For example, on Snapchat I try to make that 'newsy,' but also a fun, personal way to interact with people. Snapchat is a very informal platform," said Jackson. "On Twitter, I'm trying to provide context and analysis to different parts of a speech or what voters are telling me in the field."

When determining the proper approach, the main items to keep in mind are **demographics, style**, and **time of posts.**

Demographics. Who are you trying to reach on each site? That depends on demographic factors, such as age and gender, of users on different social media. Table 2.2 shows the demographic breakdown of top social networking sites. While there's some crossover, each site appeals to a somewhat different group. Instagram news consumers are different from other groups because they're more likely to be nonwhite, young, and female.[35] Knowing this type of data can help you tailor content to appeal to different audiences on each platform.

Style. The platform will also determine the style of content you post. Each site has distinct features and a unique culture of users. For example, Snapchat users expect visual and fast-paced stories. These stories typically include emojis, filters, and colorful text that you can draw with a finger. The style of Snapchat content could catch your Facebook followers off guard, if you were to post the same story there.

"Snap-Checking the N.H. Democratic debate. February 5, 2016. *Washington Post.*

The *Washington Post*'s Michelle Ye Hee Lee used Snapchat to report on her fact checking of two claims Democrats Hillary Clinton and Bernie Sanders made during a debate in February 2016. To view the Snapchat story, visit *bitly.com/Snapchecking.* The style of storytelling is quite different on Snapchat than other platforms.

TABLE 2.2

The demographic of users on different social networking sites.

Demographic profile of social networking site news users
% of news users of each site who are . . .

	Facebook	YouTube	Twitter	Instagram	LinkedIn	All U.S. Adults
Male	43%	57%	47%	35%	56%	48%
Female	57	43	53	65	44	52
18–29	31	38	38	58	20	22
30–49	38	30	39	28	46	34
50–64	22	23	19	12	24	26
65+	8	9	3	2	11	19
High school or less	33	34	17	28	8	41
Some college	34	41	38	41	26	31
College degree	33	25	45	31	65	28
White, non-Hispanic	65	55	61	40	65	65
Non-white	34	44	38	57	34	35
Republican	22	21	19	14	23	25
Democrat	31	29	31	40	29	30
Independent	32	31	31	27	34	31

Note: "All U.S. Adults" figures based on non-institutionalized, 18 and older U.S. adults.

Source: Survey conducted Jan. 12–Feb. 8, 2016. "News Use Across Social Media Platforms 2016" Pew Research Center, Washington, DC (May, 2016) http://www.journalism .org/2016/07/07/pathways-to-news/

"I try to adjust to Snapchat's voice, and it's just about finding how people communicate on that specific medium to keep viewers engaged and informed," says Michelle Ye Hee Lee (@myhlee), of the *Washington Post*.[36] As a reporter for the *Post*'s fact checker team, Lee has been experimenting with Snapchat to deliver political fact checking to a younger demographic.

The best social media network to share breaking news? Twitter. Nearly six in ten Twitter news users turn to the site to keep up with developing news.[37] That's nearly double the percentage of Facebook news users. This data reveals the distinct strength of Twitter as a reporting tool during live events. A constant stream of posts about breaking news on Twitter fits with the culture of that space. On Facebook, that approach, one post after another in a short time span, might leave your followers annoyed.

Time of posts.   With mobile devices in hand, people are "snacking" on social media content throughout the day. But according to research by the Reuters Institute for the Study of Journalism, there are three periods when they're more likely to engage with digital content: first thing in the morning, lunchtime, and early evening.[38] Perhaps you want to ask a question related to a story. Four-thirty in the afternoon might not be the best time, as many people are wrapping up their works days and getting ready to commute home. Of course, news never stops. So the timing of when you post certain information will depend more on whether the news event warrants it and less on the time periods when people are most active online.

As you can see, the differences based on **demographics**, **style**, and **time of posts** help to clarify the role each platform plays in the news landscape. However, this data is only one piece of the puzzle. These are general guidelines. There's no one-size-fits-all approach. So much of this is about experimentation.

In Chapter 6, we'll explore how to access your own analytics for each of your social media networks. I have created an analytics checklist for you in that chapter. This data is eye-opening. You'll be able to see the demographic of your followers and how they're responding to what you share, among other metrics. Analyzing this data is a good habit to get into, because it will alert you to whether your social media efforts are paying off. What's working? What needs improvement? It all goes back to knowing your audience so you can serve them best.

Checklist

✓ **Mobile and Social Media Strategy Analysis.** Working in teams, assess the mobile and social media activity of one news outlet and two of its journalists. For at least a month, but ideally during most of your semester, monitor the outlet's and the journalists' approaches to new media. As you learn more practical skills in future chapters, evaluate their approaches based on those additional concepts. At the end of the time period, present your findings to your classmates. Discuss what the outlet and its reporters did well and what they could do better. Provide specific examples in your presentation. Here are some suggestions to get you started:

> What's the outlet's business model? How does it make money? Reference the section of this chapter on evolving business models for guidance.

> Which platforms are the outlet and the two journalists active on? Make an inventory, and regularly check their activity on those spaces (website, mobile app, social media, and traditional print or broadcast).

> Note how they use different platforms. Is there a different approach on each social media platform? Different style of content? What is your experience with the content? Is it mobile-friendly? Is it engaging? How do they engage with followers?

> Contact one of the journalists whose activity you're monitoring or a staff member who manages the outlet's digital efforts. Chat with this person about his or her strategy, and integrate portions of the interview into your class presentation.

✓ **Discussion.** View the latest "State of the News Media" report from the Pew Research Center at *journalism.org*.

> What does the report tell us about audience news consumption habits? How about business models and economic trends in different sectors of the industry?

> How does the latest "State of the News Media" compare to the results of the previous year's?

Your Social Media Brand: Who Do You Want to Be?

3

Remember: Whatever happens in Vegas . . . stays on Google.[1]

— SCOTT MONTY, COMMUNICATIONS
CONSULTANT AND FORBES TOP 10
SOCIAL MEDIA INFLUENCERS

In this chapter, you will

- Explore how social media provides journalists the opportunity to build a brand through the type of information they share and their interactions with the public.

- Examine online presence as an extension of your reputation as a journalist. It's your digital business card.

- Discover how using social media in journalistic ways will make your brand stand out to potential employers as well.

- Learn how to conduct a social media audit and steps to build your brand as a journalist.

SOCIAL MEDIA BRANDING AND JOURNALISM

If I were to do a Google search of your name, what would turn up on the Internet? I've never met you before. But those tweets, snappy Instagram videos, and bio descriptions all add up to convey who you are. That's your brand.

What comes to mind when you hear the name Anderson Cooper? Robin Roberts? Bob Woodward? Brian Williams? The images you conjure up in your mind are their brands. And if you've never heard of these journalists, you'll probably search online, where what you come across will give you a first impression of them—of their brand.

Brand and *branding* are terms people typically associate with marketing and advertising. Some journalists turn their noses up at the idea of branding in journalism. But step away from the preconceived notion of what a brand is.

In reality, journalists have always built an individual brand based on the quality and style of their writing, reporting, and delivery, among other factors. (Bob Woodward, for instance, created a brand for himself long before the Internet and social media existed.) Journalists' brands have traditionally been tied to their affiliations with news organizations.

Today, mobile and social media allow journalists to build their own brands by sharing their work directly with the audience and fostering an informal relationship with them. Journalists don't have to rely solely on the outlet they work for to find a following for their reporting. The brand they establish though their online presence can make them a go-to source for information. In turn, this also benefits their news outlets.

You too have been establishing your individual brand. Every tweet, like, and comment is a reflection of who you are. When you apply for a job in journalism, or even an internship, you can expect hiring managers to scrutinize your social media profiles. The result of a Google search is the new resume—a digital business card, if you will. What you've posted can come back to haunt you. It also can set you apart from the competition by demonstrating you know how to use mobile and social media in smart ways, as a journalist.

Your online presence and digital savvy will be a key part of interviews for journalism jobs. I frequently hear from current and former students who share interesting information about the process. One senior who applied for a TV reporting position in a small market was given a breaking news scenario. He was then asked to write a TV story and a web version based on the scenario, in addition to crafting posts for Facebook and Twitter. A student who interviewed for a prestigious journalism fellowship had her social media accounts dissected by members of the hiring committee. They asked questions about her approach on different social media platforms as well as about how she uses mobile devices in the field. Fortunately, the students were well versed in the tools of the trade, and their online presence shined. Both were offered the positions. (Chapter 8 outlines what to expect during the job hunt and interview process.)

Now is the time to start taking ownership of your brand across all platforms. Even though you're a digital native (you grew up with these tools at your fingertips), do you know how to use them as a professional journalist? That's key.

The goal from here on out in this book is to build your journalistic skills with mobile and social media in three areas: newsgathering, distribution of news, and audience engagement. We start in this chapter by getting you going on creating a solid foundation—your own brand.

Key Points about Building Your Brand

- **Go-to source.** Journalists can use social media to build a tribe for their work. Become an audience's trusted source for credible information by providing quality content and interactions.

- **Real person.** Engage authentically and conversationally to create meaningful connections with users. Be professional, but don't be afraid to show your personality.

- **Traditional journalistic standards.** If you wouldn't say it to your audience in person, don't post it on social media. Your social media presence is an extension of your reputation as a journalist.

- **Slow and steady.** Building your brand takes time and requires consistency across platforms.

- **Digital business card.** Using digital tools in journalistic ways will make your brand stand out to potential employers as well.

DIGITAL SKELETONS: SOCIAL MEDIA AUDIT

Have you Googled yourself recently? Not at all? Now is the time to clean up your past. After all, 93 percent of managers say they review job candidates' professional social media profiles prior to hiring.[2] What they find could determine whether or not you get an offer. Fifty-five percent have reconsidered a candidate based on information they got online.

A social media audit will shed light on your digital footprint and help put your best foot forward. As part of this chapter's checklist, you'll also team up with a classmate to audit each other's profiles.

Search

First, conduct a search of your name using at least two search engines. Use Google and Bing or Yahoo, as these are the three most-used sites for searches. Odds are someone sniffing around for information about you would turn to these sites.

- Log out of e-mail accounts and clear your web browser history. This will give you a better sense of what someone searching your name encounters—what's making it to the public. Search engines tailor results based on your browsing history and other information that's part of your digital viewing. If you're logged into personal accounts and haven't cleared your history, the results may be different from what potential employers see when they search.

- Search your name. If you have a common name, enter more specific information. For example, let's say you're John Smith, a student from Champaign, Illinois, who's studying at the University of Texas at Austin. Try several different search terms, such as John Smith and Champaign, Illinois and John Smith and University of Texas at Austin, to weed out results for other people with the same name.

- Moment of truth. Don't stop at the first page of results. That's only part of your digital story. It's equally important to click on the Images, Videos, and News tabs located at the top of most search engines. You'll see content specific to your name and those three areas. When I have students conduct these audits, this is the point where I usually hear some of them cringe a bit, most commonly because the results turn up photos posted to Facebook, even if someone else tagged them. They're not necessarily inappropriate photos, but the surprise comes from the fact that these can be picked up by search engines for anyone to see.

There's typically another camp of students surprised at how little the results say about who they are. These students usually have social media accounts, but are inactive on the platforms. For aspiring journalists or journalists looking for a job, social media *inactivity* can also influence your social media brand. Your use of mobile and social media on a consistent basis will make you appear more engaged and more attractive on the job market. Odds are if it comes down to two candidates, one using social media in smart ways versus another who hasn't touch social media in a while, the former is going to get the job.

- Now, visit each of your social media pages and other digital spaces, such as a website, associated with your name. To view each as the public would, sign out of each account. Having classmates who are not friends or don't follow you on these accounts conduct searches is also beneficial. They can stay logged into their accounts on Facebook and Twitter, for instance, to check what they're able to see about you.

In addition, Facebook has a feature that allows you to view what your page looks like to other people. While signed in to Facebook, locate the Privacy Shortcuts menu button at the top right of your screen. Go to the "Who can see my stuff?" section, and choose "What do other people see on my timeline? View As." You'll see what your profile looks like to the public. To view how your profile appears to a specific person and what they can access, click "View as Specific Person" at the top of the page and type their names.

Analyze and Act

At this point, you should analyze what your searches revealed. Here are key questions to reflect on when auditing your online brand.

- **About you.** Are your bios informative and consistent across platforms? Do they tell us who you are? Does a professional photo accompany your bios?
- **Content.** What type of content do you typically share? Is it an accurate reflection of your interests as a journalist? Of your general interests? Both?
- **Frequency.** How often do you post on each platform? How often do you engage with followers?
- **Personality.** What do your posts say about you? Do we get a sense of you as a person?
- **Professional interests.** What about your professional interests? Have you highlighted your journalism skills and career aspirations?
- **Journalism skills.** Speaking of skills, do posts show any sign that you use social media for finding story ideas and sources, sharing interesting content—including your own reporting, and engaging with your followers?

If your brand doesn't reflect who you are as a journalist, there are specific actions to get you on track to building a standout online presence. More on that in the next section of this chapter.

I posted that! Now what? If you find something that you now regret sharing, deleting the post is your best option. But don't assume it will be gone for good. It will take at least a few weeks for the item to no longer be picked up in search engines. Keep in mind, people may not know the context around that photo or video you posted. So if you think it would make your grandmother cringe or question why you posted it, get rid of it.

I recommend deleting inactive accounts—those that you haven't touched in a while, as long as they're not needed as part of your professional brand. (A list of important platforms is addressed below.) Let's say you created a website in high school, but haven't updated it since. As time goes on, this will reflect an outdated version of you. If you don't plan on using this website as part of your professional work, consider deleting it. The other option: Breathe new life into an old website by using it as the centralized place to highlight your work, as we'll discuss shortly.

Some items are difficult to get rid of. Do an Internet search of the name: Vandon Gene. You'll easily discover how this self-described aspiring journalist, who worked for a Canadian news station, has made a name for himself. And not in a good way. While covering a deadly shooting in Ottawa, Gene asked CNN's Anderson Cooper to take a selfie. Cooper rejected the request, saying it would be wildly inappropriate, considering the context. But Gene, with his mobile phone recording, wouldn't back down. He continued to insist Cooper take a selfie with him. Gene posted the video to YouTube and turned to Twitter to lambast Cooper. Gene was let go from the news outlet, and that incident will forever be part of his digital business card.

This case underscores the importance of acting appropriately on and off line. Journalists are accountable to the public. Journalism relies on the trust of the public. What you post on social media can easily break that trust, undermining your reputation and that of the industry. As we discuss in greater detail in Chapter 7, crossing the line on social media can ruin your brand and your reputation, and cost you your job. Anything that would make the public question your integrity, ethics, and general professionalism as a journalist should be avoided. That's why scrutinizing your social media activity is so important.

Assume Everything Is Public

But it's only accessible to my friends. Not true.

You should assume everything you post online is in the public domain—for good. Even the strictest privacy settings on your social media accounts don't ensure your content is locked down. Everything you post is fair game. You don't have any reasonable expectation of privacy on social networking platforms. A photo of you posted behind the wall can easily be downloaded by a friend and shared with anyone.

You also have very little control over what someone else posts about you. Certainly, if a friend tags you in a photo or posts something of you that's undesirable, you can ask the friend to untag or take it down. But you can't undo the potential harm done if the post doesn't portray you positively. A few social media platforms, including Facebook, allow you to approve or reject being tagged in posts. You must first activate this feature in your account settings.

From the Newsroom

JUSTIN AUCIELLO (@AUCIELLO)

Founder, Jersey Shore Hurricane News

Freelance journalist Justin Auciello (@auciello) has carved out a niche by building a brand on social media. Around the time Hurricane Irene hit in 2011, Auciello launched a Facebook page, Jersey Shore Hurricane News, and related Twitter account, @JSHurricaneNews. Jersey Shore Hurricane News became the go-to community resource. Its popularity grew after Superstorm Sandy devastated the Jersey Shore in 2012. His social media–only outlet was a lifeline for people who needed information about their homes, communities, and loved ones.

The Facebook page has more than 245,000 followers. Auciello's work attracted a following by focusing on hyperlocal issues that many mainstream media outlets no longer covered with consistency in the months and years following the disasters. He has filled a desperately needed void in the communities. The platform was even used by the New Jersey Office of Emergency Management to communicate with people who needed to be rescued, as 911 was overloaded.

HOW DID YOU COME UP WITH THE IDEA FOR JERSEY SHORE HURRICANE NEWS?

It really started when I got on Twitter in 2007 and I saw the emergence of citizen journalists. The emergence of technology to facilitate not only the sharing of info, but also the collaboration—doing journalism by piecing together information gleaned from eyewitnesses on the ground and using that to build a report. I had been into social networking even before social media. The trigger was when I saw the potential with Twitter and began to build my personal brand as someone interested in emerging media. I started to blog about the changing media landscape and how citizen journalists could play a part.

When the moment came in August 2011, you can say I was prepared in a sense. When Irene was coming, I said this was an opportunity to create a pop-up news outlet that is two-way and can democratize news where I live, because there was nothing else that existed at that point. It caught on very quickly because of Facebook. People were desperate for information. I came in and let people know that I needed their information and I would package that with traditional journalistic methods and standards. It snowballed from there. After Irene, I had first thought this would only last for a few days, but people kept hanging around. It turned into something that was beyond just a hurricane. It turned into daily news, traffic, weather, et cetera. The takeaway is that once the community was connected to Jersey Shore Hurricane News and found value in the content, it unfolded organically.

WHAT'S YOUR EDITORIAL PROCESS? HOW DO YOU CURATE THE CONTENT AND FACT-CHECK?

On a day-to-day basis, there's about one breaking news story in this area—for example, a car accident with a fire that shuts down a major road. In a case like that, I couple content from official sources and social media users to piece together a narrative and verify information. Because I'm cynical at first and doubt everything, like any good journalist should be, I fact-check in a few ways. I get information from official sources to corroborate what I'm being told and see if anyone else on social media is sharing something similar. Giving people credit also fosters a trusting relationship, making them more likely to send content that is reliable. I give credit to contributors in order to reinforce that they're part of the team. It's a social contract. People love it and are more willing to engage in the future.

HOW CAN STUDENT JOURNALISTS BUILD A BRAND USING SOCIAL MEDIA?

Write a lot, and publish it. Create a blog where you can share your best content. Be active on social media. That's a given. But many people don't use social media for community building, so be in tune with how to do that on social media. To build a community you need a specific focus. It could be a very niche community or topic. Focus on what interests you. Know enough about the area or topic to be somewhat of a go-to expert for people.

For me, I was familiar with the Jersey shore, so that played a key role in engaging with people in such a way based on my knowledge and passion for the area. Now, people reach out to me for anything going on in this area. Stay true to the focus.

Jersey Shore Hurricane News.

BUILDING A SOCIAL MEDIA BRAND

Your brand is built over time by your behaviors. The content you post and your interactions—both good and bad—all make up your online reputation. In this section, you'll learn to how to craft your professional social media brand.

So now is a good time to think about who you want to be as a journalist. When people see your name or come across your Twitter account, what do you want them to think of? Keep that question at the forefront of your mind as you fine-tune your digital footprint.

Separate Personal and Professional Accounts?

I'm frequently asked: Should I create separate profiles for my personal and professional activity? Having only private accounts would defeat the purpose of a journalist's use of social media. These profiles would be accessible to friends only.

As a journalist, you need to optimize your profiles so anyone can follow and engage with you.

The best approach is to have one account for each platform, but it's a personal decision, and there are varying views depending on who you ask. Managing both personal and professional pages on a variety of social media platforms can be time consuming. Maintaining one account on each key platform simplifies your digital life.

In addition, what are you posting on a private personal page that can't be shared on the public one? Again, this goes back to the basic concept that everything you post should be considered public.

There's one exception: Facebook. Facebook has an option for brands—journalists, businesses, politicians, and the like—to create professional pages. This approach has advantages for a number of reasons, mainly because professional pages offer an analytics feature, something personal pages do not. In the addition, the Facebook culture is generally one where you share more personal moments with real-life friends and family. Photos of your summer vacation in Europe. A video remembrance of a family member who passed away. Sure, you may end up sharing some of this type of content with a general audience. But, simply put, some things are more private than others. For that reason, having a separate personal Facebook account is a logical choice.

The answer to whether you need to establish two separate accounts may also be determined by the policy of the newsroom where you work. According to a study conducted on newsroom social media policies, two-thirds of local television news managers said it's the policy of their station to own the professional social media accounts of reporters.[4] This type of policy is becoming common across the industry. In some cases, this means journalists are required to submit their passwords to newsroom management, and such a policy raises the question of whether employees are allowed to keep their accounts and associated followers when they leave the newsroom.

Facebook Privacy Settings

Check the privacy settings of your personal Facebook page. Recommendations for the most privacy:

- Allow only friends to see your stuff.
- Turn off the feature that allows search engines to include your personal Facebook page as part of search results.

- Enable reviewing of posts in which friends tag you before they show up on your timeline.
- Who can see posts you've been tagged in once you approve them? Limit to friends.

This policy alone may be enough to eventually force you to establish separate personal and professional accounts.

The Online Spaces You Should be in

Your professional online presence should consist of the following:

Website

A website serves as your portfolio. Create your own website to highlight your professional work and skills. It's the perfect place to publish your reporting for journalism classes. Include the website link in all your social media profiles and on your resume. When applying for jobs, the website serves as a centralized spot where hiring managers can quickly get a sense of you.

I recommend creating your site through WordPress (*wordpress.com*). I require my students, starting in their first year, to create a WordPress site. WordPress allows you to create a free account or purchase a premium plan that includes a more customized domain name. With the free version, *wordpress.com* is part of the website address. The paid version removes *wordpress* from the URL, creating a cleaner link (For example, *anthonyadornato.wordpress.com* versus *anthonyadornato.com*).

WordPress has a variety of website templates. Whichever platform you choose for a website should have built-in analytics. The analytics dashboard measures key metrics, as we discuss in Chapter 6, that you'll need to understand as a journalist. Without the analytics, it will be difficult to measure how website material is performing and what role your social media activity plays in driving traffic to your website.

- **Domain name.** A domain name is what people type into their browser to go to a site. It's your unique web address. When you set up a website, you'll be asked to select a domain name. Check whether a domain with your first and last name is available. A domain with your full name makes it more likely that your website will turn up when someone searches for you. If a domain with your full name is already taken, use only your last name. Still, no luck? Include your middle name or initial. Bottom line, keep your web address as close to your name as possible.

- **Home page.** This is the front page of your website. The welcome mat. By default, many website templates, including those from WordPress, publish posts (these are stories or blog posts) on the homepage. In your website settings, you can change the location of where your published posts appear. For example, you may want your About page to be the first thing people see when they come to your site and have your posts live on another page.

- **Site title.** A site title is important, because it's what appears in the header on a browser tab when someone visits a website. You can customize the site title in the settings section of your site. For branding purposes, using your first and last name makes most sense.

- **About page.** Include a short blurb about yourself and professional photo followed by your resume. Do not simply link to your resume or attach a file that someone has to download to view. Embed the resume in the page for easy viewing.

- **Contact page.** This is where you want to include your e-mail address and links to your professional social media accounts. Make sure you hyperlink the text. A hyperlink allows readers to simply click the text and be taken directly to the page you're linking to. Otherwise, they have to open a web browser and type in the information. This all goes back to making content user friendly.

- **Portfolio page.** Put links to your best work here. If you're just starting to get your feet wet in reporting, you may not have enough content for this page. No worries. Add this page later. It could be reporting you've done for a campus outlet, for a class, or during an internship. Include the title of the story, the outlet, and a hyperlink. I recommend listing stories on this page even if they're already published somewhere else on your website. This makes it easier for visitors to see your most compelling work compiled in one area.

- **Twitter widget.** Widgets are the featured elements typically located on the side of a website. The Twitter widget embedded on a site gives visitors a flavor of your social media activity. It displays your most recent tweets. These time-lines are interactive, so visitors can reply and retweet favorite tweets straight from your website. How you add a Twitter widget depends on the platform you use for a website (see your account's settings area).

Social Networking Platforms

Your profiles on these social networking sites should be open to the public: **Twitter**, **Facebook**, **Instagram**, **LinkedIn**, and **Snapchat**. Why these sites? They're the most frequently used by journalists and news organizations. And they're where audiences

Courtesy of Lacrai Mitchell.

Courtesy of Kelli Kyle.

Journalism students should create their own websites as a way to build their professional brands. These two websites are easy to navigate and give visitors a sense of who the journalists are. Notice the integration of social media on both websites.

are most active. (LinkedIn isn't necessarily a go-to place to distribute content, but it's a great tool for showcasing your brand, finding sources for stories, and networking for jobs, as we discuss in Chapters 4 and 8.)

Reminder: Create a professional Facebook page instead of using a personal one for your brand. To set up a professional Facebook page, go to *facebook.com/pages/create*. In the Artist, Band or Public Figure section, select the Journalist category. Enter your first and last names. In the next chapter, we dig into specifics of these social networks.

Whether you're creating new accounts or updating existing ones, make it your goal to maintain them beyond the semester. Carry these digital tools throughout your journalism studies and as you enter your career.

Video Sharing Sites

Create an account on YouTube or Vimeo. Either of these sites can serve as a centralized spot for video content you create. Video editing apps (Chapter 5) allow you to upload your finished video directly from a device to either of these sites. From there, you can embed the video in stories on a website and share to social media.

Creating Standout Social Media Profiles

Building the best version of you online begins with your profiles. Be consistent with how you present yourself—through your handles, profile and cover photos, and bios—across platforms.

Handles

Most people in the social media world know others by their handles. A handle is a username. In the professional world, you want to be recognized by your name. So when it comes to building your brand, choose a handle that is as close to your name as possible. Think @FirstnameLastname.

Username consistency also makes it easier for connections to find you in the social media sea. Ideally, when you choose a username, stick with it for all your accounts. If you previously chose a handle that has nothing to do with your brand, the good news is that many social networking sites allow you to edit it at any time.

A quick note about LinkedIn. The system automatically generates a unique link for you that doesn't include your name. You should edit your profile URL to include your name.

Profile and Cover Photos

A profile photo is the smaller thumbnail size image associated with your account. Some social networking sites also give you the option to upload a cover photo, larger images typically at the top of your profile page. Just as you would be careful to avoid errors on your resume or in a story you write, your profile and cover photos also need to be well thought out.[5] For starters, don't leave these spaces blank.

Profile Photo.   Would you go into a job interview looking the way you do in your profile photo? A single profile pic can impact the perception of you. Hiring managers are most likely to see you first in that format. As people scroll through their feeds, the profile photo is often how they determine who is sharing the content, and their perception of you impacts how they perceive that content. Choose a headshot photo that is professional and shoulders up so that people can easily recognize and see your face in the thumbnail pic.

Sree Sreenivasan (@sree), technology journalist and former Columbia University journalism professor, recommends this formula for a good profile photo:[6]

- Clear, recent close-up shot of your face
- No shots of you with a celebrity, national monument, pet, or child
- No wide shot of you at a landmark
- No hats, wigs, or sunglasses
- No tinting your photo (or putting a digital ribbon on it) in support of the cause du jour

Cover Photo.   A cover photo is an opportunity to give followers a visual sense of you as not only a journalist, but also a real person. Because of the large size of a cover photo in comparison to a profile pic, the image you choose must be of high quality. Otherwise, the photo might appear grainy. Here are some tips:

- Upload a photo that represents your work, but keep it authentic and not overly promotional. Use a photo from the field in order to highlight some of your recent reporting. Or give followers a behind-the-scene glimpse via a photo that shows the inside of the newsroom or studio.
- Think beyond your professional world. A cover photo with coffee would let me know that we have something in common. Enjoy traveling? Upload a photo of your latest destination. These types of images humanize you. Whatever you choose, make sure it's understandable to the audience.
- Avoid including text with your contact info here. Save that info for your written bio.
- Even if you have the highest Facebook privacy settings for a personal account, every Facebook cover photo is public.

Bios

Create two distinct bios. The first is a short version for your social media profiles. A longer bio will be used for your website and LinkedIn profiles.

Short Bio.   Your elevator pitch: short and sweet. You have 30 seconds to tell someone about yourself. In this case, you have a limited number of characters. On Twitter and Instagram, for instance, the character limit for a bio is 160 characters. It's more than just your followers who will look at your short bio. This bio will turn up in results when someone searches your name online.

- Think about **keywords that describe you professionally.** Try to include a few of those in the short bio. But be specific. If you cover arts and culture for a student newspaper, mention that. Don't simply write journalist or student at University of X. If you intern at a news outlet, tell us where by including the name.

- **What are you passionate about?** Drop a few hints about your interests beyond journalism. Mix in a snippet about you personally.

- **Avoid buzzwords.** There's a laundry list of words that are overused in profiles and resumes, so overused that they have little impact on the reader—words like *creative* and *innovative*.

- **Speak the social media language.** Use @mentions for specific names if possible. If your profile includes the names of your student media outlet or the place you intern, use their handles. For example, I cover life and culture for @IthacanOnline or sports intern @9News. It's important to use the proper handle for each platform. A newsroom's Twitter handle may be different from its Instagram handle (although for branding's sake, I hope not).

- It's critical to **include your website link.** Some sites have a specific section for this that doesn't count toward the character limit. Either way, every bio should link people back to your website.

- Don't forget to **include your location.**

Nancy Loo ✓
@NancyLoo

Reporter, @WGNMorningNews @WGNNews Chicago. Emmy winner. Scrabble & Social Media Nut. Oregon Duck. #ChicagonistaLIVE. #MsTech AKA #BigTiny nloo@wgntv.com

📍 Chicago
🔗 wgntv.com/bigtiny
📅 Joined July 2008

Nancy Loo's Twitter bio is personable and to-the-point. She also effectively uses @mentions and hashtags.

Longer Bio. What's your story? Here's a chance to tell more about yourself. A longer, more detailed bio can be used for your website's About page and the Summary section of your LinkedIn profile.

- **Writing in first person makes you feel more approachable.** This is *your* narrative.

- **Don't overload.** This is not the space for a list of activities and positions you've had. That's what a resume is for.

- **Show you can write.** Being able to write clearly and concisely is an important skill for journalists. Demonstrate your ability with how you craft the bio. Keep it short and succinct—maximum of roughly 200 words.

- **Tells us about your journey.** Your collective experiences in and out of school, personally and professionally, make you you. In general, this bio should highlight your professional interests, give a brief recap of experiences, and tell

ABOUT

Emily is a May 2015 graduate of Ithaca College's Roy H. Park School of Communications. She holds a Bachelor of Arts in journalism with a minor in sport studies. Emily currently works as a digital editor at Aggrego, in Chicago, Illinois. Emily creates content, manages social accounts and generates engagement on posts about news, sports and entertainment. She has previously interned at Aggrego in Chicago, Illinois, Townsquare Media in Oneonta, New York, Amref Health Africa in London, U.K. and syracuse.com in Syracuse, New York, as part of Advance Local's flagship internship program. Emily is also a former staff writer, assistant and editor of *The Ithacan*, Ithaca College's award-winning, student-run newspaper where she won a 2013 *New York Press Association* award for best sports coverage. During the 2014–2015 academic year, Emily worked as a writer/editor at Ithaca College's Office of Marketing Communications where her pieces were published in *IC View* and *Fuse* magazines. She enjoys cooking, eating and Amy Poehler.

Emily Hull's website bio is a good mix of her professional story, skills, and interests.

us something that shows you're multidimensional.[7] Personalize your story. Consider sharing what fueled your interest in journalism or how you spend your off time.

- **Show us, don't just tell.** Use specific examples to back up the claims you make about yourself. If you're interested in environmental reporting, for instance, briefly describe an issue or story you've covered.

- By the same token, **don't overhype.** Have the goods to back up your portrayal of yourself. If you interned at a TV network, don't write that you've worked for the network. That comes across as deceptive.

- Unlike your short bio for social media, **don't use @mentions here**. It's not the style of this type of profile.

Consistency

Now that you've created accounts and fine-tuned your profiles, be consistent across platforms. First, use the same profile photos, handle, and bios for each site. Revisit these profiles at least three times a year to make sure they accurately reflect you at that point in time. Rejuvenate profiles as circumstances change, such as when you get a new job or complete your degree.

Also, take small steps each day to be active on social networking platforms. Creating an online presence and then abandoning it can appear worse than not having one at all. When a journalist or journalism student has a Twitter account but hasn't posted in months or even weeks, that simply doesn't look good to the audience or a potential employer.

Come up with a routine, and it will become second nature after a while. Start by building time into your day to manage social media platforms. At a minimum, check social media platforms first thing in the morning, midday, and evening. That includes not only posting fresh content, but also engaging with followers by replying to their posts, sharing others' content, and asking questions.

What does posting regularly mean? It's different for each platform. As we discussed in Chapter 2, some sites are intended for less frequent posts. As a journalist, the type of story you're covering will also factor into how frequently you share. Breaking news warrants more updates than a feature story. There's no magic formula for how frequently you should post on each site. Much of it comes down to experimentation.

Here are general recommendations to get you started:

- **Facebook**—at least once every other day
- **Twitter**—at least three times per day
- **Instagram**—one to two times per week
- **Snapchat**—one to two stories per week
- **LinkedIn**—once per week
- **Website**—at least two stories and/or blog posts per week

Checklists in future chapters include reminders for staying active on each social networking platform and your website.

Think before You Post

Don't post to simply post. Have something valuable to share. Even more importantly as a journalist, know where to draw the line when sharing personal thoughts and details of your life. As you prepare for a career in journalism, now is the time to think before you post that type of content.

As individuals, we all have our own opinions on topics. And it has become standard for people to share those thoughts on social media. But, as journalists, we have an obligation to try to remain unbiased, fair, and objective. Apply traditional journalistic standards. Just as it would be inappropriate for journalists to place political signs in their front yard, the same standard applies to online platforms.

As noted in the social media policy for student journalists at Arizona State University's Walter Cronkite School of Journalism and Mass Communication, "actions that call into question a journalist's ability to report fairly on an issue harm not only that journalist but his or her news organization and fellow journalists."[8]

Indeed, it can be difficult to back down from posting personal thoughts about emotionally charged situations and issues, such as the 2016 shooting at an Orlando, Florida, nightclub that killed dozens of people. After the shooting, a *New York Times* editor sent a memo to staff members reminding them to avoid editorializing, promoting their political views or taking sides on hot-button issues, on social media.[9]

"Even if you personally are not involved in coverage of a particular topic, our colleagues are working hard to maintain the *Times*'s credibility and evenhandedness, and we should not do anything to make their jobs tougher. People following *Times* newsroom staffers online expect them to be well-informed and thoughtful," wrote Philip Corbett, associate managing editor for standards at the *Times*.

What Not to Share

The following items are most frequently included in news outlets' social media policies.[10] Sharing this type of personal content could jeopardize your chance of even getting an interview. Newsrooms do not want to take on the liability of having an employee whose actions, online or offline, could jeopardize the public's trust.

- Personal opinions about issues
- Political affiliation
- Religious beliefs
- Advocating on behalf of a particular cause or agenda
- Your involvement in illegal activity
- Unverified information from sources
- Internal newsroom communication
- Details of personal life beyond hobbies or interests

What to Share

As we've discussed, your social media activity should reflect your journalistic brand while also giving followers a flavor of you as a person. But what's the proper mix of professional and personal?

Consider the **80/20 rule of social media**. Keep 80 percent of your content professional related, but refrain from being overly promotional. The other 20 percent should show your personality.

In addition, the **rule of thirds for social media** is a surefire way to share the best mix of content, says Scott Kleinberg (@scottkleinberg), former social media manager at the *Chicago Tribune*.[11] One-third of the time, promote content related to your professional brand, another third of your posts should come from other sources, and the final third of the formula involves being human.

"I don't think in social media there is anything worse than following a feed that tweets the same thing all the time and never responds to your questions," says Kleinberg.[12]

Choose from this list to experiment with your own mix of professional and personal posts.

- Real-time updates while reporting in the field
- Behind-the-scenes look at the reporting process
- Links to your stories and/or blog posts
- Colleagues' stories and content from other credible sources
- Your own comments that provide context to social media posts that you share from credible sources.
- Your own questions, and responses ASAP to readers' questions
- What you're reading personally or professionally
- Hobbies and interests

Journalists' use of social media raises ethical considerations beyond what to share and not to share. For instance, liking a political candidate's Facebook page in order to stay abreast of campaign news could be misinterpreted. And is it appropriate to friend sources on Facebook? Chapter 7 delves deeper into these and many more ethical issues.

Become the Go-to Journalist

Social media affords journalists the opportunity to become a go-to source for information by owning a beat and cultivating a community online around a chosen topic. These activities define you as a brand.

Carve out a niche on a particular topic through:

- **Original reporting.** Write about stories in your local community on issues related to a beat.
- **Curating beat-related information.** Use blogging and social media activity to curate stories from other credible sources.
- **Sharing.** Use social media to share your original reporting and curated content.

Beat

Certainly, journalists must be well versed on a variety of topics. Often, they don't know what they might cover day to day. But it can also be professionally rewarding to focus some attention on one beat. Blogging and social media are ways for journalists to show they're knowledgeable in a subject area, helping to differentiate them from other reporters and sources in general.

This allows journalists to be part of a community around a specific topic. Developing these relationships will be mutually beneficial. People passionate about a journalist's given beat will turn to them first, share their work, and pass along story ideas.

It's never too early to test the waters. In my mobile and social media journalism course, students choose beats, ranging from disability to sustainability. Each student uses a combination of social media, blogging, and original reporting to build a portfolio of work around a beat. This is in addition to general assignment, or nonbeat, stories they're required to cover. The approach allows them to demonstrate their reporting versatility and an ability to dig deep into a given topic.

Curating beat-related information is an important part of the process. *Curation* is the gathering and sorting of fragmented pieces of information, and then providing analyses and context. Journalists have always served as curators of information, but it's even more critical today as people try to make sense of the overflow of content. That's where journalists focusing on a beat can be valuable. They do the work of sifting through the sea of noise and providing online communities with what they need to know. They create order among the chaos of information.

Brian Stelter (@brianstelter) is a textbook example of a journalist who created a brand and career around a specific topic. It all started from Stelter's dorm room in 2004 when he was a freshman at Towson University.[13] He launched a blog with news and commentary about news outlets' coverage of the Iraq War. He soon attracted a loyal audience, including TV industry executives. Stelter's work around a specific niche caught the eye of the *New York Times*. Straight out of college, he landed a position covering media for the *Times*. He continued to amass a following online through his social media savvy. Stelter is now CNN's senior media correspondent and host of its Reliable Sources program.

Freelance journalist Justin Auciello (@auciello) used social media to create a niche beat and community focused on the Jersey Shore area. See the From the Newsroom section above to learn more about Auciello's experience.

Blog

Writing blog posts regularly is a great way to show your enthusiasm for a beat. Your website can serve as the centralized location for these posts, along with your original reporting. Here are tips to get you started blogging about your beat.

- **Consistency.** Write a post at least twice per week.
- **Keep it tight.** No more than 350 words. Headlines should be self-explanatory and easy to understand. A headline is your promise to readers. Deliver on it. Get to the point immediately, and keep the post focused on your promise.
- **Scanning friendliness.** Online readers skim impatiently to find information. Use short paragraphs, headings, bulleted or numbered lists, and pull quotes. These elements make reading much easier, especially on mobile devices. They serve as guideposts for readers.
- **Visuals.** Use pictures, video, and graphics in your posts. Visuals make posts more engaging and also break up text. Don't simply grab an image online. You may violate copyrights (Chapter 7), and that practice is unethical. You can either ask for permission from the original source or search the Creative Commons website (*search.creativecommons.org*). Content licensed under Creative Commons can be used as long as you properly credit the source. Each piece of Creative Commons content has instructions on how to attribute the material. This is a very helpful resource if you need an image to accompany a web story or blog post.
- **Reader engagement.** Your writing should spark a dialogue. Each post should make it clear you're open to interaction. To generate thoughtful discussion, consider asking a question that invites readers to comment. Remember to respond to comments.
- **Show your style.** Writing conversationally and in first person bring readers closer to you and the content. Write as if you're having a chat with a friend.
- **Research/informational value.** Don't merely regurgitate what others are saying. Nudge the conversation along by providing thoughtful analysis. Use credible sources, and avoid sharing your opinion.
- **Link.** Hyperlinking to the sources you reference is a general rule of thumb on the web. It's a way to give a hat tip to other sources. Links also provide an easy way for readers to check out what or who you're mentioning.
- **Keywords.** Place keywords in your headline and throughout your post as often as possible. This is often referred to as search engine optimization, or SEO. Using keywords makes it more likely people searching for the topic of your post will find it. Put yourself in the shoes of someone doing an online search. What words would they search for, if looking for information on the

topic of your post? Use those. Also use these words in the tags section that appears on the back end of a website when drafting a post or story. Tags are keywords. Filling out this portion will also make your posts more discoverable to someone searching online.

- **Share.** Even if you have a following, don't expect people to constantly check your site for new content. You have to let them know. Sharing on social media is the way much of your audience will be alerted that you've posted something new. It drives people to your work and can foster interaction on social media.

- **Analyze.** How did you do? Monitoring website analytics sheds light on which posts got the most hits, how much traffic was generated from your social media posts versus people coming directly to your site, and much more. More on that in Chapter 6.

Social Media

The most effective use of social media for covering a beat or a general assignment story involves sharing, listening, connecting, and analyzing. Future chapters explore specific methods related to these four areas:

- **Share.** Spread more than just your published work. Share information from others that you find interesting, relevant, and credible. Think, does what I'm about to post provide value to my followers? When you share other users' content, give them a shout-out by including @mentions or tagging them in posts.

- **Find.** Monitor social media to find conversations and content related to your beat. These could tip you off to story or blog ideas and give you something worthwhile to pass along to followers. Conduct hashtag or keyword searches to discover what's being talked about. Twitter lists are also a fantastic tool. Twitter lists, as we discuss in the next chapter, filter your stream so that you see only tweets from users you place in a list.

- **Connect.** Become part of a community. If you're passionate about immigration, start by following people who share information about this topic and will add value to your social media streams. Consider other journalists, nonprofits, and experts in the field. Rely on your community. Listen

"Disability" Overlooked In Diversity Discussions

ADDED MAY 20, 2013, UNDER: JOURNALISM EDUCATION

THE MOST APPROPRIATE LABEL IS USUALLY THE ONE PEOPLE'S PARENTS HAVE GIVEN THEM.

There's an important part of diversity discussions in newsrooms and classrooms that needs to be addressed: disability. People with disabilities make up an estimated 20% of the population in the United States, and one in five families includes a member with a disability. Despite these statistics, in comparison to other minority groups, people with disabilities are overlooked in news coverage and classroom discussions about diversity in journalism.

This semester, I introduced the topic of disability into my diversity lesson plan in a broadcast journalism course. My goal was to expand students' understanding of diversity. I hope, as they enter the real world, they apply what they've learned. I also recently conducted a workshop at Your News Now (Syracuse) on this topic (See presentation below).

My workshop and lesson plan focus on why it's important to include disability in diversity discussions, the proper terminology related to disability, the framing of disability stories, and how journalists can include disability in news coverage.

Key takeaways

- **Terminology:** Use person-first language (notice I've been using the phrase "people with disabilities"). You should avoid terms that fail to emphasize people with disabilities as "people first." The basic idea is to name the person first and the condition second in order to emphasize "they are people first." I've worked for a disability organization the past three years. People with disabilities face unique challenges, just like anyone else. However, disability doesn't necessarily define who they are. Disability isn't something they "suffer from." That's another phrase to avoid. Also, when describing an individual, don't reference his or her disability unless it's clearly pertinent to the story.
- **Story Frames:** Disability is a way of being, not something a person "has." Journalists should avoid story frames or angles that center on pity, charity, weakness, suffering, and deficiency, among others.
- **News Coverage:** There are many ways news organizations can integrate the topic of disability into news coverage.
  *Focus on the issues impacting people with disabilities, especially unemployment and health care.

This post I wrote includes many of the important element of blogging: keywords in the headline, a visual, hyperlinks, bullet points for scanning friendliness, and data from credible sources.

"'Disability' Overlooked In Diversity Discussions" by Anthony Adornato.

and respond. Join existing conversations and invite people to weigh in. Be responsive by acknowledging audience feedback. Placing hashtags in your social media posts is a great way for others with similar interests to find you. Participating in tweet chats (Chapter 4) is also a valuable way to connect. A tweet chat is a real-time Q&A session on a topic that's regularly scheduled for a specific day/time.

- **Analyze.** What's working well? The effectiveness of your social media activity can also be analyzed by regularly visiting your analytics for each platform (Chapter 6).

Checklist

✓ **Social Media Audit.** Conduct a social media audit on yourself. Also, team up with one classmate to audit each other's online presence. Discuss your findings.

> Refer to the Digital Skeletons: Social Media Audit portion of this chapter for tips. Be sure to analyze bios, content, frequency of posts, personality, professional interests, and journalism skills.

> How would you describe your classmate's brand?

> What is your classmate doing well? What needs improvement?

> After your classmate's audit, clean up anything that doesn't reflect who you are in a positive light.

✓ **Build Your Presence.** Time to polish up and shine.

> Create a professional website. Follow the recommendations above for building a website. Establish professionally oriented accounts on Twitter, Facebook, Instagram, LinkedIn, and Snapchat. Set up an account on either YouTube or Vimeo. Remember, keep your website domain and social media handles as close to your name as possible. Invite people to like your professional Facebook page.

> Download mobile apps for each of these social networking sites.

> Create a short bio for your social media profiles and a longer version for your website and LinkedIn page. Have at least one classmate give you feedback on your bios.

> Ensure that your profile photo and bio are consistent across all platforms.

✓ **Choose a Beat.** Select a beat/niche you would like to cover this semester. Ideally, this should be an area that you plan on pursuing in your journalism career. The goal is to carry the expertise and brand you build with you when entering the workforce.

> Write two blog posts per week.

> Share them via your social media pages.

✓ **Discussion.** What are the advantages and disadvantages of having the same social media account for personal and professional activity? Discuss as a class. Also, ask social media followers what they think about this. Include your class hashtag in posts—this is an easy way for you and classmates to track the online conversation.

✓ **Reminder.** Continue working on the mobile and social media strategy analysis that was part of Chapter 2's checklist. Use what you learned in this chapter to analyze the social media accounts of the two reporters you selected for the assignment.

Mastering Social Media and Mobile Apps for Reporting

There are similarities among many social media platforms—the terms *hashtag and handle* have become a common part of our social networking language. Students, considered digital natives, know this firsthand. However, not all social media and their mobile apps can be used the same way. Certain features distinguish one social media site from another. Becoming familiar with the nuances of each platform will open the door to sharing most effectively as well as finding story ideas and connections.

SPEAKING THE LANGUAGE: THE BASICS

The list that follows includes the most common features across most social media. Integrating these features into your posts will optimize your social media content, making it more likely to stand out in the crowd. (For more on this topic, see the section on Social Media Optimization in Chapter 6.)

- **Handles,** or @mentions, are the basic way people are identified on social media. Get in the habit of including other users' handles in your posts when appropriate. They'll be notified of the @mention, increasing the odds of further engagement with your post. Be sure to double check the handle. Don't assume a person or organization uses a handle that is spelled exactly how it's named.

- **Hashtags** are used to group together posts related to a topic or event. Hashtags were born

In this chapter you will

- Learn about features of the most popular social media platforms used by journalists.

- Learn to harness those platforms for newsgathering purposes: to find story ideas, sources, and content.

- Locate reliable information from social media to enhance reporting.

- Filter and sift through all the information you have at your fingertips.

- Begin to understand how to use mobile devices and social media to plan coverage of a story and report from the field.

on Twitter. Put the # symbol at the beginning of a word or phrase you want to hashtag. The hashtag appears as a link that users can click to automatically see the larger conversation around that hashtag. Use a hashtag if there's already one for a story you're covering. They're great for live events and breaking news. People tend to search hashtags to keep up with an unfolding story. As we discuss later in this chapter, hashtags are also beneficial when crowdsourcing.

- **Tagging** enables you to link a picture, video, or other type of status update to another user. It's similar to including a handle in a post, in that a tagged person will be alerted to it. However, tagging is a separate feature from @mentioning someone in the text of your post. To tag a person, select the tagging option, start entering a username, and choose the person's handle from the dropdown menu. (Note that tagging in this sense is different from tags that you have the option of including when writing a website post. Website tags, as mentioned in the last chapter, are keywords related to a story.)

- **Geo-location** lets users indicate where they're posting from. On some platforms, the geo-location feature is called a "check-in." When you select the option, you'll see a list of places based on the location of your device. The feature is useful for journalists, particularly during breaking news, because a geo-location search can be a starting point when looking to find sources and content related to a story at a specific location. Social media users are also becoming savvy in conducting their own location-based searches. Journalists can make their work more discoverable by including the geo-location in posts about a story.

- **Notifications** on our mobile devices can be overwhelming. But, they're a critical way for journalists to monitor interactions on multiple platforms without having to constantly log in. Set up notifications on social media apps so that you're alerted when someone interacts with you, from a direct message to a comment on your post.

Now, let's examine the most used social media platforms for journalists. Each has a range of unique features, from character limits to live video options. Social networking companies update features periodically, making it all the more important to stay updated on the latest developments regarding new technologies.

Twitter

Twitter's 140-character limit is its distinguishing feature. Because of this, posts need to be crafted succinctly. The limit also impacts how frequently you share. On Twitter, unlike other platforms, it's acceptable to post a series of tweets back-to-back. A flurry of tweets, for instance, may be needed to share information on a developing story. One or two tweets simply wouldn't provide enough details or context for followers to understand a story.

Posting a series of tweets about an event or news as it unfolds is often referred to as **live-tweeting**. Tip for live-tweeting: Your first post should give followers a heads-up so they're not caught off guard. Let them know they'll see a series of posts from you and tell them why. An introductory tweet can also bring more attention to your Twitter coverage.

There are a number of **visual elements** that can be included in tweets. You can upload a maximum of four photos to each tweet. The images show up as a mini photo gallery in a tweet. It's an eye-catching feature. Twitter also has the option to share recorded video and to live-stream video through its Periscope app.

Keep in mind, some features may eat away at the 140 characters. So pay close attention to how many characters you have left when drafting a tweet. As is frequently the case with tweets, you'll have to adjust how you craft a tweet based on what you want to say and how much space you have. Twitter announced in 2016 that media attachments (still images, videos, GIFs, and polls) will no longer reduce the character count. However,

https://twitter.com/washingtonpost/lists

The *Washington Post* uses Twitter lists to organize sources for stories. The outlet also places the accounts of its reporters and interns in lists to easily see what they're tweeting. View all *The Post's* lists at *twitter.com/washingtonpost/lists*.

links still count toward the character limit. All links posted in tweets are automatically shortened by Twitter so they won't take up as much space as the original URL.

One of the most useful features of this platform is **Twitter lists**. Twitter lists filter the noise. After all, when you're following hundreds of Twitter users, it can be overwhelming to keep up with what they're saying. In fact, some people, including myself, rely more heavily on lists than the main Twitter stream. You can place a user into a specific list. Viewing a list timeline will show you a stream of tweets from only users on that list. Lists can be set to be public or private. If a list is set to public, anyone can see the list, and users will be alerted when they're placed in the list. So, make sure your lists have an appropriate name. To create a list, go to the profile page of your account, and locate the Lists section. Add users by going to their profiles and selecting "Add or remove from lists." You can add a person to multiple lists. Get in the habit of adding new followers to a list right away. It will make your Twitter life easier. You can put a user in a list even if you don't click Follow on the user's account. In this case, the user's tweets will show up only in the list feed, not in your main Twitter feed. As we'll discuss later in this chapter, lists are a great way to find sources and story ideas. As part of this chapter's checklist, you'll create several Twitter lists, including one for your beat.

Other Twitter features:

- **Retweets, replies, and likes** are forms of engagement on Twitter—ways to join the conversation. A retweet, commonly referred to as RT, is the sharing of someone else's tweet with your followers. The simplest way to do this is by clicking the retweet icon under a tweet, which brings up a screen with the original tweet. You then have the option to add your own message before the original tweet. A reply begins with the @username of the person and is a response to another user's tweet. To reply to a tweet, click on the Reply button on a tweet. Your reply will be attached to that original tweet, along with others' replies. The heart-shaped "like" icon under each tweet can serve several functions. It's a way to show appreciation for a tweet. In addition, you can "like" a tweet that you want to come back to at a later time—maybe it includes a link to an article you want to check out, but don't have the time for at that moment. On your profile page, you can locate tweets you've "liked."

- **Direct Messages (DM)** are private conversations with a user. Direct messaging can be used to contact sources without everyone seeing the exchange in your public stream. It's good for quick exchanges of information. You can then connect via phone or e-mail, if needed. There's one caveat: You can initiate DMs only with users who follow your account or who have enabled the setting that allows anyone to DM them.

- Pose a question to followers by creating a **Twitter poll**. Find this option in the main text box when composing a tweet. Type the question in the message box, enter answer options, and select the length of time you want the poll to remain open.

- Mobile **notifications for individual users** can be useful if you're tracking a particular source. By turning on the notification for the source's tweets, you'll receive an alert every time the source posts something. Turn on this notification directly from the source's profile page.

Tweet Chats

A tweet chat, also called Twitter chat, is a scheduled conversation on Twitter about a specific topic. Tweet chats are typically held at a recurring day and time. Each tweet chat has a host who leads the discussion. The host will ask participants to introduce themselves and then pose questions to those following the hashtag dedicated to the discussion. People then respond to the host's questions, tagging each response with the hashtag (and @mention, if the tweet chat has one).

Participants also interact by retweeting, replying, and liking each other's posts. Tweet chats can feel fast and furious, depending on the number of people taking part. It's a highly energizing and engaging activity. There are tweet chats dedicated to everything from multimedia journalism and AP style to yoga and agriculture. For example, #wjchat (@wjchat) is focused on all things related to online journalism. The chat takes place Wednesdays at 5:00 p.m. PT. Unfortunately, there's not one centralized site with an "official" schedule of tweet chats. Start by doing an online search for tweet chats related to your interests. As you become more active with your Twitter community, you'll become familiar with tweet chats dedicated to beats or topics that interest you. Tips for participating:

- Introductory tweet: Alert followers that you're taking part in a tweet chat.

- Use Twitter's search bar or a social media dashboard, which we discuss shortly, to filter tweets related to the chat hashtag.

- A tweet chat host usually tags the questions with Q1, Q2, Q3, et cetera. When you respond, indicate which question you're answering by including A1, A2, A3, et cetera.

- Don't forget to use the tweet chat's official hashtag (and handle, if there's one).

- Don't forget to engage with other participants and check your notifications to see who's interacting with you.

- Follow people in the chat who could provide value to your Twitter experience. Consider placing them in one of your Twitter lists.

Facebook

Signal is Facebook's discovery and curation tool for journalists. Through the Signal dashboard, you have the ability to search trends, photos, videos, and posts on Facebook and Instagram. Signal is more powerful than Facebook's general search functionality that anyone can access. Signal, available only to journalists, drills down to more specific search criteria. To request access, go to *signal.fb.com*. Sign up after you have created a professional Facebook page (part of Chapter 3's checklist).

Facebook is also ripe with opportunities to include visuals in posts. In addition to uploading photos and videos, journalists can stream live video via **Facebook Live**. The Live feature is located in the status update box when using Facebook's mobile app (Facebook is also bringing the feature to desktop computer users who access *Facebook.com*). Simply click the icon and tell people what they'll be watching. Read and reply to comments as you broadcast. The videos are recorded so people can view them once the live streams ends. You can also save the videos to your mobile device. Be authentic. The draw is that people like watching things as they happen, as they unfold organically. The *New York Times* had a bit of a hiccup while experimenting with Facebook Live. One of the outlet's first Facebook Live videos was touted as an inside look at a story pitch session. During the stream, three reporters "pitched" stories to an editor. Halfway through the stream it became clear that at least one of the stories was already about to be published. The editor asks, "Has the story been edited?" A reporter says the story is written and will be ready in a few hours. But, viewers were under the impression that this was a story pitch meeting—which happens before a story is written and undergoes editorial review. The exchange may have left astute viewers scratching their heads.

Other considerations to keep in mind:

- Facebook doesn't allow you to send **private messages** from your professional Facebook page. If you want to send messages to potential sources you find on Facebook, you will need to use your personal Facebook account (an approach that has downsides) or find another way to contact them.

- You can **schedule posts** to be published at a later time. This option is available for professional Facebook pages only. Draft your post as you normally would. Click the arrow next to the Publish button, select Schedule, and set the day and time you want the post to be shared.

- **Use restraint with hashtags** in your Facebook posts. Hashtags are not as ingrained in the Facebook culture as they are on Twitter and Instagram.

Instagram

Instagram is all about visuals. The visual should tell the story. The platform is a tool for journalists to showcase people and places at the heart of a story. A single photo can speak volumes about a story, serving as a powerful way to connect followers to your reporting.

"It's a very serene experience viewing one image at a time on your phone," said Ryan Kellett (@rkellett), the *Washington Post*'s audience and engagement editor. "That intimacy makes it a great place to follow reporters and photographers who can take you to stories they are covering."[1]

In addition to still images, you can also upload short videos. On Instagram, **less is more.** Post a few times per week, but avoid sharing consecutively in a short time span—that goes against Instagram's "language." Instagram's focus is on the visual components of a post, so keep the text portion concise. **Hashtags are king** on Instagram. Use them in every post.

One of the limitations of Instagram is that **clickable links aren't allowed in posts**. However, links placed in your Instagram profile are hyperlinked. There's a simple and common workaround if you want to provide people with a story link. Add the hyperlink to your bio, and then, in the post, direct followers to your profile for a link to more information. NBC News takes this approach frequently. For example, when it shared this photo of a woman mourning the death of a loved one in the terror attacks at Istanbul Atatürk Airport, it referred followers to the link in its profile.

Filters are Instagram's calling card. Use caution with filters. An image should reflect the reality of what a journalist sees in person. Filters can distort reality. If applying a filter communicates something other than reality, that's unethical in journalism. The safest approach is to avoid the use of filters.

Additional Instagram tips:

- **Signal** can be used to find content and sources on Instagram. No surprise here, since Facebook owns Instagram. Through the Signal dashboard, search Instagram for photos and video related to specific hashtags, associated with specific public accounts, or tagged in locations around the world.

- With the Layout app by Instagram, create a **photo collage.** Layout lets you combine multiple photos into a single image—a picture narrative—without having to post photo after photo (an Instagram "no-no"). After you download the app, you can access the collage feature directly through the Instagram app.

- You can **connect Instagram to other social media accounts.** Each time you upload a photo or video to Instagram, you'll have the option to share to each of the social networks you've enabled. But when you share from Instagram to Twitter, the visual isn't embedded in a tweet. Instead, the tweet will include a link to your Instagram post. This is cumbersome for users. Placing an image or video directly into a tweet is more likely to catch people's attention and prevent them from having to click elsewhere. Think user friendliness!

NBCNews. Instagram Post.

nbcnews
Istanbul, Turkey
Following

892 likes   46m

nbcnews A mother mourns outside a forensic medicine building close to Istanbul's airport on Wednesday, a day after a coordinated terror attack blamed on ISIS left dozens dead, scores wounded and blood streaked throughout the arrivals hall of #AtaturkAirport.

#Istanbul's governor said Wednesday that the death toll had climbed to 41 — including at least 10 foreigners and 3 dual nationals, with 37 of those 41 identified so far. Tap the link in our profile for more coverage on the attack (📷 @Kilicbil / @afpphoto / @gettyimages)

#Turkey #IstanbulAirportAttack #NBCNewsPics #IstanbulAttack

Add a comment...

This single photo on NBC News's Instagram captures a heartbreaking moment. Hashtags and @mentions are used to make the content more discoverable and to credit the photographer.

LinkedIn

LinkedIn, launched in 2003, is a different animal from other social media platforms. It's a professional-oriented social networking site. LinkedIn is much more than just a place to hold your resume, though. You can connect with potential employers and tap into its features to find a job or internship. In the final chapter, we explore how to make the most of LinkedIn for building a professional network and job hunting.

LinkedIn is a research treasure trove for journalists. **Advanced People Search** is a tool to find sources, from experts to former and current employees of a company. The search tool allows you to drill deep based on specific criteria including location, education, nonprofit interests, and employment history. Once you click on a potential source's profile, you'll see if anyone in your LinkedIn network knows the source. Connections can help you get past "no comment." Having something in common can be a starting point to get someone to talk. That's where the **Find Alumni** search function can be useful as well. Use this search area to locate alumni of your college or university based on their expertise as well as where they live and work.

Follow **Company pages** to stay updated on changes at specific companies. Search for companies related to your beat or located in your city, and then click Follow Company to get regular updates on hiring, promotions, departures, and job listings. Company pages also list current and former employees. When covering sensitive stories about a company, former employees can be more willing to talk than current ones. LinkedIn's search tool lets you search for these "formers."

Discover what's trending. **LinkedIn groups** are a way to track the latest chatter related to a beat. Monitor groups related to your reporting interests in order to find story ideas and sources.

Other LinkedIn tips:

- **Who's Viewed Your Profile?** You can see who's checking out your LinkedIn profile. The Who's Viewed Your Profile feature works both ways though. If you enable the feature in your account settings, other users will also be able to see when you have looked at their profiles. That could tip people off if you're working on an investigative or sensitive story. If you decide to turn off this feature, you'll no longer see who has viewed your profile either.

- Request to be added to the **LinkedIn for Journalists group** on the site. The space is for journalists to learn more about industry news and how to use LinkedIn as a tool to uncover sources, story ideas, and scoops. LinkedIn also holds monthly webinars for journalists. Journalism students can join in on these tutorial sessions. Checkout the LinkedIn for Journalists group for webinar details.

- LinkedIn is an ideal space to **share news about your professional developments**, such as awards and job changes, and periodically you can post your stories to LinkedIn. However, this is not the platform to post constant updates from the field.

Snapchat

Snapchat is becoming more than just a chat app to send friends photos—likely a selfie or two—that "disappear." An increasing number of journalists and news organizations are testing the app to engage a younger demographic. After all, Snapchat is the dominant platform on which young people "hang out."

NBC News correspondent Hallie Jackson, *hallienbc* on Snapchat, frequently uses the platform to engage in fun ways with her followers. Jackson says Snapchat is a space that's underutilized by most of the news media: "If you look at the numbers of how 18-25 year-olds get news from Snapchat, people are stunned. This is our future audience. You have to be engaging now with this demographic. You need to bring them into the tent early because in 10 or 15 years they'll stick with our brand if we engage them now. You're cultivating a relationship that has the potential to last."

Snapchat has a very different "language" than any other social networking platform. Stickers, emojis, and text drawn with your finger are the norm. It's fun and a bit unorthodox, even by social media standards.

Now, the Snapchatter lingo. A **Snapcode**, the Snapchat logo with dots around it, is your unique identity. Sharing your Snapcode image with followers on other social media sites is an easy way for them to connect with you. Open Snapchat, point the camera at a Snapcode, and then press and hold on the screen. Voila, you're Snapchat friends! Snapchatters can also find each other by conducting a username search.

Each photo or video you share is called a **Snap**. You can send Snaps directly to individual users. Snaps sent in private messages disappear in 10 seconds. Snapchat's **Story** feature is the most useful element for journalists to reach a broad audience of Snapchatters. Each Story contains a series of Snaps. Every time you create a Snap (a photo or video), you then add it to "My Story." Each Snap that is part of your story disappears 24 hours after it's published. Before adding a Snap to a story, you can add text by drawing on the screen with the pen tool or by typing a caption the traditional way. You also have the option to add emojis and stickers. To view stories from people you follow, swipe left from the open screen. Swiping right will show any one-on-one conversations with Snapchat friends.

From the Campaign Trail: Covering a Presidential Primary with Snapchat

Two of my students "took over" NBC News's Snapchat to cover the 2016 South Carolina Republican presidential primary. NBC News promoted the Snapchat takeover on its Twitter feed and politics blog. While logged into the NBC News account from my iPhone, the students took Snapchatters to polling locations, campaign headquarters, and candidate rallies. To view the Snapchat Story from the campaign trail, visit *bitly.com/NBCSnapchat*.

Ready to step up your Snapchat game? Here are some quick tips based on our experience in the field.

- Ideal number of Snaps per story is 10–15.

- Start with a video introduction to set the scene.

- When you're finished with a Story, wrap it up with a video. This is an ideal time to promote coverage elsewhere, such as on your outlet's website or your Twitter feed.

- Mix up the Story by varying the order of photos and videos.

- Add descriptive text and location-based filters to provide context to what you're showing. Keep text short. If you think some users will need a bit longer to digest what they're looking at, adjust the length of time a photo appears (10-second max) on the screen.

- Many Snapchatters don't turn on the audio to videos unless they're given a reason to. When you record someone talking, write a caption. Consider using a quote.

- Cross-promote your Snapchat coverage on Twitter and Facebook. Share your Snapcode image with followers, and include your Snapchat username in the message. Snapchat allows you to save individual Snaps and entire Stories to your mobile device. To promote your Snapchat Story, consider sharing one of the Snaps to Facebook or Twitter.

@NBCNews. Twitter post. February 20, 2016.

Photo by Anthony Adornato.

More Snapchat pointers:

- Find **geo-filters** by swiping right after recording a Snap. A geo-filter, customized based on the location you're Snapping from, appears as a sticker overlay on your Snap. For instance, if you're snapping from New York City, you'd have the option to select a filter designed for that city. Your geo-location setting for the app must be enabled in order to see this type of filter.

- There's a **10-second limit on video clips**. If you're interviewing people specifically for Snapchat, the trick is to get them to complete a statement in under 10 seconds, or else they're going to get cut off. You have the option to delete the clip and rerecord the Snap interview. But, that could be cumbersome and awkward depending on who you're interviewing.

- **Who watched your Story?** Snapchat has limited analytics compared to other social networking platforms. (See Chapter 6 for a detailed breakdown of analytics.) Nonetheless, the data is interesting to monitor. You can see how many times your story was viewed and by whom. Go to your Story, and click on the three horizontal dots next to it. A list of your Snaps appears. For each Snap, you'll see an eyeball with a number next to it. That's the number of times each Snap has been viewed. Tap on an eyeball to see the names of Snapchatters who viewed it.

Social Media Command Center

Keeping tabs on all your social media accounts by opening each app and tracking alerts may seem like a lot to juggle. Streamline the process by creating your own social media command center. Tools such as TweetDeck, owned by Twitter, and Hootsuite let you **monitor multiple social media streams** from a single dashboard. The real power on both dashboards comes with Twitter. TweetDeck and Hootsuite allow you to keep eyes on different parts of Twitter at once. Organize lists, @mentions, direct messages, keyword and hashtag searches, and other elements all in one dashboard. These different elements show up in multiple columns.

Unlike on TweetDeck, you can connect multiple social media accounts to Hootsuite. Open up the Hootsuite dashboard to view posts from different social media accounts, including Instagram, Facebook, and LinkedIn. From the dashboard, you're also able to create and share posts to any of the connected accounts. Hootsuite also has a mobile app.

One feature of interest for journalists is the ability to **schedule posts** through these dashboards. Scheduling posts works best with feature and evergreen stories. The *New York Times*, like other newsrooms, schedules multiple runs of tweets highlighting enterprise stories.[2] One word of caution: If there's breaking news during the time a prescheduled post is supposed to go live, cancel the post. It will look awkward if a scheduled post with a feature story from the archives shows up among posts about breaking news.

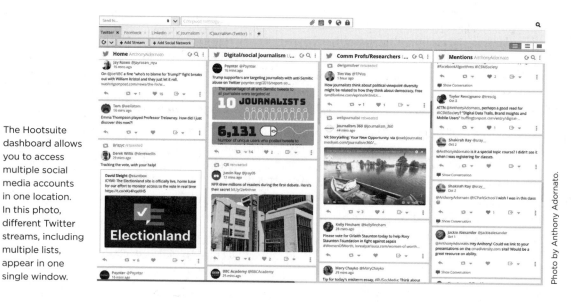

The Hootsuite dashboard allows you to access multiple social media accounts in one location. In this photo, different Twitter streams, including multiple lists, appear in one single window.

Photo by Anthony Adornato.

SOCIAL NEWSGATHERING: STORY IDEAS, SOURCES, AND CONTENT

There's more than meets the eye with social media platforms. On the surface, they're a place to share and interact. But social media has also added a new layer to the newsgathering process. As was first introduced in Chapter 1, social media is a valuable newsgathering tool for journalists in three ways:

- **Tips line.** To find story ideas.
- **Sources.** To find sources for a story.
- **Content.** To find information for a story. This often includes user-generated content or crowdsourced information.

Now that you're fluent in the basic language of each platform, in this section we explore how to tap into the wealth of material and voices on social networks. Journalists have never had so much information at their fingertips. Unlocking social media's potential for locating story ideas, sources, and content is much like being a detective. You need to understand where and how to listen, monitor, and search.

Verify, Verify, Verify

Is the unbelievable video you found too good to be true? Is that source credible? Never assume the images or people on social media are who or what they appear to be. Locating *reliable* information is key. In Chapter 7, we explore how to identify misleading content and sources.

Social media complements and enhances, but doesn't replace, traditional reporting skills. The quality of your stories is only as good as the quality of information you gather, whether it be online or offline. As the old cliché says, garbage in, garbage out.

Social Listening

The term *social listening* is just what it sounds like. Social listening refers to the practice of monitoring social media to discover what's being talked about by citizens and others, such as public officials. It's a way to uncover potential story ideas, content, and sources as well as monitor conversations in real time about a current story. Fine-tune your listening skills to filter out the background noise and find what's important.

Create Lists.   Lists are king. Twitter lists are perhaps the best way to wade through a tsunami of information and keep your finger on the pulse. They act like an office water cooler. A basic go-to list for any local journalist should be local newsmakers. Place the accounts of local officials, companies, nonprofits, and community leaders in this list. This stream is a local tips line. Journalists should also consider making lists for beats, local law enforcement, industry peers, and other journalists at their outlets. The options are endless. Tend to these lists periodically. Weed out unhelpful sources and add new ones. Accessing Twitter lists through a social media dashboard, such as TweetDeck or Hootsuite, is the easiest way to view those streams in one central location.

@indiancreekfarm. Twitter Post. March 27, 2016.

Indian Creek Farm @indiancreekfarm · Mar 27
Well we can't just sit around and worry about the peach crop #springweekend #farmcountry #localfood #twithaca

0:30

↩   ⇄ 2   ♥ 5   •••

Michael Tkaczevski
@Mike_Tka
⚙ Following

.@indiancreekfarm Has the mild winter put peach crop in danger? Local reporter, I'd like to speak with you about this. Tweet me back! Thanks

While "listening" to sources on Twitter, a student journalist came across a tweet from a farm mentioning issues with its peach crop. He then reached out via Twitter to the farm and eventually produced a multimedia story about the issue.

If you don't want to tip someone off that you're monitoring him or her, private lists are a handy tool. Henk van Ess (@henkvaness), a reporter and researcher, used a private Twitter list of Dutch bankers to break a story about mass layoffs. Van Ess noticed a series of unusual tweets from people on the list. [3] A banker posted, "Hate unscheduled meetings." The chatter of bankers on this list stopped for about four hours. Then, a banker wrote, "Sometimes you must leave behind what you love the most." A tweet from someone else on this list had mentioned the name of the restaurant where the supposed meeting had taken place. So, van Ess called the restaurant and confirmed that there was a meeting of bankers at that location. By combining the individual tweets, a collective narrative became clear, and he was able to turn to traditional reporting skills to break the story. "Thanks to my list, these subtle hints were not drowned in a timeline full of friends, family and strangers, where I might have missed their implications."[4]

Subscribe to Lists. You can also follow public lists created by others. There are a number of ways to locate public lists. Start by visiting social media profiles of trusted users to see if they have public lists. After subscribing to someone else's list, you can see it in your lists area and watch that stream.

Search. You can locate public Twitter lists by doing an online search with the following search structure: *site:twitter.com/*/lists/followed by keywords*. For example, if you wanted to see if anyone created a list related to the Paris terror attacks, you would type the following in a search engine: *site:twitter.com/*/lists/ paris attacks*.

The search results include a list created by the *Wall Street Journal (https://twitter .com/WSJ/lists/paris-attacks)*. More than 80 people subscribe to this list made up of *Wall Street Journal* reporters covering the Paris attacks and the aftermath. This list is also a great example of how to curate sources during a breaking news situation. Add sources who are sharing information about the incident, including journalists, witnesses, and officials.

Official Accounts. Whether by going directly to pages or via lists, make it a habit to monitor the social media accounts of traditional sources, such as city government, police departments, and local politicians. How journalists receive information from these more traditional sources is evolving. These types of sources, as we discussed in the first chapter, now bypass news outlets in many cases, because social platforms allow them to share information directly with the public. News outlets are no longer the sole gatekeepers, controlling the flow of information.

The Boston Marathon bombings was a case in point. The Boston Police Department turned to Twitter to share the latest information. And, officials, such as politicians, are increasingly making major announcements and commenting on issues through social media rather than holding traditional press conferences or issuing press releases.

Local nonprofits, another traditional source that previously had to rely on journalists to get the word out to the community about their work, also heavily utilize social media. Checking nonprofits' social media pages is a great way to find evergreen story ideas.

Grassroots Groups. Groups are ripe with story ideas and sources. There are a variety of groups on Facebook and LinkedIn. Groups are different from pages because they aren't designed to be "official" profiles of entities such as public offices and businesses. Rather, groups are grassroots online communities where people come together around a common cause, issue, or activity. This includes groups to memorialize victims, and those dedicated to communities such as mothers who breastfeed and parents who have children with disabilities. For these niche communities, the groups act as news feeds and places for discussion about issues that impact them. One of the biggest daily challenges for journalists is finding people to interview who are directly impacted by an issue. These "real" people humanize stories. Telling a story through their eyes helps the audience better relate to an issue. Groups are a perfect place to find these sources.

Some groups are closed. To be part of them, you have to request access. Be transparent. If you're joining the group as part of your job as a journalist, rather than for personal reasons, be sure to use a professional account that clearly states in your profile that you're a journalist. If you ask questions to the group as part of a fact-finding mission for a story, always make clear you're a reporter working on a story. As NPR's ethics handbook states, this approach should be used in all online spaces:

> Just as we do in the "real" world, we identify ourselves as NPR journalists when we are working online. So, if as part of our work we are posting comments, asking questions, tweeting, retweeting, blogging, Facebooking or doing anything on social media or other online forums, we clearly identify ourselves and that we work for NPR. We do not use pseudonyms when doing such work.[5]

In Chapter 7's exploration of mobile and social media ethics and policies, we address the ethical concerns of contacting sources through social media and how to properly use information from these platforms.

Social Searching

A boy crawls into a gorilla enclosure at the Cincinnati Zoo. A Boeing 777 crashes while attempting to land at San Francisco International Airport. A power plant in central New York catches fire.

In all these cases, journalists tracked down sources and user-generated content on social media to paint a picture of what was unfolding at the scene. How would you search social media to locate information?

A basic search would include keywords, hashtags, and the name of a location at the center of the story. That's a good starting point. Like any good detective though, a journalist needs skills to drill deeper. Utilizing a myriad of advanced search methods depending on the situation can uncover a treasure trove of details. Advanced sleuthing by **location**, **keywords**, and **time** will take you past general search results.

Location. Through location-based searches, journalists can zero in on a specific spot where a story is unfolding. And this type of search pinpoints social media posts in the area even if people don't use keywords in their posts. The search relies on users having their geo-location turned on and their accounts public, so not every post from that location will turn up in a search.

Some platforms, such as Twitter, have advanced search tools through which you can select a location and search for posts within a certain radius around that location. You can also filter deeper by looking for people who have included images or keywords in their posts at a specified location. In the case of the landing at the San Francisco Airport, you could start by typing San Francisco, CA, into the location box and then entering keywords such as "crash landing" or "emergency landing."

A more sophisticated method of conducting a location search is by using a geocode, the longitude/latitude coordinates for a location. Many location searches through social media platforms tools don't allow you to pinpoint down to street level. That's where geocode searching comes in handy. You can "zoom" to the location of a house or building. In Google Maps, navigate to the location you want to search. Right click on the pin on the map, and select What's here? That's where you'll find the longitude/latitude data. You can then copy that into the Twitter search bar.

A geocode search for tweets at or around the Cincinnati Zoo would look like this:

- Cincinnati Zoo's geocode is *39.144765, -84.508574*
- In the main search box of Twitter, use this search format: *geocode:39.144765, -84.508574* (delete spaces after punctuation)
- To search a radius around that location, add the miles or kilometers after the geocode, as follows: *geocode:39.144765,-84.508574,1mi*
- To search for posts with keywords within that location, add the keywords to the beginning. For example, *gorilla geocode:39.144765,-84.508574,1mi*

Another method of conducting a location-based search is by finding people who have checked in on social media to a spot. The check-in feature tags a post with the location a user selects. Some platforms, including Instagram, allow you to search by check-in location. So you could, for example, locate people who have checked into the San Francisco Airport or Cincinnati Zoo. And from there, see if they're posting anything related to a news event. Keep in mind, just because someone checked into a location on social media doesn't necessarily mean the person is physically at that location. People can check into these places even if they're not at them.

ProPublica's Justin Elliott (@JustinElliott) tapped into Instagram's location tagging when he was working on a story about Texas congressman Jeb Hensarling.[6] After Hensarling became chairman of the House Financial Services Committee, his political action committee held a fundraiser at a Utah ski resort. Elliott searched for Instagram photos tagged at the St. Regis Deer Valley Resort, the location of the event. "I went through the photos and looked at each user and tried to figure out if they were a lobbyist or lobbyist family member," said Elliott.[7] He was able to locate at least one photo of a lobbyist who attended the event.

There are apps, including Banjo and Geofeedia, that help simplify location-based searches by pulling in posts from multiple social media platforms. When I was searching for information about the landing at San Francisco Airport, I opened up the Banjo mobile app and typed in "San Francisco Airport." A map displayed the airport, and social media posts made at and around that location were marked by pinpoints on the map. I clicked on each pin to see what users from Facebook, Instagram, and Twitter posted in real time. A man who was on the flight tweeted out a dramatic photo minutes after he came down the plane's evacuation slide. I turned to Twitter, typed in his username, and was able to follow the ordeal.

Keywords. Think about a combination of keywords that will capture content specific to what you're looking for. If you're getting results that aren't relevant or you're getting too many results, pivot. Adjust keywords. Sometimes that requires creating more complex searches or thinking more simplistically.

When you're searching for content from the scene of a story, put yourself in the shoes of people there. How would a witness—not a journalist—craft a post? What would the witness say? "Imagine what your perfect source would tweet, or what you yourself would tweet in that situation, and search for the words that would probably be in it," said Daniel Victor (@bydanielvictor), of the *New York Times*.[8]

Me and *my* are keywords journalists should add to searches, Victor noted in a blog post about how he tracked down sources for one particular story.[9] The *Times* got word that there had been reports of conflicts on airplanes because Hasidic Jewish men didn't want to be seated next to women other than their wives. He was able to find 13 possible sources on Twitter through keyword searches using *me* and *my* along with other terms related to the issue. All five passengers quoted in the story were found through Twitter searches.

"If tasked with finding these sources, most would probably start with words like *Hasidic* and *flight*. But that search is horribly noisy to the point of uselessness," said Victor. He adds that some people might not know the term *Hasidic,* so they may use the words *Jew, Jewish,* and/or *orthodox* combined with the word *flight.* He added those words, along with *me* and *my,* to his search. Bingo. They were used in all of the sources' tweets.

In other situations, especially for nonbreaking news stories, find sources by searching social networking platforms for keywords they might use in their profiles. Looking for someone in the aerospace industry to interview for a story? You could type *aerospace* into the keyword box on LinkedIn and your zip code in the location section. Need to interview a school bus driver? Type *school bus driver* and your city into the search bar of a site.

Another trick is to take the keyword search outside of a platform. Turn to Google. Use advanced search phrases to find public social media posts and profiles. Below are two of the most helpful, yet somewhat unknown, search formulas. Copy and paste the following into Google; then edit the site name and keyword(s) accordingly.

- To search by keywords in posts, *site:twitter.com "keyword(s)" OR "additional keyword combination"*

  Example: *site:twitter.com "cincinnati zoo gorilla" OR "child falls cincinnati zoo gorilla"*
- To search by keywords in bios, *site:twitter.com bio:*keyword –inurl:status*

  Example: *site:twitter.com bio:*neurosurgeon –inurl:status*

Finally, the online platform Storify can be an effective tool to curate posts across many social networking sites. From a single dashboard, search keywords for posts in Twitter, Instagram, Facebook, YouTube, and other platforms. You can drag posts into a section of the site that saves them for future viewing.

Time. Filtering posts by a specific time period can be another way to sift through posts and locate valuable information. After running a Google search with any of the search formulas mentioned above, select the advanced filter for time. Search for posts sent since a date, between two dates, or on a date. Some social networking sites also have this feature.

A time-based search could have been used after the Cincinnati Zoo incident to narrow down the flood of posts to only those sent on the day of the incident. Or, you could use this feature to see what visitors to the zoo are saying in the days following. Zoo visitors provided firsthand accounts of what unfolded that day by posting to social media as it was unfolding. Videos recorded on mobile devices showed the boy being dragged by the gorilla and screams of people around after he crawled into the animal's enclosure. These images were broadcast by news outlets around the world.

Organize Listening and Searching

Social media dashboards, such as Hootsuite and TweetDeck, are not only handy for posting content. They also simplify the listening and searching process. On the dashboard, create a separate column for each Twitter list, keyword(s) search, hashtag search, and location search. Even in a breaking news situation, all this can be set up in a few minutes. You can even filter these columns to show text-only posts or those with visuals. When you no longer need a stream, simply remove it from the dashboard. Monitoring these streams from one location is more efficient. It saves you the headache of clicking around a million different places.

CROWDSOURCING: SOCIAL COLLABORATION AND CURATION

One way to bring the audience into the newsgathering process is through crowdsourcing. The term *crowdsourcing* was coined in 2006 by Jeff Howe (@crowdsourcing), then editor of *Wired* magazine. Crowdsourcing is the process of turning to a large group of people to solve a problem or contribute to a project. Social media provides the avenue to collaborate with a "crowd."

Crowdsourcing is different from searching for user-generated content that has already been created. In crowdsourced journalism, reporters make a specific request from the audience. It's an open call to gather a range of content including photos, data, and comments about an issue. This social collaboration, in which you invite people to participate in the reporting process, reinforces the concept of journalism as a conversation. Collaboration through crowdsourcing harnesses the collective power of the audience.

Crowdsourcing: Harnessing the Power of the Audience

Journalists crowdsource all types of stories, from general assignment reports to long-form investigative pieces. The potential benefits of crowdsourcing are these: The audience can suggest angles to a story, provide eyewitness accounts, and provide information that otherwise would be difficult to locate. It also makes them more invested in your work.

Here are a few ways, fun and serious, news outlets are doing just that.

- Where are the best sledding spots? During a major snowstorm, WNYC, New York City's public radio station, posed that question to social media followers. The station created an online map for people to pin their favorite sledding spot, comment about the location, and upload photos. The map was embedded within a page on WNYC's website. WNYC shared the link via social media. The station also asked followers to share their sledding photos on social media platforms and tag the images with #nycsledding.

- ProPublica journalists frequently tap into the wisdom of the crowd. For a story about medical errors, they launched community crowdsourcing long before publishing a story.[10] Their efforts included a Facebook group where people could share stories and a questionnaire for patients and their families. These provided hundreds of sources (not only patients but also experts) and tips.

- The *New York Times*' health reporter, Elisabeth Rosenthal (@nytrosenthal), wrote a blog post, on the *Times*' website, about the difficulty in getting an estimate for the cost of a hip replacement surgery. In that post, she asked readers to join the discussion if they'd had hip replacement or another procedure. More than 500 people responded to the callout. Those sources became the launching point for Rosenthal's series, "Paying Till it Hurts," about the costs of medical care.[11]

How do you make a callout happen? Every crowdsource effort has five steps, according to NPR's Serri Graslie (@sgraslie).[12]

- Hone the question(s). Be specific about what you're asking the audience.

- Write the pitch. Be clear how the information will be used and why it's important. Test out several different drafts.

- Share it. Reaching a broad audience by posting to social media is an obvious approach. But don't forget about niche communities, such as Facebook groups.

- Review the responses. Analyze data, and contact sources if needed.

- Write the story. Think about how to integrate the data into the story and how you'll present it. Remember to thank contributors and share the final product.

Properly setting up your call to action is critical before sharing it. Spend time upfront thinking through the crowdsource request. This will help make sure you get the most useful data. After the fact, it may be too late.

To start, creating a specific hashtag dedicated to a crowdsourced effort can be effective. Have people tag their posts with this hashtag, if you're asking them to share images or comment about a topic. This is an easy way to filter posts. Consider using Storify to collect answers submitted across social media platforms.

Polls and surveys are perhaps the most effective and frequently used tools in crowdsourcing. Some social media platforms have the option to create basic polls. The information you gather from those is limited though.

To get more robust data, use Google Forms to create surveys. After building a survey, share the link to it on social media platforms. Peoples' answers are automatically fed into a searchable spreadsheet accessible through Google Forms.

ProPublica almost always uses Google Forms in crowdsourcing. In the case of the medical errors investigation, as patients and providers responded, reporters began to spot patterns, story leads, and sources. "Our questionnaires are one of our most valuable sourcing tools, because they turn a jumble of stories and comments, from a range of social networks, into structured data that our team can sort and annotate," said Blair Hickman (@amandablair), who worked on the ProPublica project.[14]

Keep questionnaires short and concise. It shouldn't take someone more than a few minutes to respond. Ask for demographic information. If you're interested in sorting the results by demographic data—such as age group or section of your city—include those questions in the survey. Give people the option to contact you via e-mail or phone, particularly for more sensitive stories. Some members of the crowd may have newsworthy information but may be reluctant to share it via a survey. Include at least one opened-ended question that allows participants to write anything additional. This is the equivalent of asking people at the end of an interview if they'd like to say anything else. A source may be sitting on a key piece of information that can really bring a new angle to a story. Include a section for people to submit their contact info. This is important if you need to follow up with a source. Finally, have your colleagues test the survey. Get their feedback in terms of the clarity and order of questions as well as the length. Don't forget to check how the survey works on a mobile device.

NPR Asks: Exploring Fear of Black Men in America

We're kicking off a challenging conversation about race, focusing on whether a fear of black men fuels tensions in communities and between individuals, and we want to hear from you. Are you a black man who has ever felt as if your presence has elicited fear in others? How has that affected you?

Or are you someone who has been in a situation where you've felt anxious because of the presence of an African-American man — maybe in a way that you've been uncomfortable with? Where do you think that comes from?

We want to hear about your experiences on either side (or both sides) of this story. Please fill out our questionnaire below:

* Required

Which describes your experience? *

○ I've been in situations where I've felt anxious because of the presence of a black man.

○ I'm a black man who has experienced the irrational fear of others simply because of who I am.

○ Both of above describe my experiences at different times in my life.

○ Other: _____

Please tell us about your experiences.

What is your race or ethnicity?

Would you be willing to share your experience with our audience? *
We would have to identify you. No anonymous sources here.

○ Yes, I'd be willing to tell my story on NPR.

○ No thanks. I just felt like sharing.

If you said yes, how may we contact you?
Please share your name, email address and phone number.

NPR.

NPR Morning Edition
March 20, 2015 · 🌐

We're kicking off a challenging conversation about race, focusing on whether a fear of black men fuels tensions in communities and between individuals, and we want to hear from you. Are you a black man who has ever felt as if your presence has elicited fear in others? How has that affected you?

Or are you someone who has been in a situation where you've felt anxious because of the presence of an African-American man – maybe in a way that you've been uncomfortable with? Where do you think that comes from?

We want to hear about your experiences on either side (or both sides) of this story. Please fill out our questionnaire below:

NPR Asks: Exploring Fear of Black Men in America
Click here to share your experiences.
DOCS.GOOGLE.COM

👍 Like   💬 Comment   ↪ Share   </> Embed

➕ 278   Top Comments ▾

NPR Morning Edition. Facebook post. March 20, 2015.

Fostering Dialogue: NPR's Identity and Culture Unit crowdsourced when reporting about the topic of racial tension. The NPR team used Google Forms to create a survey and then shared the survey link with its social media followers.

Reporting What You Gather: Vetting and Visualizing the Data

Once you collect information, it's time to vet and then visualize the data, presenting it in an easy-to-understand way for readers. Interview the data. Approach it with a critical eye. There are inherit limitations in asking people to self-report. They may be outright dishonest. In other cases, a lapse in memory may be to blame for an inaccurate answer to a question.

If you have doubts, contact the source. Use old-school interviewing skills. Ask more questions to try to determine if the source is reliable and if what the source has submitted is valid. That's why getting contact information is so critical.

You may also be able to verify without contacting a source. For example, if you were to ask followers to report how much snowfall they received in their neighborhood, you could easily corroborate a claim of five feet. A simple check with a meteorologist would indicate whether this was possible or not. You could also look at the snowfall totals that other people in that location reported. Throw away bogus data. These approaches are no different from the approaches you would use to vet information gathered offline—in documents, databases, or through interviews. The same rules apply here.

Now, bring the data to life. A journalist's job is to curate information, make sense of data. Sift and sort to decide what stands out. What story is the data telling you? What's the news value? The trick here is to decide which information to use and how to present it.

SNOW SHOVELING SAFETY

DO NOT...

STRETCH TO WARM UP
BEFORE SHOVELING

SHOVEL SNOW
WHILE SMOKING

LIFT WITH
YOUR BACK

WORK UNTIL
TOO EXHAUSTED

SHOVEL
AFTER EATING

WEAR LAYERS THAT CAN
BE EASILY REMOVED

IF OVER THE AGE OF

40

SHOVELING ACCOUNTS FOR
NEARLY 100 DEATHS EACH YEAR

BE PARTICULARLY CAREFUL

CLEAR SNOW AFTER EVERY FEW INCHES RATHER THAN WAITING UNTIL IT STOPS FALLING

Matthew Merlino, matthewmerlinodesign.com

Matt Merlino created this infographic to accompany a story about snow shoveling safety.

Weave the information from crowdsourcing efforts into the narrative of a story. Let the audience know how the information was gathered. Including the number of people who responded can add context. Was it 15 or 150? In most cases, the data you receive will not be representative of a general population. People who respond through social media are themselves a subsection of society.

Data visualization through the use of infographics can complement the written narrative. An infographic is a visual representation of factual information. The goal of an infographic is to present information in a highly visual format that enhances the audience's ability to understand the content. This multimedia element brings the data to life.

Journalists have access to a wealth of data through crowdsourcing efforts and online databases. Infographics have become essential components in journalism to highlight data. The best infographics show, and don't overwhelm the audience with data. Infographics can include a host of features such as charts, graphs, word clouds, and pull quotes from sources.

With online tools, journalists are able to create their own infographic components for their reports. Infogr.am and Piktochart are web-based platforms where you can easily build interactive infographics. Then, embed them in stories and share on social media.

Reuben Stern (@sternreuben), of the Reynolds Journalism Institute at the Missouri School of Journalism, said an awesome infographic is the combination of useful information and good design. Stern offers these tips for building infographics:[15]

- Is the information worth visualizing? Can it be more easily visualized than explained in written form? The best infographics tell stories that could not be effectively communicated any other way.

- Do you have enough details to create an effective visual presentation? Two pieces of data usually aren't enough to merit an infographic. You can simply mention in the text of the story the difference between two data points.

- Did the data come from reliable sources? Scrutinize data and sources.

- Is this something people would want to know? Just because you have data, you don't necessarily have to include it in an infographic. In other words, don't create an infographic simply because you have data. On the same note, if the data is too complex or confusing to explain in an infographic, leave it out.

- Be mindful of basic design elements. A clean design can help information shine. Start with a headline in a larger font than the headings that follow. Color can be used to call attention to parts of a graphic. Choose an infographic format appropriate for the information at hand. A chart or table is best to show how different things compare to each other. But a map would be needed if you want to show where things are located.

From the Newsroom

BLAIR HICKMAN (@AMANDABLAIR)

Adjunct Professor, New York University and Columbia University

Blair Hickman is a journalist and teacher who specializes in crowdsourcing, audience engagement, and innovation in journalism. Hickman was the audience editor at The Marshall Project, a non-profit, nonpartisan newsroom covering America's criminal justice system. Prior to that, Hickman worked at ProPublica on crowdsourcing investigations into patient harm and unpaid internships.

TELLS US ABOUT YOUR ROLES FOCUSED ON AUDIENCE ENGAGEMENT

It's an interesting field because the responsibilities can vary so widely from newsroom to newsroom. As ProPublica's community editor, I managed our Twitter, Facebook, and Tumblr pages and experimented with other platforms. A big portion of my work at ProPublica was crowdsourcing for long-term reporting projects. I was part of the health care, education, and financial teams. Because these were investigative pieces, we had a long time to work on the stories. This enabled the newsroom to see the fruits of deep user engagement.

For our series on patient harm, we launched a Facebook group for people who had been injured in hospitals and their loved ones to speak out. We also created a specific callout for doctors in order to bring them into our reporting

process. We were building sources and trust through our engagement. A lot of the doctors provided expert advice for the investigation. For this investigation, it started with a reporter already having a story idea and then turning to the audience for help. But, sometimes it begins with a general idea and then the audience can help to determine if the story is newsworthy or what the story is, as was the case with an investigation we conducted into unpaid internships. (Read more about ProPublica's patient harm project: *bitly.com/PatientHarm*.)

At The Marshall Project, much of my job was centered on audience development, growing our audience. Engagement was at the heart of that strategy. For example, we created a partnership to host series on criminal justice in an effort to expose us to new communities interested in the topic of our reporting. The interesting thing about that was figuring out what type of content was important to potential audience members in order to onboard them as regular readers.

HOW DO YOU BEGIN THE CROWDSOURCING PROCESS FOR A STORY?

It's important to understand that crowdsourcing is a subset of audience engagement. Crowdsourcing is a task that you ask the audience to do. A lot of people get excited about the tools, and they start there. But, a crowdsourcing project needs to start well before that. What's the story we are trying to tell and what is the info we need to collect? Do you want them to pick out a story? Do you want them to contribute

(Continued)

(Continued)

to a story you're already working on? Do you want them to send you personal experiences? Knowing what you want and who you are trying to target is the first step.

And after that, it needs to be research that will help you decide the tools you need. Of those people you're trying to reach—where do they live online? Sometimes you can just use the built-in audience you already have, such as if you want your audience to vote on story ideas. But, if it's sharing personal experiences, that audience research is key to making sure you're reaching people on the right spaces. That will drive your distribution strategy for a callout. It's about understanding them as people and their media consumption habits.

A good example is the patient harm story. We knew we wanted to reach doctors as well as patients and loves ones. First thing we did was launch a Facebook group, and we noticed that doctors weren't contributing. So we called a few doctors and a lot of them felt they would be attacked if they spoke out in this group. Through that research we were able to come up with a strategy specifically for medical professionals. That meant launching a page with content targeted to doctors as a way to facilitate engagement. Then, once we got them to that page, there was a call to action asking them to fill out a survey.

WHAT ARE THE CHALLENGES INVOLVED WITH CROWDSOURCED REPORTING?

Verification and the time needed to go about that process are two challenges with crowdsourced reporting. Any time you get a personal story through a callout, there are extra steps involved, and that takes time. When you talk to a "traditional" source, you typically try to vet them before you conduct the interview. You know their background, and there are cues you can pick up on during an interview to help you gauge whether they're telling the truth. In addition, you can ask them in person if they have documents or other information that backs up their claims.

With crowdsourcing, that's a bit trickier. You can and must verify these things. But it takes time to go through all the submissions, call people, ask them questions, and attempt to verify the information they submitted. In the meantime, however, you're exposing yourself to more themes and a better grasp of an issue than if you're simply reaching people by telephone. That's a great advantage of crowdsourcing.

WHAT ADVICE DO YOU HAVE FOR STUDENT JOURNALISTS?

Students need to get in the habit of sharing. Many students aren't initially active on social media. If they are, a lot of times, it's simply for personal reasons. A key to engagement and crowdsourcing is frequent interactions, posts, and callouts. I tell students they need to be able to share valuable content during the reporting process. It's also important to understand your audience. Many fields have done a better job than journalism of getting to know communities. It's important to have information about who you are trying to reach so you can develop the best strategy.

Checklist

✓ **Social Media Lists.** Create three Twitter lists: one for your beat, one for newsmakers in your region, and one for sources that will keep you updated on the latest mobile and social media journalism trends. Place at least 15 sources in each list. For the list related to mobile and social media journalism, consider the accounts I recommended you follow in Chapter 1's checklist. On my Twitter account (@AnthonyAdornato), I've created several lists that may be helpful. You're welcome to subscribe to any of my lists. The Mobile/Social Journalism list is my go-to spot to see what's being talked about in digital journalism

✓ **Tweet Chat.** Participate in one tweet chat related to a beat that interests you or to journalism in general. You may want to jump in the web journalism chat (#wjchat/@wjchat) that takes place Wednesdays at 5:00 p.m. PT. Engage! Respond to at least three of the host's questions. Retweet and reply to other participants. After the tweet chat, use Storify to create a summary of your experience. Pull in tweets from the chat and write a narrative around them. After you're done, tweet the link to your Storify reflection. Use the hashtag and Twitter handle of the tweet chat.

✓ **The Workout.** No pain, no gain. Flex your mobile and social media muscles. Get in the habit of carving out time every day to manage your social media. Remember, posts must be spread out during the week. It's all about consistency. By the end of each week, you should have

> 15–20 tweets and a combination of 10 retweets, replies, and likes

> 3–5 posts on your professional Facebook page

> A few posts to LinkedIn

> A few posts to Instagram

> Two tweets about class discussions and/or readings that you found interesting. Tell followers why and include your class hashtag.

> Followed a handful of people on each platform. On Twitter, make it a goal to follow at least five new people every week, at least as you begin to build your professional brand.

✓ **Crowdsource.** Create a callout, preferably for a story you're currently working on. Or work in groups to create a callout specifically for this checklist item.

> Build a questionnaire using Google Forms.

> Share the link and callout request to social media. (This may have to be done multiple times.)

> Analyze the data you collect.

> Create at least one infographic with crowdsourced information. Consider using Infogr.am or Piktochart to produce the infographic(s).

> If the crowdsourcing is part of a story you're working on, embed the infographic(s) in the online article. If not, write a blog post reflecting on what you learned from the crowdsourcing experience. Also, include the infographic(s).

✓ **Reminder.** Continue working on your mobile and social media strategy analysis, first assigned as part of Chapter 2's checklist. Have you been keeping up with your blog posts (Chapter 3's checklist)? At least two per week? Don't forget to share them to your social media sites.

From the Field: The Mobile Journalist

In this chapter, you will

- Explore the use of mobile devices and applications to gather, produce, and distribute news content—without having to be tied to a physical newsroom or carry around bulky equipment.

- Learn how to create a mobile journalist go-bag with accessories that will allow you to gather quality content with your device.

- Learn how to create a digital-first story pitch, preparing you to develop a plan to use social media and mobile devices while covering stories.

Photo by Anthony Adornato

A journalist uses an iPhone to record video and broadcast live reports from the 2017 U.S. Presidential Inauguration.

A video recorder. A still camera. An audio recorder. A computer. A phone. A rolodex. A single mobile device serves all these purposes—and more—nowadays. It's no wonder mobile devices are the go-to tool for modern journalists.

From the palm of his or her hand, a reporter can easily gather, produce, and share stories to any platform from nearly anywhere. No need to cart around clunky equipment. Streaming live from the field, for instance, used to require a lot of gear and a small army of people including a reporter, a videographer, and a live truck operator. Now, reporters simply open an app to bring people live to the scene.

Mobile devices and apps simplify the process of getting content from the field to the audience, most notably on social media. Not to mention, journalists can engage with followers on the fly. You see, then, why mobile devices and social media go hand in hand. You can't discuss one without the other. Imagine how cumbersome it would be to take photos or record video on traditional devices and then post that content on social media. A single mobile device gives journalists the flexibility to get the job done quickly and efficiently.

In addition to streamlining workflow, mobile devices have made it possible for a journalist to accomplish tasks traditionally carried out by a team in the field. Armed with a mobile device, a single reporter fills the roles of one or two others. In most cases, a reporter doesn't need a photographer or a videographer. This is not limited to reporters in smaller markets. Even those who work in major markets are flying solo in the field with only a mobile device.

Yes, you have to be skilled at doing it all. Welcome to the world of a *mojo*, or mobile journalist.

DIGITAL-FIRST MINDSET: MOBILE AND SOCIAL FIRST

By now, you should have a solid understanding of the digital-first mindset, introduced earlier in the book. Digital-first means mobile and social media first. A digital-first approach requires journalists to use mobile devices to share and engage with audiences on social media prior to publishing on other platforms, such as a website. A news outlet's website is important, of course, but it's increasingly becoming the secondary spot to publish information. It all goes back to the audience's news consumption habits—mobile and social.

Planning Your Story: The Digital-First Story Pitch

In newsroom editorial meetings, journalists "sell" the stories they would like to cover. A story pitch has to be convincing and well thought out. Journalists must be prepared to answer key questions before an editor decides which story they'll be assigned. The art of pitching story ideas takes time to hone. Done right, it can build your credibility and reliability with colleagues as a solid journalist.

A well-crafted pitch has always addressed the following:

- **Story focus.** What's the angle of the story? Is it focused enough so people will understand the point after watching or reading it?

- **News peg.** Who cares? Why is the story important to your audience at this point in time?

- **Sources.** Does the pitch include a mix of sources to provide a comprehensive story? Does it include "real" people, those directly impacted by the issue or topic? You can humanize a story by integrating the narratives of "real" people, instead of only experts and officials.

- **Data/background info.** What other information, such as scientific research results or statistics from government databases, are needed to provide context and illuminate the issue at the heart of a story? This type of information can back up claims made in a story.

- **Visuals.** How will you tell the story in a visually compelling manner? What visuals do you expect to gather in the field? Which multimedia elements (video, still images, infographics, etc.) are appropriate for this story?

There's a missing component to this traditional story pitch formula. It doesn't include a game plan for using mobile devices and social media. Every story pitch today needs to be digital-first. A digital-first pitch outlines how you'll use mobile devices and social media for newsgathering, distribution of content, and audience engagement.

You'll recall from our discussion in Chapter 1 that those are the three areas in which new media has impacted journalism, opening up new ways to report and engage. For each story pitch, then, include the following elements to not only sell the story to editors, but also stay focused in the field.

- **Newsgathering.** How do you plan to use social media to find sources and content for the story? You may have already been tipped off to the idea because of something you saw on social media.

- **Distribution of news.** Sharing as you go. What's your plan for keeping the audience up to date on social media? Which platforms will you focus on for this story? Which visual elements can you capture and share with your mobile device?

- **Audience engagement.** How can you bring the audience into your reporting process?

TABLE 5.1

Use this toolbox to create your own digital-first pitch for stories. Start by selecting one item from each category.

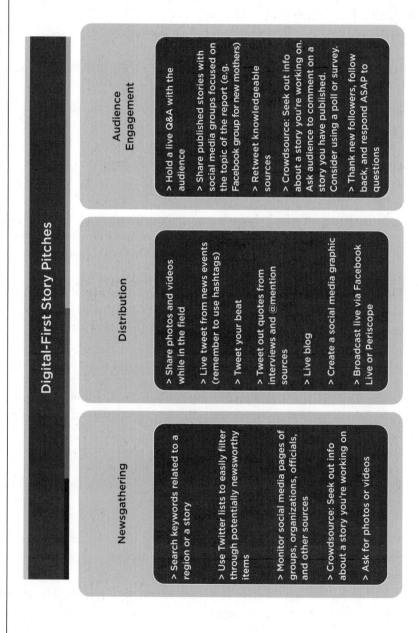

Digital-First Story Pitches

Newsgathering

> Search keywords related to a region or a story

> Use Twitter lists to easily filter through potentially newsworthy items

> Monitor social media pages of groups, organizations, officials, and other sources

> Crowdsource: Seek out info about a story you're working on

> Ask for photos or videos

Distribution

> Share photos and videos while in the field

> Live tweet from news events (remember to use hashtags)

> Tweet your beat

> Tweet out quotes from interviews and @mention sources

> Live blog

> Create a social media graphic

> Broadcast live via Facebook Live or Periscope

Audience Engagement

> Hold a live Q&A with the audience

> Share published stories with social media groups focused on the topic of the report (e.g. Facebook group for new mothers)

> Retweet knowledgeable sources

> Crowdsource: Seek out info about a story you're working on. Ask audience to comment on a story you have published. Consider using a poll or survey.

> Thank new followers, follow back, and respond ASAP to questions

Courtesy of Anthony Adornato.

Mobile and social media should be embedded in every one of these stages of the reporting process. Table 5.1 serves as a guide to help you brainstorm digital-first pitches. Create your own digital-first checklist using the items in the toolbox. For every story, explain how you will use mobile devices and social media for newsgathering, distribution of content, and audience engagement.

To start, consider picking one toolbox item from each of the three categories. Over time, it will become second nature to integrate more of these elements into your reporting mix, depending on time constraints and the type of story. Notice how some items in the toolbox overlap several categories. For example, asking followers a question isn't just a form of audience engagement; it also could be used as a newsgathering technique.

Different Types of Stories, Different Approaches

What you choose from the digital-first toolbox will depend on the type of story you're covering, for instance, a breaking news story versus a feature story. A breaking story will require more frequent posts, and you may choose to stream video live to bring people to the scene.

For a feature story, you'll want to post less frequently and might consider crowdsourcing or a live Q&A, approaches that wouldn't work as well in a breaking news situation. The type of story determines the approach, including which "channels" (Facebook, Twitter, etc.) you'll use. And, in turn, the channel will dictate certain norms, such as the frequency of posts.

Of course, for a journalist, there's no typical day. You never know what you'll be up against in the field. Even the most well-thought-out plans may have to be thrown by the wayside. So, you have to be flexible to change your plan in an instant depending on the situation.

Take the case of journalists covering a sit-in held by a handful of US congressional Democrats. The Democrats sat on the floor of the House chamber for 26 hours as they tried to convince the Republican House majority to hold votes on gun-control measures. The sit-in took place shortly after the deadly Orlando nightclub shooting in 2016, so this was a high-interest story.

The video feed from inside the chamber was turned off, because the House went into official recess. But the sit-in continued. News outlets depend on the feed to monitor House business and to record the video for use in reports, if needed. This is also the feed C-SPAN uses to broadcast congressional proceedings on air. When the feed went dark, journalists used mobile devices and social media to cover the sit-in. The real-time reporting tools included live-tweeting, live-streaming video, and live-blogging.

Only a few journalists were in the House chamber at that point. So many outlets turned to social media to locate content from lawmakers who were using Periscope and Facebook Live to "broadcast" live from inside the chamber. The live-streaming done by lawmakers was used by C-SPAN and other outlets. They not only shared the content on social media but also used the video streams as part of their on-air broadcast and website coverage.

By quickly choosing the right approach and tools for this type of event, journalists were still able to get the story. Flexibility was key.

LIVE
2:42 pm ET

Periscope Video

C-SPAN
c-span.org

ALERT DEMOCRATS STAGING SIT-IN ON FLOOR OF U.S. HOUSE

C-Span.org.

C-SPAN used Periscope and Facebook Live to cover a sit-in on the floor of the US House of Representatives.

Covering News in Real Time

When covering news in real time, there are three tools you should consider. A combination of live-tweeting, live-streaming, and live-blogging can keep the audience informed during breaking news and other types of ongoing news events.

- **Live-tweeting.** Tweeting as events unfold creates a narrative to keep followers up to speed. Answer key questions for the audience. Keep the 5 W's in mind (who, what, where, why, and when). When live-tweeting breaking news, it's imperative that journalists don't leave the audience hanging. For example, if you were to write that there's an active shooter on a campus, people expect that you'll then follow up ASAP with what you know and don't know. Include a hashtag related to the news event, so your coverage becomes part of the larger conversation.

- **Live-streaming.** Streaming video through Facebook Live or Periscope can bring people to the scene in ways other social media posts can't. There should be a reason why you're live-streaming though. Don't simply use technology for technology's sake. Tell people what they're looking at, and provide a recap periodically, as new people will continue to join the stream. Use your ethical judgment when deciding what to stream. In dangerous or unfolding situations, be mindful that you could broadcast a worst possible scenario.

- **Live-blogging.** Live blogging is a series of frequent posts on a single webpage dedicated to an ongoing news event. The page contains posts with short bursts of information, each with a time stamp so readers can see the series of events. The posts are in reverse chronological order, with the latest one showing at the top. Live-blogging was first used by technology journalists to cover Steve Jobs's keynote addresses at the MacWord conventions. Today, journalists live-blog to report on a range of developing stories, including breaking news and trials. For instance, during the House sit-in by Democrats, the *Atlantic* created a live blog on its website. A team of *Atlantic* journalists posted short bursts of text, sometimes including photos and video, as they received new information about the sit-in. A live blog can be set up as a page within a news outlet's website or through another platform, such as the microblogging site Tumblr. For student journalists, one way to experiment with live-blogging is to select a campus event and create a Tumblr page to live-blog about it. Each year, Educational Technology Day, held at Ithaca College, attracts educators from all over the northeast. As a learning drill, my students live-blog the day's event at *edtechday.tumblr.com*. They're assigned a shift, with three people each hour posting updates using the Tumblr app and several people throughout the day acting as editors for the live blog.

Appelbaum, Yoni. "A Sit-In on the House Floor Over Gun Control". June 22, 2016. *The Atlantic.*

From the Newsroom

NEAL AUGENSTEIN (@AUGENSTEINWTOP)

Reporter, WTOP-FM
Washington, D.C.

Neal Augenstein became the first major-market radio reporter to use an iPhone as the primary tool to produce news stories in the field. The Newseum recognized Augenstein's innovative work in mobile journalism by displaying his iPhone 4S as an artifact representing this new era of reporting.

WHEN DID YOU REALIZE THE POTENTIAL OF USING ONLY A MOBILE DEVICE FOR REPORTING?

When I started at WTOP in 1997, I used to go into the field with two cassette recorders.

(Continued)

(Continued)

The cell phones we carried were as big and as heavy as a bowling ball. By 2000, I was carrying a laptop, cameras, microphones—all that gear. Whenever I did something in the field, I would spend a lot of time waiting for the laptop to start and then transferring my clips onto the laptop. I thought, wouldn't it be cool if we could speed up this process.

Eventually, in 2010 when the iPhone had been out for a bit, I remember reading about an app that could do multitrack editing. So, I was quick to test that out. With that, I could do all the things I needed. It allowed me to record interviews, edit them, add my voice track and a track of natural sound, and then send the report via e-mail to the newsroom. Being able to do that on a single device was what I was looking for.

WHAT ABOUT THE QUALITY OF THE SOUND?

At the time, I remember thinking to myself that the quality needs to be good enough for broadcast.

I found that by the time the pieces get edited and go through the audio processing at the station, the sound quality recorded on an iPhone was the same to a listener as that recorded on traditional equipment. I said to myself, "Let me see if anyone notices." This was February of 2010. No one has ever said, "Are you recording on different equipment than coworkers?"

HOW DO YOU USE YOUR IPHONE WHEN YOU FIRST ARRIVE ON A SCENE?

When I arrive on the scene, I immediately look for images that I may not be able to capture again, such as a house burning. I can record a 10-second video, tweet it out with what I know at that point, and then follow up with the latest information. I can also snap a couple of photos and then tweet them out. Then I record an audio or video interview with the public information officer for the fire department, for example. I prefer video interviews, because they allow me to have both video and audio elements. If I only need audio for a report, I simply strip out the video during the editing process.

YOU'VE CAPITALIZED ON THE BENEFITS OF MOBILE REPORTING. WHAT ARE THE CHALLENGES? HOW DO YOU OVERCOME THEM?

The biggest limitation of the iPhone is that the microphone is very susceptible to wind—even a breeze. The answer to that is a simple mic windscreen that I always have. Slip it over the bottom of the iPhone, where the mic is located. It may look silly, but I've covered hurricanes with it and it worked perfectly. Also, charging is very important. I carry two charging bricks with me so I can keep reporting in the field with the charger attached to my device if needed. I'm always charging in the car and in the newsroom.

ADVICE FOR BUDDING JOURNALISTS?

Envision different ways of telling stories. What's the best way to tell a particular story? Some of the most exciting things right now are new ways to engage audiences. Realize and accept that social media storytelling is critical on this front. If someone is looking at social media and sees you're covering a story in a unique way, that pays off in the long run for your brand and that of your outlet.

For example, I covered the reopening of the Watergate Hotel. What I wanted to do is tell the story in photos with detailed captions—something that would do well in a gallery, something someone could thumb through and enjoy. I took a whole bunch of close-ups that showed details, and then I processed them all in black and white on my phone. It got me excited to tell this story and ended up being an effective storytelling format— better than a standard video package. Because of the engaging user-experience of someone flipping through the photos, they would likely remember this piece and share it.

WORKING REMOTELY

Your "office" as a journalist is, well, just about anywhere. Odds are you won't be returning to the newsroom to write and "file" most stories. The news needs to get out now on multiple platforms, and you have the tools do that from the field. Mobile devices allow mojos to be "mobile" in more than one sense. They give them the flexibility to produce stories with a single device and set-up an "office" anyplace.

In this section, you'll learn how to make the most of your mobile device to gather, edit, and distribute news. With the proper production apps and techniques, you can capture quality content while working quickly under deadline.

Photo by Anthony Adornato.

A typical mobile journalism go-bag contains the following:
1. selfie stick
2. mini tripod
3. iOgrapher filmmaking case
4. iPad Mini
5. iPhone
6. XLR cable
7. headphones
8. iRig Pre XLR adaptor
9. microphone
10. car charger
11. portable charger.

Equipment and Accessories

Before you head into the field, organize the essential equipment and accessories. They can all fit into one backpack—a journalist's go-bag. Most newsrooms will issue many of these tools of the trade when you're hired. If you're a freelancer or student journalist, you can build your own toolkit inexpensively.

There are dozens of mobile apps and a big market for smartphone accessories, but the bottom line is keep it simple. That's the mojo mantra. Weighing yourself down with equipment and accessories defeats the purpose of a mojo. Here are the essentials to get the job done:

- **Mobile device with network connectivity.** You're not going to get very far without a mobile device, smartphone, or tablet that has a network connection. No surprise that the devices of choice for journalists are the iPhone and iPad. Other devices simply don't compare to the functionality and versatility of Apple products for multimedia reporting. Many Apple iOS editing apps also offer features such as multitrack video editing, which is critical when producing professional-quality content.

  No matter the device, it must have network connectivity through Wi-Fi or a cellular network connection. Network connectivity is obviously needed in order to carry out tasks in the field, such as sending content back to the newsroom, posting to online platforms, and live-streaming. If you're using a smart phone, you'll almost always be connected via your cellular data plan. Keep in mind, the signal strength will vary depending on where the story takes you.

  If a tablet, such as an iPad, is your device of choice, there are a couple of ways to connect to a network. You can either purchase a data plan, if that's an option through the provider, or find a way to connect to Wi-Fi. Connecting to Wi-Fi available in public places, such as coffee shops and libraries, isn't always a reliable option. You never know where you'll be, and you don't want to waste time trying to find Wi-Fi you can tap into.

  A portable Wi-Fi hotspot can do the trick. There are two choices for portable hotspots. Many providers give you the option to turn your smartphone into a Wi-Fi hotspot for an additional fee. This is often referred to as "tethering." Or, you can purchase a standalone mobile hotspot.

- **Portable chargers.** The last thing you need is for your device to go dead in the middle of a story. A device's battery can drain quickly when it's getting such a workout in the field. A portable charger is a lifesaver. They cost as little as $15. Plug a mobile device into it, and you can work as the device charges. Don't forget about a car charger—another great way to charge on the go.

- **Monopod/tripod.** One of the limitations of using a mobile device is that, depending on the situation, it can be difficult to get steady video shots by hand. Overcome this challenge by using a tripod or monopod. A tripod has three legs, whereas a monopod is a single pole.

Traditional tripods are heavy and bulky. There are mini tripods made for mobile devices that can fit into your bag or even your pocket. These smaller tripods and monopods give you the stability and flexibility you need in the field. There are many different brands. Recommendation: the JOBY GripTight GorillaPod tripod (around $20). Manfrotto also sells a variety of mini tripods and monopods that work well with mobile devices.

Selfie stick? Yes, include it in your kit. The selfie stick can be handy for getting different visual angles, such as aerial shots, and recording reporter stand-ups.

Mini tripods help provide stability for shooting video and photos. In the photo on the right, the iPad Mini is placed in an iOgrapher Filmmaking Case, which is attached to a mini tripod.

- **External microphone and adaptors.** The quality of audio recorded on a mobile device is quite good overall. But there are times when an external microphone is needed to get professional-quality audio, such as while interviewing someone in a location with background noise.

  Not a problem. With a special adaptor, you can connect handheld or lavalier microphones to a mobile device. Recommendation: the iRig Pre XLR adaptor (around $40). Simply plug the battery-powered adaptor into your device's headphone jack, and then plug into that an XLR cable attached to the mic. These adaptors also have a spot where you can plug in headphones to listen to the audio. There are also microphones that plug directly into your mobile device, but many of these do not have a headphone jack, making it impossible to monitor audio while recording. Also, throw a mic windscreen in your bag. You'll need that on windy days.

- **Headphones.** The type of headphones you use to listen to audio is important. Avoid earbuds. Instead, toss into your toolkit a pair of headphones that cover your ears. These do a better job of blocking out background noise, so you can hear more accurately the audio coming into your device.

- **Optional gear.** Bringing along a laptop isn't a necessity, but it can make the job of writing stories in the field much easier than tapping on your device's keyboard. If you'd rather leave the laptop at work or don't have one, consider a portable Bluetooth keyboard. The portable keyboard makes it possible to type stories quickly on your mobile device. There are also many other attachments on the market for mobile devices. Some mojos use mini lights and camera lenses that attach to their mobile devices.

Production Apps

In Chapter 3 we discussed the social networking platforms you should be active on as a journalist. If you haven't yet, be sure to download the apps for each of those platforms: Twitter, Facebook, Instagram, LinkedIn, and Snapchat.

In addition to those, you need production apps that allow you to edit photos, video, and audio. This section highlights the best apps for journalists for these purposes. I've also noted top recommendations in each category below based on my experience using the apps in the field, my students' use of them as part of my classes, and feedback from journalists. Keep in mind, the availability of each app depends on the type of device you use.

Don't wait to test out apps for the first time in the field. Do this well before you use them to cover a story. Experiment with different apps to find which is the best fit for you. As you do this, think about how quickly each app allows you to produce quality content. Shareability is also key. It's important that the content you produce within the app can be easily sent to colleagues via e-mail, uploaded to platforms such as YouTube or Vimeo if needed, and shared to social media platforms.

Mojo Checklist

Preparation begins well before you head to a story. There's nothing more frustrating than having something go wrong in the field that could have easily been prevented. So don't wait until you're in the field to complete this checklist. Store this mojo checklist in your go-bag.

- Do you have all the gear you normally use? Mic(s), headphones, monopod, et cetera.
- Do you have enough memory on your device(s)? Check your device settings for this information.
- Are your devices charged? What about your portable charger? Did you remember your car charger?

- Do you have batteries for equipment that needs them?
- Do you have all the cords for your devices?
- Do you have all the social media and production apps on your phone that you'll need to get the job done?
- Have you tested the mic(s) you plan on using?
- Have you searched for locations where you can tap into Wi-Fi, if you need it? Certain apps pinpoint on a map where public Wi-Fi spots are located.
- Recharge and repack as soon as you get home or back to the newsroom.

There's an App for That

- ◆ Video
- ◆ Photo
- ◆ Audio
- ◆ Social Graphics

The go-to mobile production apps.

To quickly snap a photo or record a video to post on social media, you can simply use your device's camera and then share via social media apps. But for more highly produced reports, such as radio wraps or video packages that will be embedded in a web story or aired in a newscast, the production apps listed here are essential.

Video

Some video apps allow multitrack editing—the ability to mix a combination of reporter voiceovers, natural sound, sound bites, and visuals (video and photos). Others do not give users this type of flexibility, limiting the production level of video packages. The following apps have a variety of options to share your finished product, including e-mailing, posting to social media, saving to your device, and uploading to Vimeo or YouTube.

- **iMovie.** iMovie is my go-to video editing app. It's an easy-to-use app for video stories that require a combination of visuals and audio tracks. You can create a traditional TV style news package with this app. It's also simple to produce stories that include visuals, interviews, and natural sound, but no reporter track. There's a lot of flexibility within this app. The app has two tracks for video and two for audio and is packed with many of the same features as traditional desktop video-editing software. You can trim clips, split clips, detach audio from video, and much more.

The iMovie app allows layering of video and audio, among many other features.

- **Videolicious.** Videolicious is perfect for quick turnaround videos, such as breaking news updates from a scene and social media teases about a story. Select visuals from your mobile device in the order you want them to appear in the video. You then have the option to open the mic and use a forward-facing camera to record your voice or a stand-up shot. As you narrate, you tap the screen when you want the next visual to appear. The free version of Videolicious doesn't include more advanced editing options, such as trimming video clips or adjusting audio levels of natural sounds. However, the premium version, used by many newsrooms, including those of the *Washington Post* and the *Los Angeles Times*, comes with additional editing features. Journalism programs can get free access to the premium version by contacting Videolicious.

- **Voddio.** This app was one of the first used by journalists to produce video and audio stories on mobile devices. Voddio has multiple tracks for audio and video. My students and I have found there is a steeper learning curve with this app than with iMovie, its closest competitor. Voddio isn't as intuitive as other apps, and it's a bit more complicated to layer tracks. Voddio includes a feature in which you can write a script and then record the audio from the same screen.

- **Filmic Pro.** This app also offers multitrack editing options and has advanced editing features. In addition, Filmic Pro has manual controls typically seen on traditional video cameras. Open the app to record video, and you're able to lock focus, exposure, and white balance. It also gives you the option to monitor audio levels as you record.

- **Vimeo and YouTube Capture.** After producing a video, it's recommended you upload it to Vimeo or YouTube. Either one of these video sharing platforms should serve as the central place to house your videos. Most video production apps allow you to upload the finished video directly to these platforms with a few taps. The other option is to save the finished video on your mobile device, open either the Vimeo or YouTube Capture app (the main YouTube app allows you only to view videos, not upload them), and upload the video directly from your device's camera storage. After you upload to YouTube or Vimeo, it's easy to share the video to social media or embed it in a web story.

    Recommendation: iMovie, Videolicious, and either Vimeo or YouTube Capture.

Photos

The cameras on most mobile devices now include basic photo editing features such as cropping and color adjustment. Typically, that's all you'll need as a mojo. There are a range of photo apps that provide more sophisticated editing features. You can snap photos from within these apps or import from your device's photo storage. Posting photos to social media sites, saving to the device's photo storage, and e-mailing are also standard features.

- **Adobe Photoshop Express.** Don't expect this app to be as powerful as the desktop version of Adobe Photoshop. Photoshop Express is intended for easy touch-ups. Use it to adjust hue, color, brightness, white balance, and a handful of other elements. Compared to the traditional Photoshop software, there's not much of a learning curve with this app. Simplified tools give users the effects and changes they want without much effort.
- **Snapseed.** This app is a good fit for both novice and more skilled still photographers. Snapseed has more than a dozen different editing tools from basic to more advanced, most of which include different adjustments. One advantage of Snapseed is that it allows you to selectively adjust parts of a photo. Snapseed also saves your adjustments as reeditable layers (or "Stacks" in Snapseed-speak). The Stacks tool lists every edit you have applied, making it easy to remove one or more.
- **Camera+.** Like almost every photo app out there, Camera+ includes a variety of filters and editing tools. The main advantage of Camera+ is that you can shoot in manual mode from within the app. This approach allows you to manually control the exposure, focus, and white balance to get the best image. Camera+ also has a stabilizer that automatically takes the shot when your hand is most stable.

    Recommendation: Adobe Photoshop Express (although you can't go wrong with any of these three apps).

Audio

The built-in audio-recording feature on mobile devices does a fine job of recording audio, and most allow you to monitor audio levels as you record. However, they're limited in the ability to edit beyond a simple trim of the audio. To produce audio reports, you'll need an app that offers multitrack editing. With all of these apps, the audio files can be e-mailed and shared on social media, among other locations.

- **Ferrite Recording Studio.** Ferrite is aimed at journalists and podcasters, in terms of functionality and workflow. You can record interviews and voiceovers, rearrange tracks, make finely tuned edits, change volumes, and mix ambient and natural sounds into a report. While recording within the app, you can monitor audio levels. This is the go-to app for Neal Augenstein (@AugensteinWTOP), a reporter for all-news WTOP-FM and wtop.com in Washington, DC. Augenstein was one of the first major market reporters to use only a mobile device for reporting. Since 2010, he's been doing all field production and reporting on an iPhone.

- **Voddio.** Before switching to Ferrite, Augenstein used Voddio, one of the original multitrack audio and video editing apps. Voddio's layout and functionality aren't as intuitive as those of Ferrite. "The learning curve is fairly steep—the swipes, hidden menus, and ducking audio are not terribly intuitive," Augenstein wrote on his website, iphonereporting.com.[2] In addition, the Voddio software is infrequently updated, which may explain why it crashes so frequently.

- **Hokusai Audio Editor.** This multitrack audio editor is straightforward. The interface is simple and makes it easy to quickly edit tracks side by side or mix them together. Live "scrubbing" means you can hear the sound under your fingertip as you make your adjustments. You can also monitor your sound while recording.

- **SoundCloud.** Once you finish an audio story, SoundCloud is the ideal spot to upload the file to. Like Vimeo and YouTube are for videos, SoundCloud can be a centralized place for your audio reports. From SoundCloud, you can embed the audio clips directly into a web story and share via social media, among other options.

Recommendation: Ferrite Recording Studio and SoundCloud.

Storage and File Management

"Storage is very important if you're going to be a mobile journalist," said Allissa Richardson (@ProfAlliRich), a journalist and professor of mobile journalism. "Things happen and things get lost, and you don't want to be the one who had the exclusive and now it's gone."[3]

With the **Dropbox** and **Google Drive** apps, storing and managing files on mobile devices is as easy as doing it on a computer. Dropbox and Google Drive allow you to access and upload files from any device—mobile, laptop, and desktop computer. You can move raw materials and finished audio, video, and written stories from your device into any one of these apps. That provides an easy way to share content with coworkers. Simply create a shared folder in Dropbox or Google Drive, and drop in the content you want others to have access to.

There's an App for That

There are all sorts of apps that make a journalist's life easier. Here are a few other recommendations.

- **Call Recorder.** Record a phone interview and easily import the audio file to any one of the video or editing apps to use as part of a story.

- **5-0 Radio Police Scanner.** Ideal when tracking breaking news in the field. Take the police scanner on the road

with you. This app allows users to listen live to local, national, and international police, fire, and ambulance radio traffic.

- **Banjo.** This app provides an easy way to locate social media posts in real time at a specific location. Type a location in the search bar, and posts from that spot will be displayed on a map. This can be useful in breaking news situations to locate witnesses and images from the scene.

Dropbox and Google Drive are connected to many of the multimedia apps highlighted above, giving you the option from within each app to transfer content directly to Dropbox and Google Drive. As an alternative, you can save a finished report to your device and upload it to Dropbox or Google Drive. In most production apps, you can also import content stored in your Dropbox or Google Drive accounts.

It's important to note that Google Drive typically compresses uploaded video files, decreasing the quality. Dropbox is a better option for video.

If your device is running low on storage in the field, these apps can be a lifesaver. Move content from your device into one of these two apps to free up space. After moving the item, such as a photo, you can delete it from your device. It will remain wherever you transferred it to, Dropbox or Google Drive.

The Documents feature in Google Drive is useful for writing web stories or a broadcast script that can then be shared with colleagues.

Shooting and Editing Video

Regardless of the app or equipment you're using, maintain the basics of videography, audio reporting, and photography. Don't throw traditional production skills out the door simply because you're using a mobile device.

Despite all the new gadgetry, reporting is still about the fundamentals of storytelling. Quality is still king. Shaky video and inaudible interviews, for example, are what distinguish a novice from a professional. Maximize what the device can do well, and recognize its limitations. Minimize what it can't do well.

One benefit of mobile devices, beyond the mobility and simplicity of producing content, is that they can be less intrusive for interviews. Any TV reporter will tell you that the biggest barrier to getting someone to talk is the camera. A mobile device can make that experience less intimidating for interview subjects.

"When you're filming someone who is a bit of a nervous contributor, or a member of the public who hasn't had media training, they can clam up a bit when they've got a big camera in their face, as they feel overwhelmed. But if you're doing it on the phone, it's much smaller and an object they're used to, so they're definitely much more relaxed and forthcoming in interviews," said BBC reporter Dougal Shaw (@dougalshawBBC), who uses an iPhone and Filmic Pro app for video.[4]

Follow these rules when shooting and editing mobile video:

- **Airplane mode.** Put your device in airplane mode to prevent incoming calls or messages from interrupting the audio or video you're recording.

- **Horizontal or vertical?** There's much talk in the industry about whether video should be shot holding the device horizontally or vertically. There's no correct answer. It depends on the platform. If you're shooting for a TV broadcast or web story, the general rule of thumb is to turn your device horizontally when you shoot video. The video will fit the orientation of those types of screens. As mobile consumption continues to grow, though, news outlets are turning to vertical video to optimize their content for viewing on phones. Snapchat and Facebook Live, for instance, are designed for vertical video. "What we're trying to do is make sure that we're producing video that works specifically for each platform, so we don't expect one video that we produce is going to work across our site, across social networks, across devices," said Mica Gelman (@mbgelman), senior editor and head of video at the *Washington Post*.[5]

- **The basics.** The same video journalism basics you would use with a traditional camera apply to shooting video on a mobile device—most of the time. With vertical video, breaking some of the rules actually gives the mobile audience a better experience.

  - Record a sequence of shots around specific actions, events, or locations. Wide, medium, and close-up shots are key to building sequences. A series of shots that don't seem to fit together can often leave viewers with a sense of disorientation. A sequence of shots related to a specific subject creates a seamless progression. When that sequence ends, you're ready to start a new one. You have to get the appropriate series of close-up, medium, and wide shots in the field in order to be able to edit sequences.

  - Don't stay in the same spot for all your shots. Move around the scene to get different angles as you shoot sequences. Different positions give the viewer different vantage points.

  - Always get a sequence of video clips of people you interview. These will be needed to cover voiceovers in which you mention a specific person. Even if you aren't producing a video package with a reporter voiceover, you can still use this video to cover portions of a person's interview. In my experience, this is the one item many new video journalists forget to shoot in the field.

  - The rule of thirds is a foundational composition principle of videography and photography. Imagine your screen is divided by straight lines into thirds horizontally and vertically, with four points where the lines intersect. Where those lines meet, you should try to position the primary subject of your image. Most mobile devices have the option to superimpose the rule of thirds grid onto the camera screen. On an iPhone or iPad, go to the device settings to turn on this feature. With vertical video, break this rule. It's best to put the subject, particularly people you interview, in the center of the screen.

- ○ Hold each shot for about 10 seconds, or as long as an action requires. There's nothing worse than looking through raw footage and realizing you didn't get enough of a particular shot to use in a story.

- ○ It's tempting to move a mobile device more often than you would move a traditional camera. But avoid the urge to pan and tilt unless it's absolutely necessary. There should be a reason to record these types of shots. For example, to show how tall a building is or how long a line is.

- ○ When recording a stand-up for a package or a social media post, capitalize on what's happening around you to bring people to the scene. Show and tell. Using the front-facing camera can give viewers an in-the-moment intimate experience with you and the story you're covering. You can also use a monopod, tripod, or selfie stick to shoot a more traditional stand-up.

- **Zoom with feet.** Don't use the zoom controls in the camera. The resolution quality is degraded when zooming manually. Instead, when you want to get a closer shot, walk closer to the subject.

- **Steady shots.** It's always preferable to use a tripod or monopod in order to avoid shaky video. If that's not possible to get the shots you need, bring your arms and hands close to your body, and lean against something to stabilize the camera.

- **Lighting.** One challenge of shooting with mobile devices is finding the proper lighting. You have to rely on natural lighting most of the time. For starters, avoid shooting into the sun. When recording interviews, the sun should be behind you so that it acts as natural light on the subject. In low-light indoor situations, turn on as many room lights as you can and open shades or curtains. When recording interviews indoors, bring subjects to a window, and have them face it so the natural light fills their face. Never shoot into windows. The window should not be behind the subject. The same principles apply for reporter stand-ups—position yourself so that you're facing the sun or other dominant light source.

- **Play back at the scene.** Watch your video and make sure you have usable audio before you leave the scene. Be sure to play back interviews right after you record them—while the person is still with you. That will make it much easier to rerecord in case there's an issue with the quality of audio or video.

- **Editing.** When editing multitrack video stories, use the same methods as you would with a desktop editing system. First, lay down your audio (voiceover tracks and sound bites), and then layer video on top of those elements. When possible, build sequences by editing together a series of related shots. Avoid jumping from one video clip to another that's unrelated to the action in the previous one. The sweet spot for total video length for social media is 40–60 seconds; for websites, it's 60–90 seconds. Remember to include a lower-third, or title, graphic the first time we hear from a person you've interviewed. Place the person's name on the upper line and title on the bottom line. It's also customary to include a lower-third graphic at the beginning of a package to describe what the story is about. Place the description on the upper line and the location on the bottom line.

Recording and Editing Sound

Getting good audio is also vital for video. It's as important as the visuals. Whether you're producing a video package or an audio-only story, here are recommendations to capture professional quality audio.

- **Airplane mode.** You don't want the audio to be interrupted.
- **Monitor with headphones.** Always listen to the audio as you're recording. Remember, ear buds are not a substitute for headphones. Headphones give you the best sense of what's being captured on your device.
- **Don't cover the device's mic.** Know where your devices microphone is located so you can make sure your hands aren't blocking it while recording audio.
- **Get close.** The closer you get to an interviewee, the better the audio will be. This is particularly important if you aren't using an external mic. Ask the person to speak louder if needed.

- **Step away from noise.** When interviewing someone, you should try to find a location in which background noise will not interfere with the audio. For example, let's say you're covering a public meeting in an auditorium and want to interview people after it ends. Find a spot away from the crowd of people talking after the meeting.

- **External microphone.** Overcome many audio challenges by using an external microphone. If you're recording an interview in a loud environment, you'll want to use an external mic. In this type of situation, you can't rely on the built-in mic to capture quality audio of the person you're interviewing. Plug the mic into your device before launching any apps to make sure it's detected. If you're recording in a loud environment and have no external microphone, a pair of standard headphones can come in handy. They usually come with a microphone that can make a huge difference. Use a wind screen when needed.

- **Natural sound.** When capturing natural sound—such as fire truck sirens or demonstrators chanting—the built-in microphone usually is all you need. Connecting an external mic to record natural sound can be cumbersome if you need to move around quickly at the scene. When recording natural sound in windy conditions, however, an external mic with a windscreen is recommended. The built-in microphones on mobile devices are usually overtaken by wind noise.

- **Phone interviews.** There are two ways to record audio from phone interviews. You can use an app, such as Call Recorder, that saves calls as an audio file on your device. You can import the file to a video or audio app in order to edit. The other option, one recommended by Augenstein, is to have the sources record the call with their device. Augenstein has interviewees open the built-in voice app on their device, hit record before the conversation begins, and then e-mail him the file directly from the app once the call is over. He's even created a short video tutorial that he sends to sources prior to this type of interview.

- **Voiceovers.** Always use an external microphone for voiceovers. Hold the mic about six inches away from your mouth to prevent a popping sound. Record voiceovers as audio files using the device's voice recording function. There's another option recommended by journalist and mobile media trainer Ivo Burum (@citizenmojo). For voiceovers in video packages, Burum films the voiceover instead of audio-recording it.[6] This provides all the files you'll use as video clips when you start to edit. Burum advises holding your hand over the camera when you record tracks this way. The clip will be all black and easier to find among the video files. You then pull only the audio portion of that clip into your project sequence.

- **Play back at the scene.** Again, just as you do with video, get in the habit of doing this so you don't get burned with bad audio.

- **Editing.** With the proper app, editing audio-only stories is straightforward. Place voiceovers, sound bites (also referred to as *actualities* in the radio industry), and natural sound on separate tracks. This layering approach makes it easy to locate and adjust the key audio elements. For example, typically Track 1 contains all voiceovers, Track 2 is dedicated to sound bites, and the third track has any natural sound. Natural sound under voiceovers and sound bites should be adjusted so as not to overpower the other audio. The audio levels of voiceovers and sound bites should be consistent, so one isn't any higher or lower than any other. After exporting your finished piece, listen to it to make sure the audio sounds the way you want it to.

Still Photography

Photographs shot on mobile devices have even proved worthy of the *New York Times'* front page. In a 2013 front-page feature of New York Yankees player Alex Rodriguez, the *Times* used a photo taken by professional photographer Nick Laham. However, Laham didn't use any professional equipment. He snapped photos of Rodriguez with his iPhone—and in the Yankees' locker room bathroom. Latham then edited the photos through Instagram. The *Times* was one of the first major newspapers to publish a front-page photo taken with an iPhone.

With reporters able to capture quality images on a mobile device, some professional news photographers have found themselves out of a job. For example, in 2013, the *Chicago Sun-Times* let go its entire photography staff of 28 people.[7] Its reporters then received iPhone photography training to start producing their own photos and videos.

Here are the fundamentals of shooting still images on mobile devices.

- **Composition.** Traditional composition techniques will help you take eye-catching shots. Composition has to do with the position of the subject and the angle at which the photo is shot. As we discussed with shooting video, follow the rule of thirds. Place your main subject at one point where horizontal and vertical lines intersect. Also, use your foreground and background to

Photographer Nick Laham captured this *New York Time*'s front page photo with his iPhone.

The New York Times.

place objects or scenes in relation to your main subject. For example, placing a tree in the foreground of a photo with a person who is the main subject will provide depth of field and make the image more multidimensional.

- **Zoom with feet.** Just as with video, zooming with fingers degrades the quality of the visual. Move closer to a subject to avoid making your picture look pixelated and blurry.

- **Stay still.** The steadier your mobile device is when you're taking your shot, the clearer your image will be.

- **Lighting.** Use available light as you would with video. Bright light sources should come from behind the camera. Don't set the flash to automatic. Turn it on and off as needed. Manual flashes can often blur photos. iPhone and iPad cameras have a feature called *high dynamic range,* or *HDR.* HDR lets you produce a quality image when taking photos that have high-contrast light sources, such as a bright blue sky and a dark-colored building in the same shot. In HDR mode, your device combines three different exposures of the same photo to create one properly exposed image. You can turn HDR on directly from the device's camera.

- **Set focus and exposure.** The device will automatically adjust focus and exposure. Exposure refers to the amount of light in a photo. To get a better-quality photo, take control by adjusting these two elements. With the camera open, just tap on the screen where you want to set the focus and exposure. The camera does a good job of handling the rest. But, if you still want to adjust the exposure, move your finger up and down the screen to brighten or darken a photo. You can also lock focus and exposure. Press and hold on the screen to lock in settings. The words "AE/AF lock" will be displayed. To remove the lock, just tap anywhere else on the frame. Whenever there are significant changes inside the frame, your focus and exposure settings will be lost unless they're locked.[8] These techniques work with shooting video as well.

- **Shoot in burst mode.** The burst mode allows you to take multiple photos in the matter of seconds. Simply hold down the shutter button and the device will start taking photos one after another. It's an easy way to capture the perfect action shot.

- **Landscape or portrait?** Horizontal photos typically work better for web stories, which means you'll want to hold your device horizontally. For social media, the portrait orientation works better.

- **File size.** When transmitting photos back to the newsroom through e-mail or another service such as Dropbox, you might be given an option to select a photo size. When possible, maintain the original size of the photo. "Small" photos generally will not look good on websites.

- **Minimize use of filters.** Filters raise ethical concerns. Using them can alter a photo's editorial content. A photo with a filter applied to it should accurately portray what a journalist saw when taking the photo. In addition, filters can degrade the quality of an image, especially when the size of the photo is increased.

Mobile-First Workflow: A Digital Juggling Act

Today's do-it-all journalists must have the flexibility to report, write, shoot, edit, post to social media and web, and—if they work for a radio or TV station—produce a broadcast story. Workflow is all about coordinating and planning how to tackle the list of tasks.

It's a process that can be messy, chaotic, and exhilarating—a digital juggling act of sorts. With practice, workflow will become second nature. You'll create your own routine. Here are the key workflow considerations:

- **Plan.** Planning the workflow process starts before you get to a scene. What content does your newsroom expect from you? How will you get content back to the newsroom, if needed? That's where Dropbox or Google Drive come in handy. Some newsrooms also have their own upload systems and general plans for workflow that you'll become familiar with. All the apps you need should already be on your device and equipment in your go-bag. Follow the tips on the Mojo Checklist.

  What about social media platforms? Which platforms are appropriate for the story? Have a grasp of each platform your newsroom has and how they rely on you, the reporter, to provide content for those platforms while in the field. There are newsroom social media accounts and then your professional ones. You obviously will manage your own. However, for a newsroom's accounts, there are two approaches: centralized and decentralized. In the centralized approach, only certain staff members, usually a digital team, have access to an outlet's social media accounts. In this approach, the team members often rely on reporters' posts to their own professional social media accounts from the field, particularly during breaking news the reporters cover. They'll reshare that content from the outlet's main accounts. In other newsrooms, more commonly at smaller outlets, the process is decentralized. Many newsroom staff members manage the outlet's accounts.

- **Prioritize.** Triage the situation when you're in the field. What are the most critical elements you need to gather for a story? Capture those right away, because you might not have another chance. Workflow priorities will differ depending on the type of outlet you work for. Most TV stations still have their reporters shoot and edit video packages using standard cameras and computer editing software. That's in addition to using mobile devices to gather and post content for social media posts and web stories. A TV reporter, then, has to decide if recording certain video on a mobile device is the best approach. If the reporter needs a clip for a traditional TV broadcast, it might make more sense to put the phone aside for a bit and record with the video camera.

- **Publish.** Sharing content on different platforms takes place throughout the reporting process. It can be as simple as a few taps to get a photo or video on social media. Or it may require using a production app to create an audio or video component. Keep it simple. Avoid having to transfer audio or video files to another device for editing and publishing. That takes up valuable time.

Workflow in Action

Let's say you're sent out to breaking news, a house fire. You have to make lightning-fast decisions. Your workflow might look something like this.

- **Initial post.** Alert Twitter followers that you're heading to a house fire and will update them when you arrive on scene.

- **Follow through on your promise: Share as you go.** With your iPhone, you snap photos and video of firefighters battling smoke and flames. You also record interviews with a witness and the fire chief. You share the latest details in a series of tweets that include photos. In your tweets, you @mention the fire department's Twitter account. You then open the Facebook app and use Facebook Live to stream video from the scene. You show people what's unfolding. We hear your voice giving us tidbits of information. Your decision to stream live was based on the fact that the fire chief told you everyone made it out of the house without injuries.

- **Newsroom's counting on you.** A social media editor back in the newsroom is monitoring your posts and sharing your information on the outlet's main social media accounts. She retweets your flurry of tweets, creates a Facebook post with the latest details and photos you shared on Twitter, and sends out a breaking news alert to mobile app users.

- **Multimedia web story.** After four minutes of live-streaming on Facebook, you call the newsroom to let colleagues know you're about to write a 300-word story for the website. You spend the next 15 minutes drafting the story and editing a short video clip. You use the iMovie app to piece together video clips and portions of your two interviews, upload the finished video directly from your iPhone to YouTube, and then embed the video in your story.

- **Audience engagement.** You also have several Facebook comments you need to respond to, as neighbors in the area saw your live stream and are looking for more information. A Facebook follower claims crews had difficulty locating nearby fire hydrants because they were buried in snow from last week's storm. This could be an important element to the story. You track down the fire chief to ask about this and update followers.

- **Feeding content to the newsroom.** The social media editor in the newsroom needs your photos and raw video so she can create some additional content for the outlet's social media accounts. No problem. You have the Dropbox app on your phone. You simply place the video and photos from your mobile device into a shared folder on Dropbox. Collaborators with access to the shared folder can retrieve the content from any device.

- **Not done yet: Continue updating.** You update your web story and social media accounts throughout the afternoon until the scene is clear. Once you're confident you have all the information you'll get from the scene, you head back to the newsroom. You work at an outlet that prints a newspaper three days a week. The print version doesn't come out tomorrow, so you're off the hook this time around for writing a story for the newspaper.

- **Analytics.** During the next morning's editorial meeting, the social media editor discusses social media and website analytics. Your tweets received a lot of engagement, and your web story was the second-most viewed for the day. Your Facebook Live video had three dozen views.

Sound like a juggling act? You have to go in with a game plan, yet be flexible enough to change that plan on the fly. That's always been the case with reporting. Hang on for the ride. Time to flex your mobile and social media muscles.

Mojo Reporting from the Presidential Campaign Trail for NBC News

Little sleep. Lots of coffee. Plenty of planning. It was a whirlwind three days for Ithaca College journalism students who covered the South Carolina Republican presidential primary for NBC News in February 2016. Armed with mobile devices, our team crisscrossed South Carolina, providing content for the network's broadcast, digital, and social media platforms. Students got a real lesson in how to cover a major news event for multiple platforms.

Coordinating with NBC News producers, correspondents, and technical staff based in New York City and on the ground in South Carolina, we created a fluid workflow plan. Because of the nature of a major story like this, with many moving elements, we were in constant contact via phone and e-mail. Often, plans changed quickly depending on the news at a certain location and what the network needed from our team. Here's a glimpse into how we covered the primary.

- We used traditional video cameras for footage that was included in two packages that aired on *NBC Nightly News*. Our team transferred the raw footage from cameras to a laptop computer and then uploaded the video through Latakoo. Latakoo, used by NBC News and other outlets, is an online video transfer system that lets you send high-quality video from a desktop or mobile device. Once the video is in the system, all NBC News staff can access it from any location. One of the biggest challenges was finding a strong enough Wi-Fi connection to upload the video files, since at times we were in more rural areas.

- Another group of students took over NBC News's Snapchat account and the NBCBLK Instagram account for a day. NBCBLK focuses on culture and news from the perspective of people of color. Logged into NBC News's Snapchat account from my iPhone, two students were responsible for creating a Snapchat story with at least one new Snap an hour. For NBCBLK's Instagram, our assignment was to produce short video clips with people of color reflecting on the election. All those clips were shot and edited using iPad Minis and iMovie. The clips, along with a profile photo for each interviewee, were uploaded to a shared Dropbox folder. We also e-mailed short descriptive text about each person to the NBCBLK producers in New York City, who uploaded the content to Instagram.

- Students produced several multimedia stories for the NBCBLK website. Here too, iPad Minis were used to snap still photos and record and edit the videos. All content was uploaded via Dropbox, and the text of the stories was e-mailed to producers. Some of the content used for the Instagram takeover was repurposed for the web stories.

Checklist

✓ **Website Tutorials.** For video tutorials on how to use the production apps mentioned in this chapter, visit the book's companion website, *MobileandSocialMediaJournalism.com*.

✓ **Mobile-First Discussion.** You're a reporter assigned to the story below. How would you use a mobile device and social media to cover this story? Use the toolbox in this chapter as a guide (Table 5.1) to think through newsgathering, distributing information, and audience engagement. And discuss with your class what the workflow from the field might look like.

Shortly after arriving to work at 8:00 a.m., you hear on the police scanner that a train has derailed. You head to the scene, which is 30 miles north of your newsroom. By the way, you're able to listen to the police scanner anywhere, thanks to an app that gives access to hundreds of law enforcement scanners across the country. You arrive to see a crowd of onlookers at the scene. You see that several of the train cars are toppled over, and traffic in the area is at a standstill. The train is operated by CSX.

✓ **Teaching Moment.** This is your opportunity to teach your class! Each student leads a 10-minute class presentation/discussion about a current topic related to the use of mobile devices and social media in journalism. These teaching moments can be spread out over the course of the semester. This book and content from online sources mentioned in Chapter 1's checklist, such as Nieman Lab and MediaShift, can serve as starting points for ideas. Post a preview of the topic to the class Facebook page (if there is one), tweet about your teaching moment using the class hashtag, and write a blog entry about it. Topics might include how a news outlet uses new media in a novel way, an ethical issue related to the use of social media in journalism, and ideas on how journalists could use a particular mobile or social media tool.

✓ **Get in the Mojo Groove.** Time to practice mojo newsgathering and production. Use several different video apps to produce videos for a campus or community story.

> iMovie: Produce one video that includes a voiceover and sound bites, and another that uses only sound bites to tell the story. Upload both to either Vimeo or YouTube, and share to social media. Use subtitles in at least one of these videos.

> Snapchat: Produce a Snapchat story while in the field. Follow the tips for Snapchat stories in Chapter 4.

✓ **Cover It Live.** Pick one event being held on campus, and use a combination of live-tweeting, live-streaming, and live-blogging to report about it. Use Tumblr to create a live blog that multiple people can contribute to.

✓ **Scavenger Hunt.** Your workout this time around is in the form of a scavenger hunt. Complete the following tasks in no more than an hour. Use your class hashtag for each tweet. Think like a reporter. Double check your facts and spelling of names. Offer an introductory tweet to followers in which you explain the posts that will soon follow.

> **Professor on the street (not a professor you know).** Photo of and quote from a professor on campus. Ask the professor what role social media plays in our society today. Be sure you include the professor's title and department.

(Continued)

(Continued)

> **Student on the street.** Photo of and quote from a student. Ask the student where he or she gets news and if he or she uses social media to keep up on the news. Be sure you include the student's year in school and major.

> **Little-known fact.** Photo of something you think many people might not know about your campus. Include a description of what you're showing people.

> **School spirit!** Photo of and quote from someone you don't know revealing school or civic spirit.

> **Twitter video from a scenic spot on campus.** Explain what you're showing people.

> Respond to at least two tweets from classmates also taking part in the scavenger hunt.

> Finally, create a Storify that contains all your own tweets and several of your favorite tweets from classmates. In the Storify, write a short narrative reflecting on the experience and what you learned.

✓ **Reminder.** Continue working on your mobile and social media strategy analysis, first assigned as part of Chapter 2's checklist. Have you been keeping up with your blog posts (Chapter 3's checklist)? At least two per week? Don't forget to share them to your social media sites. Finally, in order to maintain consistent social media activity, aim for the following each week.

> 15–20 tweets and a combination of 10 retweets, replies, and likes

> 3–5 posts on your professional Facebook page

> A few posts to LinkedIn

> A few posts to Instagram

> Two tweets about class discussions and/or readings that you found interesting. Tell followers why, and include your class hashtag.

> Follow a handful of people on each platform. On Twitter, make it a goal to follow at least five people every week, at least as you begin to build your professional brand.

From the Field: Social Media Engagement and Audience Analytics

Y ou want to make sure you're putting your energy into publishing social media content that isn't a waste of your time—or the audience's. After all, people are bombarded with content on social media. For reporters, it's critical to understand how to cut through all this noise on social media and provide valuable content that your audience will engage with.

Think about it. What makes you stop to read a social media post? What is it about a post that attracts your attention? There are a number of things you can do to make sure people don't simply scroll past your social media posts. It all comes down to what you share while reporting and how you craft your posts.

WHAT DO I POST WHILE REPORTING?

Journalism is no longer about simply publishing a story for a news outlet's website or producing a video package for your station's 5:00 p.m. newscast. The story you cover is all about an ongoing conversation with the audience via social media platforms. Stories have lives of their own, and news consumers have grown accustomed to finding out pieces of information throughout the day.

That's why sharing information during your news reporting process is important. Think about your social media feed as a faucet of information. You provide drips of information throughout the day. All those drips help the audience engage with you, the story, and your news outlet.

Providing valuable, engaging, and consistent content will make you the go-to source for news.

In this chapter, you will

- Discuss the type of content to share while reporting in the field, how often to share it, and on which platforms in order to engage with the audience.

- Discover the role of social media optimization (SMO) and analytics in today's newsrooms.

- Explore how to post valuable content using SMO best practices and then how to analyze the effectiveness of social media activity.

- Understand how journalists' social media activity is a key driver of traffic to news outlets' websites and their overall brand.

Social Media Optimization

Not all social media posts are viewed equally. The practice of social media optimization (SMO) can help posts stand out. SMO has become a commonly used term in newsrooms to describe how posts are crafted and published for maximum audience engagement. Keep the fundamentals of SMO in mind when thinking about what you'll share during the reporting process.

A tweet or Facebook post that is social media optimized is more likely to lead the audience to share, like, and comment—that's engagement! In addition, as we discuss later in this chapter, these posts can attract attention to news outlets' websites. Journalists' and news outlets' social media activities are becoming a key driver of traffic to outlets' websites.

With people spending more time on mobile devices and social media platforms, their first point of contact with news is often on social media. People go directly to websites less and less often, as we first discussed in Chapter 1.[2] Instead, compelling social media posts are leading people to an outlet's website for more information.

This tweet and Facebook post are examples of social media content optimized for maximum engagement. Both posts use compelling visuals, @mentions, and hashtags.

Makes sense, right? How many times have you scrolled through your social media feeds, seen an interesting post, and then clicked on a website link to get more information? This is becoming a more common way for people to visit websites, rather than directly opening a web browser and typing the URL.

Chip Cutter (@ChipCutter), a former Associated Press business reporter who works as a content editor for LinkedIn, says the key to mastering SMO is to "share so frequently that you are considered an expert, ensure every post has a high-quality image attached and write headlines that start conversations."[3]

The following SMO techniques can make your posts stand out from the rest.

Visuals

Including photos or videos is an easy way to catch social media users' attention. Unlike posts that include only text, visuals related to your story fuel engagement by bringing a story to life. They bring the audience to the scene of the story. In addition to uploading a single photo, Facebook and Twitter allow you to create photo galleries. Galleries can be effective if you have a series of compelling photos.

Social Media Graphics

One way of creating engaging social media posts is by incorporating graphics. More and more news outlets are using social media graphics, because they're not only eye-catching in a sea of posts, they also allow you to include more information than is possible in a single tweet.

As you see in the photo, NPR used social media graphics to create a list of the latest information during its coverage of the deadly nightclub shooting in Orlando. The *New York Times* frequently produces social media graphics that include a powerful quote from a story. Adobe Spark Post and Canva are apps that allow users to quickly create these visuals for social media.

NPR ✔
@NPR

Mass Shooting At Orlando Gay Nightclub: What We Know n.pr/1YjiMkl

WHAT WE KNOW: ORLANDO NIGHTCLUB SHOOTING

- 50 people killed, 53 injured
- Shooter identified as Omar Mateen
- Shooting began at 2:02 a.m., ET., at Pulse, a popular gay nightclub
- At least 30 rescued following hostage situation with shooter
- Deadliest mass shooting in U.S. history

JUNE 12, 2016 10:59 AM ET

n p r

RETWEETS 2,035   LIKES 726

11:03 AM - 12 Jun 2016

2K   726

@NPR. Twitter Post. June 12, 2016.

Data scientists at Twitter analyzed the content of millions of tweets from verified users in the United States to understand what resonates best with followers interested in news and other industries.[4] Tweets that include photos were 35 percent more likely to be retweeted, and those with videos were nearly 30 percent more likely retweeted.

Research from the American Press Institute also shows that Facebook posts with an embedded photo got the most likes, comments, shares, and link clicks.[5]

Simply uploading photos or a video isn't enough. It's important to give your audience context about the visuals. In the text of your post, provide information about what you are showing them.

Tagging and Mentioning

Most social media platforms allow you to tag locations, individuals, and brands (such as companies, politicians, and organizations).

Tagging the location of a news event can be valuable as people search for information related to that particular place. For example, drivers stuck in traffic because of an accident may decide to search social media using the name of the road, exit, or town they are on or near. If you were covering this story, your posts are more likely to turn up in search results if they're tagged with the location.

You also can tag individuals and brands in your posts as well as in photos, assuming the individual or brand has an account on the platform. Users will be alerted to let them know they're tagged, and this will increase the likelihood that they interact with your posts. You've probably experienced this yourself when family and friends tag you in social media posts. There's a tendency for people to share or comment on posts that they are tagged in. You see the ripple effect here. Your post has the potential to reach many more people than just your followers.

This is also the case when using the @mentioning feature in the text portion of your posts. Many social media platforms allow tagging and/or mentioning. To create an @mention, you include the @ sign followed by the username. Just as happens with tagging, an individual or brand @mentioned in your posts will receive an alert and is more likely to engage with your content.

For example, the *Denver Post* will @mention pages of restaurants that are involved in stories. Without this @mention, readers might not see the posts, especially if they don't follow the newspaper's social media accounts. According to Twitter, news organizations that tweet 20 percent fewer URLs and 100 percent more @mentions grow followers by almost 20 percent.[6]

The bottom line: Get in the habit of tagging and @mentioning sources and subjects that are part of your stories. Remember, we're not just talking about people. Tagging and mentioning companies, schools, or organizations can be highly engaging. Find their usernames on social media platforms early in the reporting process, and then include their social media handles in your posts.

Hashtags

A hashtag is the # symbol followed by the subject or keyword of your post. The use of hashtags can help your social media content become part of a larger conversation and reach more people than just those who follow you. According to Twitter, including a hashtag can double engagement for individual journalists and boost it 50 percent for news organizations. Avoid vague hashtags. Instead, hashtag words that are specific to a story.

Determine if there's already a hashtag that's commonly used for the story you're covering. If so, use it. If not, you can hashtag keywords such as the names of individuals, places, and things. People often do hashtag searches related to news stories, particularly in breaking news situations. Avoid using too many hashtags in a single post. It can be difficult to read and annoy readers.

Your use of hashtags can be an effective way for your posts to become more visible. If you're covering a developing story and posting consistently, the use of hashtags can attract attention to your reporting. It's a chance to let others know you're providing valuable information.

Links

Social media is increasingly becoming the first place users learn about news. It's where they will continue to follow developments. While your blasts of details on social media helps the audience see a story unfold, links to information provide them with additional perspective.

Think of content on your news outlet's website that you can link to in social media posts. You may be covering an ongoing issue that you have reported on before. That's a perfect opportunity to share your outlet's previous reports on the topic while you work on gathering the latest developments.

Once your stories are published on your outlet's website, be sure to share those links. When you share links to your stories, also include a photo from the story to help attract attention. Sharing links to your stories can significantly increase the number of people who view your stories.

Optimize This!

Using the social media optimization techniques outlined in this chapter, write three tweets for the following scenario and then discuss your approach with classmates.

A fire at an apartment building in a downtown section of your city has forced 50 people out of their homes. The city fire department sends 25 fire fighters to put out the fire. Shortly after arriving on the scene, you learn that the tenants will not be able to go back in the building for at least 24 hours. The fire chief tells you, at this point, the extent of damage to the apartments is not known. The Red Cross arrives on the scene to assist the displaced tenants with temporary housing.

More info on optimizing. On his website, Jeremy Littau, a journalism professor at Lehigh University, describes seven different forms Twitter optimization can take: breaking news, developing news, standard news, commentary/analysis, factoid, questions, and clickbait. To learn more about these types of tweets, visit *bit.ly/OptimizingTweets*, where you'll also find a class exercise created by Littau.

Writing for Social Media and Mobile Devices

A combination of photos and videos, tags and mentions, hashtags, and links can provide a powerful social media post—one that is rich in content for the audience. But, it's critical that quality writing does not get lost in the mix.

Writing is a fundamental of good journalism. Social media optimization techniques must be accompanied by solid writing. The kind of writing that is clear, concise, accurate, and balanced.

Also keep in mind how people consume news. In a survey conducted by the Associated Press and the American Press Institute, 78 percent say they used their smartphones to get news during the past week.[7] That number continues to increase. They not only engage with news while swiping through social media feeds but also read articles on their mobile devices.

This impacts how journalists craft social media posts and write stories that will be viewed on mobile devices. Reading text on mobile screens is more difficult than reading on larger screens, and the information it conveys is more difficult to comprehend. The size of the screen limits the amount of information that can be displayed.

In addition, there are so many distractions. People tend to multitask while on a mobile device. They may not have the time, let alone patience, to read an entire story.

You can make it easier for the audience to locate, understand, and engage with information by writing in a specific style for both social media posts and stories that will likely be read on mobile devices. Let's start with social media posts.

Social Media Posts

- **Critical info first.** Sharing the most important information related to a story should be top priority. This approach is particularly important during breaking news and developing stories. The "who," "what," "where," "why," and "when" are often the first pieces of information your audience needs. Avoid sharing details on social media until they are confirmed, despite what information other journalists or outlets are sharing. Accuracy and verification trump speed—that urge to be first.

- **Short bursts, multiple posts.** Brevity is key. Short bursts of information on social media are more digestible than longer posts. On some platforms, such as Twitter, you don't have a choice because of the character limits.

  "Twitter is a powerful tool for writers. With its 140-character limit, it's like an electronic editor that forces us to find a focus and make every word count. It's a verbose writer's friend and worst enemy—a constant reminder that it's often harder to write short than it is to write long," wrote Mallary Jean Tenore (@mallarytenore), a journalist and managing editor of the Poynter Institute's website.[8]

  The downside to brevity is that it can be difficult to communicate the full context of what you're sharing. Don't leave unanswered questions for the audience. You can provide this context by sharing multiple posts that give followers the information they need.

- **Start a conversation.** Social media writing is more informal than traditional news writing. We're having a "conversation" with our followers. Asking a question, including a short quote from a source you just interviewed, and writing in active and descriptive language can help foster interactions. In addition, giving followers a behind-the-scenes look at your reporting process is a unique way to engage them. Show them what it takes to get a story.

  Coming across as a "real" person can help build a relationship with the audience, making them more likely to engage with your work. Show some personality when appropriate. Creating your own distinctive writing voice on social media can be an effective way to connect with followers. The American Press Institute's analysis of news outlets' Facebook posts found that posts using a casual voice received more likes on average.

- **Don't overhype.** Clarity works better than being clever or obscure in tweets, wrote Michael Roston (@michaelroston), senior staff editor at the *New York Times*, in an article for Nieman Lab.[9] Making a story out to be something it isn't or overhyping a story is inappropriate.

- **Follow AP style.** Your social media posts should adhere to correct grammar, spelling, and punctuation. This conveys a level of professionalism and credibility. It's common to abbreviate words in social media posts. The general rule of thumb is to follow the *Associated Press Stylebook* abbreviation guidelines.

Mobile-Friendly Stories

- **Short and shareable headlines.** The mantra "every word counts" has always been familiar to journalists. It takes on new significance when it comes to crafting headlines that will be viewed by mobile users. Succinct headlines are critical.

  BBC News has a best-practice guideline to help its journalists write and create compelling content with mobile-first in mind.[10] BBC News recommends headlines of no more than 55 characters. A headline with more than 55 characters can appear lengthy on the top of a mobile screen.

  In addition, think about "shareability." After users read an article, they may want to share it on social media or e-mail it to a friend. The article headline typically becomes the text of the social media post, making it all the more important to keep the headline concise.

- **Front-load stories.** Get to the point. Place the most important information at the top of the story. Under the headline, include a compelling one-sentence summary of the story followed by the most important information. BBC News has a rule that readers should be able to get the key points of a story within the first four paragraphs. Readers who can't find the key information within the first few paragraphs can get frustrated and leave the page.

  In addition, creating a Key Points section between the headline and main body of the story can be useful for readers. With a few bullet points, summarize the main points of the story in this area.

Hurricane Matthew hits Haiti

By Max Blau, Holly Yan and Steve Visser, CNN

🕐 Updated 9:40 AM ET, Tue October 4, 2016

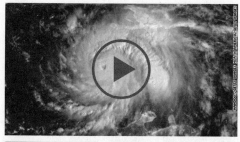

 01:11   ▶ 01:38

Hurricane Matthew taking aim at Haiti, US East Coast

How are hurricanes named?

How t hurric

Story highlights

Forecasters warn that Hurricane Matthew is "extremely dangerous"

The Category 4 storm made landfall in Haiti Tuesday

Editor's Note: Are you affected by Hurricane Matthew? If it is safe for you to do so, WhatsApp us on *+44 7435 939 154* to share your photos, experiences and video. Please tag #CNNiReport in your message.

(CNN) — Hurricane Matthew pounded western Haiti Tuesday morning, packing winds of 145 mph as it made landfall.

The "extremely dangerous" storm has already killed at least three people, caused cruise ships to change course and prompted officials to declare states of emergency.

Collision course for Cuba

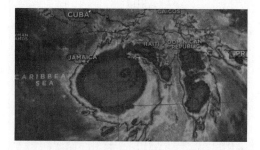

After passing through Haiti, forecasters expect Matthew to churn toward Cuba, where it is expected to move near the eastern coast Tuesday afternoon. The storm could dump up to 20 inches of rain in some isolated parts of the country.

Watches and warning

Hurricane warning is in effect for:

• Haiti

• Cuban provinces of Guantanamo, Santiago de Cuba, Holguin, Granma and Las Tunas

• Southeastern Bahamas, including the Inaguas, Mayaguana, Acklins, Crooked Island, Long Cay and Ragged Island

• Central Bahamas, including Long Island, Exuma, Rum Cay, San Salvador and Cat Island

• Northwestern Bahamas, including the Abacos, Andros Island, Berry Islands, Bimini, Eleuthera, Grand Bahama Island and New Providence

Hurricane watch is in effect for:

• Cuban province of Camaguey

Source: National Hurricane Center

This is a series of screenshots of a CNN story on a mobile device. The story includes mobile-friendly features—the use of "Story Highlights" at the top, lists, visuals to break up text, and headings—that make the content easily digestible on a small screen.

Source: Blau, Matthew, & Yan, Holly. "Hurricane Matthew hits Haiti," October 4, 2016. CNN.com.

- **Bite-sized, "snackable" chunks.** Many people scan before they decide to read, especially mobile users. Headings, bullet points, and lists in the body of a story provide visual cues. Think of them as guideposts that give readers an idea of how a story is segmented out. They allow readers to instantly see where certain information is located and help them decide which portions to read.

  According to a study by Jakob Nielsen of the Nielsen Norman Group, people read online pages in an F-shaped pattern.[11] Much of what was learned in this study can be applied to mobile viewing. The first paragraph is typically read in its entirety. From there, readers scan and skim. They scroll along the page for visual cues. Headings, bullet points, and lists create "snackable" content, bite-sized chunks of information that are more easily digestible than lengthy text with no visual cues.

- **Keep it short.** Keep the length of the story and paragraphs short. Stories should be no longer than 500–600 words. If background information is needed, think about putting these details in a list rather than eating up multiple paragraphs. This can help trim the length of the story.

  Paragraphs of no more than a few sentences are typical of traditional newswriting. This approach is even more important on mobile. Lengthy paragraphs act as speed traps, slowing down readers. A paragraph viewed on a desktop computer will appear about double the length when viewed on a mobile device.

Beyond the "Final" Story: Continuing the Conversation

You've worked all day on a story, sharing information on social media and then publishing a multimedia package online. Don't consider this the final draft of the story.

This may only be the beginning.

Social media allows journalists to get instant feedback on stories and social media posts. The audience is active, interacting with stories in new ways. It's common for the audience to turn to social media platforms to share their thoughts about stories.

These conversations might be reactions to your story, or they could be general comments about the topic at the center of your report. Journalists need to monitor these conversations.

The feedback may serve as a source for follow-up coverage. Perhaps it will provide a different angle to your initial story. The fact that a story or issue generates significant social media reaction could be reason alone for follow-up coverage.

Make sure you're not just reading the feedback, but also responding.

Scott Kleinberg (@scottkleinberg), former social media editor at the *Chicago Tribune*, says not responding is "the digital equivalent of someone ignoring you—someone standing in front of you and not answering you when you talk."[12] Kleinberg adds, "You wouldn't like that in real life, and you wouldn't like that in social media."

Journalists must set aside time in their workdays to maintain these conversations. Your social media followers will appreciate the interaction. It's a two-way dialogue that can strengthen the connection with readers and viewers.

Journalists who interact with their followers are viewed as more credible and rated more positively than journalists who use Twitter solely to disseminate news and information, according to a study conducted by Hope College journalism professor Mi Rosie Jahng and Lehigh University journalism professor Jeremy Littau.[13]

Certainly not all comments are going to be positive. In your reporting career, you'll encounter a healthy dose of criticism. Sometimes it's constructive. Other times, it's of no value.

How, and if, you respond to criticism on social media will likely depend on the language and tone of the comments.

Steve Buttry, a former journalist who conducted social media training in newsrooms across the country, encouraged responding to criticism that is hostile or disrespectful.

"Some of them may think you're not listening, and you change their view by answering respectfully," Buttry wrote on his website, The Buttry Diary.[14]

However, he said, if a respectful response encourages a troll, don't engage long.

Checklist

Sharing as You Go. This is the first of two checklists in this chapter. They're broken up into two because you'll have to complete the tasks in this checklist before you can be effective in using the second checklist, which focuses on analytics.

You're now ready to share information with your audience as you report from the field. You should have a social media game plan for every story before heading out the door. Digital-first story pitches (outlined in Chapter 5) combined with the tips in this chapter will help you brainstorm what to share during your reporting on a particular story.

Creating your own social media checklist will give you an organized approach to using social media while reporting. Remember, posts should be social media optimized. For example, they'll include @mentions, hashtags, and visuals—items that lead to increased engagement.

Repetition and experimentation are key. After repeatedly testing out different approaches, sharing as you report will become second nature. You'll also learn what works and what doesn't.

Here's a sample checklist of items to complete for your next story.

✓ **At least four tweets related to your story.** Give your audience meaningful information. Ideas we've discussed: Use quotes from sources, ask a question about the story, provide a behind-the-scenes look. When possible, include @mentions, tags, and hashtags. Using Adobe Spark Post or Canva, produce a social media graphic for one of the tweets.

✓ **One post to your professional Facebook page.** Use the same engagement tactics you used for Twitter. However, Facebook and Twitter require different approaches to the number of times you post. The general rule is that Twitter is intended for quick, more frequent bursts of information. Fewer posts are more effective on Facebook.

✓ **Video tease.** Produce a 30- to 45-second video that gives the audience a preview of your story, and then share it to your professional social media platforms. Experiment with Videolicious or the iMovie app. You can upload videos directly from those apps to YouTube or Vimeo, and then share to your social media accounts. For a future story, switch it up. Create a Snapchat story or use Twitter's video feature. To view a great example of a video tease used during a breaking news story, check out this tweet from NBC News's Jacob Soboroff (@jacobsoboroff): *bitly.com/VideoTease.*

✓ **Photos.** Share two photos to your Twitter account, professional Facebook page, and Instagram. Provide information about what you're showing followers. When possible, based on the platform, consider creating one gallery with the images rather than separate posts.

✓ **Mobile story.** Publish a 500- to 600-word multimedia story to your class website or your personal website. The story should be intended to be viewed on mobile devices. Use the strategies for writing mobile stories—short and shareable headlines, front-loaded key information, bite-sized chunks—and keep it short. Include a photo gallery with images you take on a mobile device. In addition, embed a one- to one-and-a-half-minute video produced with a mobile video app. Share the story on your social media platforms.

From the Newsroom

BRIAN FOSTER (@FOSTERDIGITAL)

Managing Editor of All Platforms

KMBC-TV (ABC, Hearst Corporation)
Kansas City, Missouri

YOUR JOB TITLE INCLUDES "ALL PLATFORMS." WHAT EXACTLY ARE YOU RESPONSIBLE FOR?

At KMBC, the managing editor of all platforms oversees the content we push out on KMBC-TV, KMBC.com, our apps, and social platforms. So that means I'm making sure that the right "type" of content is going out on each stream. What are we leading with on the air? What sort of video content are we pushing out on Facebook? Where are we placing that slideshow on the app? I'm also making sure the content is accurate, well-written, and well-edited, among other factors. In addition, I oversee the assignment desk—we call it the hub of content at KMBC-TV—and the digital employees.

WHICH SOCIAL MEDIA PLATFORMS ARE REPORTERS AT YOUR STATION EXPECTED TO BE ACTIVE ON? WHAT RECOMMENDATIONS DO YOU HAVE FOR JOURNALISTS TO MAKE THEIR SOCIAL MEDIA POSTS RESONATE WITH AN AUDIENCE?

We have social media guidelines that I developed, in conjunction with other managers, to help ensure reporters are active on social media. Our reporters are responsible for keeping their Facebook and Twitter feeds updated throughout the day. We also suggest they be active on Instagram, though that isn't a requirement at this point.

(Continued)

To ensure your social media posts resonate with the audience, they need to be compelling, genuine, and happen with regular frequency. A quick story: One of our anchors went home after work and recorded a Facebook video, talking about what a tough night it was. Two firefighters died in a fire. It was genuine. It was real. The video ended up going viral. View the post at *bit.ly/KMBC-TV*.

WHAT ROLE DO ANALYTICS PLAY IN YOUR DAY-TO-DAY TASKS?

Monitoring analytics is critical to understanding what works. We use Google Analytics to track our website page views, sessions, and video views, among other key data. We also keep a close eye on Real-Time Google Analytics, which allows us to monitor activity as it happens on the website or app. (For example, you can see how many people are on your site right now and which pages/content they're interacting with.)

Facebook Insights and Twitter Analytics are our go-to sources to track engagement on those platforms. Sprinklr is a tool we use to populate posts on our Facebook and Twitter accounts.

IS IT WORKING? MEASURING THE SUCCESS OF YOUR MOBILE AND SOCIAL MEDIA ACTIVITY

How do you know if your mobile and social media activity is successful? Is the audience engaging with your content? Analytics help journalists answer these questions. After all, what's the point of all your tagging, @mentioning, tweeting, and Facebook posting if you're just talking to thin air?

Analytics have long played a role in newsrooms. News outlets have constantly monitored the number of people who are interacting with their news products and how they're interacting with the content.

The more we know about our audience, the better we can serve them. Analytics allow journalists to understand

- What the audience cares about.
- If we're reaching our intended audience.
- How the audience is finding our content.
- What the audience does once it sees our content.

Traditionally, TV newsrooms have used Nielsen ratings to measure the success of newscasts. TV newsrooms pay close attention to not only the number of people watching specific newscasts, but also the demographic of those viewers and how that compares to the competition.

Print outlets have traditionally tracked key data such as circulation (the number of copies circulated to the public) and readership (the number of readers).

> *"Having a better understanding of data really helps you be a better storyteller as a journalist more than anything else,"* says Michael Roston (@michaelroston), *part of* the New York Time's *social media team.*
>
> *"It used to be that reporters were focused on satisfying editors, but I think a lot of reporters these days should be thinking more about how they're going to connect with an audience, and if you have a better idea of what does and doesn't work with that audience, ultimately you're going to do a better job of telling them stories."*[15]

The front of the *Democrat & Chronicle* (Rochester, New York) newsroom is called Mission Control. Monitors feature digital metrics that show how stories are resonating with readers in real time. "The metrics are among the tools we use to determine the direction of digital coverage and what might play well on the front page of our print edition," said Karen Magnuson (@kmagnuson), editor and vice president of news at the outlet.

TV news ratings as well as newspaper circulation and readership remain important metrics in newsrooms today. But they're now just one piece of a much larger puzzle. As people consume news differently, it's no surprise that journalists are rethinking measurement.

Website analytics provide additional insight. News outlets track website metrics, such as the number of people who visit the website, the type of stories they view, and how long they stay on the site.

With the emergence of social media, measurement has become even more complex. It no longer makes sense to rely only on old metrics. Audiences are active on new platforms. This requires journalists to use different ways of finding out if the time they spend sharing information and engaging social media users is actually paying off.

We'll discuss where you can find analytics and how to make sense of the numbers. It's easier than you think! First, let's talk about the role of social media and web analytics in newsrooms.

How Newsrooms Use Social Media and Web Analytics

The path many people take to get their news is quite different from ten or even five years ago. Social media is increasingly their first point of contact with news. From there, links in social media posts lead many news consumers to a news outlet's website. And they're likely using a mobile device at this time.

You can see then that social media and website analytics go hand in hand. This relationship between social media activity and website traffic is closely monitored in newsrooms.

In fact, Facebook drives at least 40 percent of traffic to news sites.[16] That percentage is even higher—upwards of 50 percent and more—when you look only at people using mobile devices. Among the top 50 news sites, at least 39 now get more site traffic from mobile devices than from desktop, according to findings from the Pew Research Center.[17]

Cory Haik (@coryhaik), former executive director of emerging news products at the *Washington Post*, saw this trend firsthand. Opening a web browser and entering a URL to a news website is becoming a thing of the past. "People won't type in WashingtonPost.com anymore," said Haik.[18]

Recognizing that you can no longer expect people to come directly to your website, the *Washington Post* ramped up its social media strategy to draw in viewers. The *Post* was aggressive in distributing its content via social media networking sites.

The efforts paid off. For the first time, in October 2015, more people visited the *Washington Post*'s website than the *New York Times*'. The *Post*, like other outlets, used social media optimization techniques to engage with the audience, which ultimately drove traffic to its website.

Remember the approach: Catch users' attention with compelling social media posts, and they'll be more inclined to find out more on the website. And once they get to your website, the content needs to be easily viewed on a mobile device.

By tracking the referrals, or how users get to a website, news outlets are able to determine how much traffic can be attributed to the social media activity of journalists and the outlets' social media accounts.

In addition to website analytics, there are social media analytics that can help journalists gain insight into how users are engaging with specific social media posts. The analytics checklist in this chapter outlines how to view website and social media analytics.

The insights gained from analytics are used in a number of ways, including these:

- **User experience.** Website analytics allow newsrooms to determine the types of devices readers are using while visiting their websites. We know people nowadays are increasingly viewing websites using a mobile device. This information is important, because it shows that newsrooms need to test how their content looks on multiple platforms, such as desktop computers and mobile devices. The BBC News recommends always previewing stories for how they look on mobile devices, and, once a story is published, checking to make sure the story looks eye-catching, clean, and readable on every platform it's on.

- **Editorial decisions.** Analytics also help guide editorial decisions. According to a study of news editors conducted by Missouri School of Journalism, the majority of online newsrooms use analytics to make decisions about which stories to cover, where stories are placed on their websites, and how the stories are presented.[19]

It's not uncommon for story selection to be based on how well content is performing. If a story or topic generates interest or buzz—a spike in traffic and engagement—journalists may be more likely to be assigned to it.

The same approach holds true in TV newsrooms. A survey of local TV newsrooms found that popular, or trending, topics on social media factor into which stories are covered in newscasts.[20] However, news is about giving people what they need to know, not necessarily what they want to know. So relying too heavily on trending social media content may mean other, more important, stories are lost in the mix.

Social media analytics also shed light on what followers are most engaged with in social media feeds. Posts that are most interacted with can help journalists understand what works and what doesn't on social media platforms. If a post didn't receive much engagement, you might ask yourself what it is about that post that left the audience uninterested.

- **Employee evaluations.** This last point makes many journalists cringe. Imagine having your reporting skills based on how many views your story gets or how many social media followers you have. An increasing number of newsrooms are using analytics to evaluate their newsroom staff members.

  In the survey conducted by the Missouri School of Journalism, nearly a fourth of online news editors reported that they use web metrics as part of the performance evaluation of their employees. At some news outlets, the compensation of journalists is tied to the number of stories they write and/or the amount of clicks their stories generate. This reflects the increasing impact of the use of analytics in their news work.

Pitfalls of Analytics

It's no surprise that the use of web and social media analytics has caused debate within the journalism industry. Relying solely on analytics to shape newsroom decisions has its pitfalls.

Take, for example, newsrooms that evaluate journalists based on web metrics. In an effort to get the most clicks, journalists may feel pressure to turn out stories that are more entertainment driven or trivial rather than of sound news value.

Journalists should question whether those stories are really worth pursuing. Are you chasing the story simply because it will drive traffic to the website? Does the story provide meaningful and relevant information to your community?

An emphasis on the number of clicks and page views can also lead to the use of clickbait. Clickbait is a story headline or social media post that is sensational or misleading, and is used in an effort to entice people to click on a link. Clickbait posts can be deceptive by including suspenseful language and leaving out key information.

Clickbait undermines your credibility and that of the journalism profession. It leaves the audience frustrated after clicking on a story that didn't live up to the hype.

"I try to be really careful about not posting something that I can't deliver," says Irene McKisson (@irenemckisson), of the *Arizona Daily Star*. "You lose trust that way really fast."[21]

Evaluating journalists based on the number of stories they produce or clicks those stories generate can be problematic in other ways as well. Churning out story after story may not leave time for enterprise and investigative reporting—types of stories that can take months or more to research and write.

The late journalist David Carr explored this topic in his *New York Times* column, "Risks Abound as Reporters Play in Traffic."[22] It's not just entertainment news sites or digital start-ups, such as Gawker and BuzzFeed, that are turning to analytics to measure reporters' performance. Carr discusses how traditional media outlets are also playing the analytics game. Newhouse Advance Publications, which operates about a dozen local news websites and newspapers, started requiring reporters at the *Oregonian* to post new articles at least three times a day. As Carr notes, it was part of a digital-first initiative to increase page views by nearly 28 percent in one year.

Another pitfall of the use of analytics is relying too heavily on quantitative data to determine the success of a journalist's work. Not everything can be counted. Narrative descriptions are as valuable as short tweets and @mentions.

For example, monitoring comments and the tone of comments on stories and social media posts is an important way to learn about which stories are resonating with the public.

And one of the most important ways to measure success in journalism is by the positive impact it has in society. Did your newsroom's reporting get a corrupt official fired? Lead to new legislation? Put a crook in jail?

These are questions that can't simply be answered by watching the numbers.

Analytics Tools

Now that you have an understanding of how newsrooms use analytics, it's time to familiarize yourself with the tools of the trade. There are a variety of analytics platforms that gauge audience activity on websites and social media.

Many analytics dashboards are free and share common features like those described below. Some newsrooms, such as NPR, have built their own analytics dashboards designed for staffers to learn more about how people are connecting with their work online.

Where do you find useful data?

Facebook Insights

Facebook offers detailed analytics for professional pages, such as those of journalists and news outlets. Keep in mind, Facebook Insights analytics are not available for personal accounts, making it all the more important to create a professional Facebook page on which you share content. (See Chapter 3 for information about setting up a professional page.)

The Overview tab gives you the most important data about your page, including new page likes, post reach, and engagement for the time period you choose. From the Overview page, you can dig deeper into the data. For example, select a date range to see if you had more engagement one week versus another, or check to see which posts are receiving the most engagement.

Analytics Tutorials

For video tutorials of each of the analytics platforms described in this chapter, visit the book's website: *MobileandSocialMediaJournalism.com*.

Here's a breakdown of key data on Facebook Insights.

- **Likes.** The Likes section is straightforward. It shows the page's fan growth, or the number of people who have liked it. Use the date selector to view the number of likes from the last week, month, or other time period. As you hover over the graph, you can view the number of likes you had on a particular date.

- **Reach.** Total Reach indicates the total number of people who have seen any content associated with the page. Post Reach indicates the number of people who have seen a particular post.

  But how do you know if they're actually interacting with your content, instead of just viewing and scrolling on? The Engagement portion of this dashboard helps you determine the number of people who liked, shared, or commented on your posts.

- **Page views.** This portion gives you the total number of times your Facebook page was viewed during the time period you select. This is where you can also see the areas of your Facebook page that people visit most, including your timeline, info, and photos tabs.

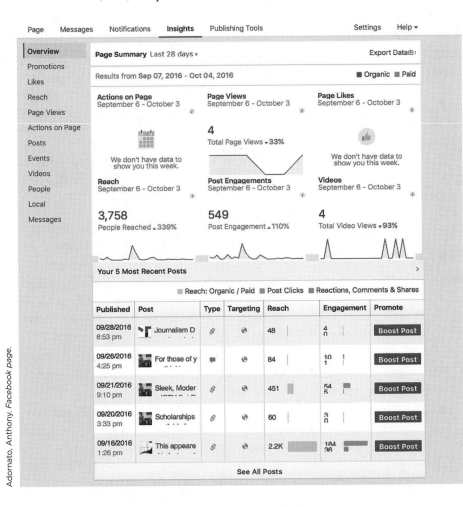

Facebook Insights
Overview page

You can also view data about external referrers, the number of visitors who came to your page from a website other than Facebook. For example, someone may click on a link to your Facebook page that was posted elsewhere, such as in a tweet. You can see the number of external visitors and which sites they came from.

- **Posts.** When should you post to Facebook? The Posts section provides valuable information about when those who like your page are on Facebook. On the top of this dashboard, you can hover over each day of the week to see when they are most active on Facebook.

  Which posts are performing the best? Toggle over to Post Types to find out the type of posts that receive the most engagement, for example, those that include photos or videos versus text-only posts. Below this portion, you can view how individual posts are performing. This portion of Insights can help you determine the type of content that is most appealing to followers of your page.

- **People.** Finally, you'll find a demographic breakdown of the people who like your page. You can also dig deeper to determine if you're reaching your target audience. Toggle over to People Reached and People Engaged for detailed data on those who are viewing and engaging with your content.

Twitter Analytics

All Twitter users can access the analytics dashboard directly from their profile page or by visiting *analytics.twitter.com*. The Home section of the Twitter Analytics dashboard provides a summary view. You can quickly view your highlights for each month. The monthly summary reports include a breakdown of top tweets, how much you tweeted, the number of new followers (and the number of people who unfollowed you!), the number of people who saw your tweets, and the number of people who viewed your profile.

Toggle over to the Tweets and Audiences tabs to dive deeper into the data. You can select any date range. Here are the key Twitter metrics you should be familiar with:

- **Top tweets.** Top tweets are those that have the most impressions. The Home section of Twitter Analytics lists the top tweet for each month. In the Tweets section, you can view a list of top tweets for the time period you choose.

- **Impressions.** Impressions are the number of times users saw a tweet. On the top of the Tweets section, there is a graph that gives a day-by-day breakdown of impressions. You will see spikes in the graph that indicate days with the most impressions. What did you post on those days that increased impressions? Could it have anything to do with the time of day you posted?

  Beneath the graph, you can view the number of impressions specific tweets received. Ask yourself what it is about those tweet(s) that could have contributed to the increased number of views.

- **Engagements.** The engagement data indicates whether Twitter users interacted with your tweets. For each tweet you can see the total number of engagements. Just click on the tweet you're interested in, and it will expand to show you more detail. You'll see engagement broken down even further, into retweets, favorites, clicks on photos or video, replies, link clicks, follows, and more.

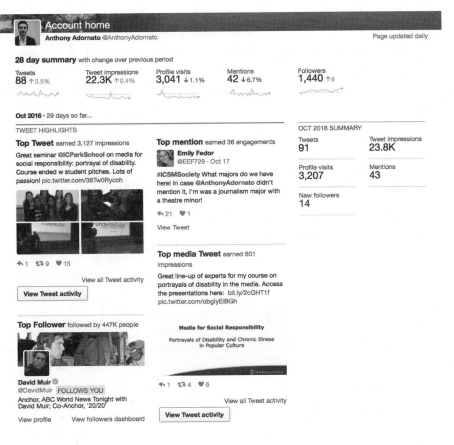

Adornato, Anthony. *Twitter page.*

Twitter Analytics
summary page

- **Engagement rate.** This is one portion you'll want to pay close attention to. Engagement Rate indicates the number of people who did something with a tweet, as a percentage of everyone who saw it. Your content caught their attention, prompting them to not just scroll past it.

  You know you're doing something right with tweets that have a higher engagement rate than others. You can find the engagement rate of your tweets by clicking on the Tweets tab in Analytics. On this page, you'll also see a breakdown of the types of engagement (likes, retweets, replies, and more) with all tweets during the time period you select.

- **Audiences.** Finally, just like Facebook Insights, Twitter Analytics provides a snapshot of your audience. This section helps you better understand who follows you. Based on their location and gender, among other demographics, you can gauge whether you're sharing information relevant to your followers.

Website Analytics

Google Analytics is one of the more popular tools to track website activity. WordPress also has an analytics dashboard for websites built on that platform. As you can imagine, there are many other analytics tools.

Adornato, Anthony. *Wordpress page.*

The analytics
dashboard on
WordPress

Regardless of the platform, below are the common features of website analytics tools most frequently monitored by newsrooms. Most analytics tools allow you to drill down the following metrics by specific time periods, such as day or week.

First, a note for student journalists. I recommend you build your own professional website using WordPress (as noted in Chapter 3). The website can act as a central location for stories you produce while in college. From there, you can share via social media. This approach allows you to practice viewing and analyzing your own website analytics on WordPress. Most of the following metrics are available through WordPress's analytics dashboard.

- **Unique visitors.** Unique visitors are the number of visitors who accessed pages on the website within the time frame you are examining. This does not count people who visit multiple times from the same device. If a page was viewed 100 times by 50 different visitors, the 50 people represent the number of unique visitors. But if the same person visits the website from two different devices, such as a laptop and a mobile device, that would count as two unique visits.

- **Page views.** Page views are the number of times a page was accessed. This includes multiple visits by the same person. It is one of the most commonly used metrics, because it gives an indication of which stories or pages on a news website are viewed the most—and least. Sometimes this information is listed as Top Posts or Top Pages.

- **Session duration.** Session duration, sometimes called "time on site," is the average amount of time visitors spent on the website. Analytics tools can also calculate the session duration for a particular page. Most visitors to news websites spend one to two minutes before clicking off the site. Pages with short session durations should be reviewed, because it could mean the content, story layout, or site design are not resonating with viewers. Even a slight change to a headline or placement of a more compelling visual at the beginning of a story can make a difference.

Related to session duration is bounce rate, another important number to pay attention to. The bounce rate is the percentage of visitors who leave a site after visiting just one page. Generally, the lower the bounce rate, the better.

A high bounce rate, however, doesn't necessarily mean visitors were unsatisfied with what they saw. Visitors might leave the site after viewing only one page because they found the information they were looking for.

- **Source.** How did a visitor end up on your website? Source data, sometimes called referrals or referrers, provides this information. Direct traffic refers to visitors who arrived by typing in your site's URL. But, as we've discussed, increasingly social media is a key driver of traffic. That's where this metric really becomes handy.

  Most website analytics tools monitor which social media platforms are driving traffic to your site during a given time period. They show you how many visitors clicked a link on a social media platform and ended up on your site—for example, a link in your Facebook post or a tweet. Sites other than social media that refer visitors to your website are usually also listed.

  Source information is a valuable tool in determining if there's a correlation between your activity on social media and the number of people visiting your website. (Test this out for yourself by using the analytics checklist at the end of this chapter.)

  The source section also shows the number of people who came to your site after conducting an online search using keywords. Keywords are the words visitors typed into a search engine that led them to your website. This normally means your website ranked high in the search results for the keywords they typed.

- **Technology.** Many website analytics tools provide data on the number of people viewing a site while using a desktop, mobile phone, and tablet. Some platforms even give a breakdown of the brands of devices visitors used, such as an iPhone or an Android phone. Monitoring the types of devices people are using while viewing your site is critical. The data helps a newsroom ensure a positive experience for website visitors. Newsrooms can test how their website functions on each type of device and catch potential viewing problems that may cause a visitor to click off the site.

Report, Share, Experiment, Measure, Adjust

You've analyzed the numbers. Now what? This isn't the end of the story.

The process of producing compelling journalism and engaging with audiences on various platforms is a never-ending cycle. For any story in a given day, the cycle might go something like this: Report on a story, share information along the way, experiment with new ways of sharing content on social media, measure whether it worked, and adjust accordingly.

The rulebook on social media is not yet set in stone, so testing out new approaches to posting is critical for journalists who want to thrive. "The 'go big or go home' mentality works a lot better than 'what if I screw it up,'" says Erica Smith (@ericasmith), of the *Virginian-Pilot*.[23]

Armed with this data, news outlets and journalists can adjust their techniques in areas where they believe the numbers aren't as good as they should be.

Posting content to social media at different times of the day and testing out different types of visuals and styles of writing are common ways newsrooms try to determine what sticks most with the audience.

Some newsrooms also perform A/B testing. A/B testing is the sharing of two different social media posts for the same story and measuring the results. In other words, you compare data for the first post (A) with data for the second one (B) to see which performs better.

"It's a lot of figuring out the time of day and what people are thinking about at that time of day, week, season — (and) what type of content we are going to give them," says Leia Mendoza, online editor for engagement at the *Omaha World-Herald*.[24]

The goals of a news organization will also determine which data is most important and how they adjust their strategy. Analyzing data is a way of helping achieve goals. For example, the *New York Times'* goal of driving loyal visitors to its website is much different than that of BuzzFeed, which has said publicly they care about as many shares as possible.[25]

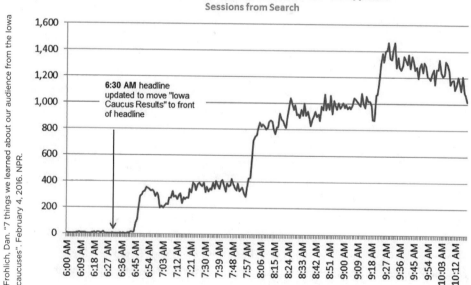

By monitoring analytics, NPR was able to measure the effectiveness of a change in the headline of a story about the Iowa caucuses in February 2016. The original headline was, "How It Happened: 6 Things That Explain the Iowa Caucus Results." NPR then placed "Iowa Caucus Results" at the beginning of the headline. The headline tweak was intended to match what people looking for information about this story would type into a search engine (also known as search engine optimization, or SEO). After the edit, traffic to the story skyrocketed. It was NPR's second-most viewed story of the day.

Checklist

Making Sense of the Data. These terms and all the numbers may seem overwhelming at first. How do you make sense of it all? The following checklist will help you focus on analyzing the most important metrics. It's easier than you may think. You simply need to know where to look, what numbers to look at, and some key questions to ask. At the very least you should check analytics on a weekly basis. Checking data daily is ideal, but not realistic for most reporters. Most newsrooms have a digital team that monitors analytics daily.

It's best to use this checklist during the course of a semester in which you are posting content on your professional website and are also active on social media. I recommend you first complete the items from the earlier checklist in this chapter. Then, the following analytics checklist will allow you to gauge the effectiveness of your posts from the previous checklist.

During each week, for at least six weeks, keep a diary answering the questions below. At the end of this period, write a one-page memo that summarizes what you learned from keeping track of your analytics. Students typically notice that when their social media activity is consistent and social media optimization tactics are used, they receive the most traffic to the stories posted on their websites—and that traffic typically comes from social media, not direct visits to the websites. Just as new outlets are learning, social media activity is a key driver to websites and the overall brand.

✓ **Facebook Insights.**

> Which posts received the most engagement (likes, shares, clicks, and comments)?

> What's unique about those posts versus others? For example, did they include images and @mentions that could have led to increased engagement?

> How many people "like" your page?

✓ **Twitter Analytics.**

> Which tweets have the highest engagement rates (retweets, likes, replies, and clicks)?

> What's unique about those tweets versus others? For example, did they include images and @mentions that could have led to increased engagement?

> How many total followers?

✓ **Website analytics.**

> Notice any days with a spike in traffic? What may have contributed to the increase in views? Is there any relationship between your social media activity that day and the spike in traffic?

> What are your top visited posts? Anything unique about those posts that made them the most visited?

> Where is your website traffic coming from? How many visitors from each referrer or source? Pay close attention to the number of visitors from social media.

> How many total visitors to your website?

Social Media Ethics and Policies

It's important to remember the iPhone is just a tool. It helps you gather and transmit the information faster. It doesn't replace at all the old-school journalism, the ethics, the context; there's not an app for that. Those are things you have to learn in school. Now, as quickly as information can be spread with these devices, it's more difficult than ever to retract bad information. So, reporters using these tools should think twice before hitting send.[1]

**— NEAL AUGENSTEIN,
REPORTER AT WTOP-FM
IN WASHINGTON, D.C.**

NEW ETHICAL DILEMMAS

Social media challenges, and blunders, are the focus of increasing discussions in newsrooms, in the media, and on the social media platforms themselves. Misinformation—rumors, fake photos, posts from unreliable sources—can spread like wildfire on social media. Journalists and news organizations have taken the bait, reporting inaccurate information gathered from social media.

Unfortunately, we've seen this in case after case.

A young man wrongly identified as the suspect in the Boston Marathon bombings. An image supposedly taken inside the Paris nightclub minutes before a deadly attack at that location. A picture of a giant wave slamming into the Statue of Liberty during Hurricane Sandy. All these went viral on social media. None of them was accurate. Yet, many journalists reported them as if they were.

In this chapter, you will

- Consider the common ethical dilemmas journalists are confronted with relative to social media.

- Discover emerging issues, including the blurry line between journalists' professional and private "social media lives," the verification of user-generated content, and the appropriateness of "friending" sources.

- Explore how newsroom social media policies address these issues.

- Apply traditional journalism ethics to guide your social media activities.

A major challenge facing journalists is balancing the pressure to publish quickly, particularly during breaking news, while upholding traditional news values. Speed versus accuracy. Often, these are two competing values. Vetting information and sources takes time. In the sea of "noise," traditional journalistic ethics and values, such as verification and accuracy, are more important now than ever.

And then there are newsroom staff members who have come under fire for how they respond to audience complaints. Rhonda Lee, a meteorologist with KTBS-TV in Shreveport, Louisiana, was fired in 2012 after responding to viewer comments on the station's Facebook page, including one that referenced her as "a black lady" who "needs to wear a wig or grow some more hair."[2]

In a statement, the station's news director said that Lee repeatedly violated procedures for responding to comments on social media. This was one of the first cases to draw widespread debate not only on how best to respond to disparaging remarks, but also on how newsroom social media policies address emerging issues.

The use of social media by journalists raises a host of ethical and professional dilemmas addressed in this chapter:

- The blurry line between professional and private social media lives
- Contacting sources via social media
- Interacting with the audience
- Verification of user-generated content
- Copyright and proper attribution of user-generated content
- Correction guidelines: handling inaccurate or false information reported on social media
- News outlets' "ownership" of their journalists' social media accounts

NewsLab
November 4 at 12:29pm · ⊙

A timely reminder that your social media posts really can get you in trouble. "We remind our journalists frequently to avoid even the appearance of support for any sides of this election," said the news director.

Wendy Bell WTAE ✓
on Wednesday

I have removed a post that I initially placed here on Monday. I sincerely apologize for that post about the Wilkinsburg mass shooting and the restaurant employee whom my husband and I encountered. I now understand that some of the words I chose were insensitive and could be viewed as racist. I regret offending anyone. I'm truly sorry.

👍 1,665   💬 2,015   ↱ 231

'Good Morning Cleveland' anchors Jackie Fernandez, Somara Theodore let go after social media posts
Channel 5 news director Jeff Harris would not speak directly to the reason why...
CLEVELAND.COM | BY JOEY MORONA

👍 Like   💬 Comment   ↱ Share   </> Embed

When Journalists Become the News: Wendy Bell (left) was fired from a TV station in Pittsburgh, Pennsylvania, following controversial remarks she made on Facebook. Bell, who later apologized, sued the station. Comments on social media also cost two Cleveland journalists their jobs. They were fired after tweeting about waiting in line for tickets to a Hillary Clinton event featuring Jay Z.

CHARTING AN ETHICAL COURSE: APPLYING JOURNALISM ETHICS TO SOCIAL MEDIA

As journalists and newsroom managers navigate these new ethical dilemmas, what is acceptable social media behavior can sometimes seem ambiguous. That's where journalism ethics play a critical role in guiding decisions.

The foundation of journalism rests on key ethical principles that include truth, verification, fair and balanced coverage, and avoiding conflicts of interest. Applying these principles to social media informs what is and what is not appropriate conduct for journalists. Ethical decision making should occur at every step of the journalistic process—newsgathering, distribution of news, and audience engagement. In abiding by ethical principles, journalists best serve the audience and uphold the integrity of the profession. Straying from this course can erode trust with the public and undermine the credibility of the profession.

> *"No matter if your tablet is made of stone or glass, it is the words that matter. Are they right? Are they fair? Are they honest? Are they true?"*[4]
> — Scott Pelley (@ScottPelley), *CBS News*

Professional journalism organizations have established ethics guidelines that have long been the basis for newsrooms' policies. The Society of Professional Journalists (SPJ) Code of Ethics is widely used in newsrooms and journalism classrooms. In 2014, SPJ adopted a revised code of ethics to address contemporary issues. Prior to this, the code was last revised in 1996. It had become outdated. The code's principles, such as minimize harm and act independently, are central to good journalism, but the explanations following those principles were rooted in an age prior to the existence of social media.[5]

Below are some of the revised explanations associated with each of the four key principles that have always been at the heart of the code. Note how these can be applied to mobile and social media journalism. (Read the complete SPJ Code of Ethics at *www.spj.org/ethicscode.asp*.)

- **Seek Truth and Report It**

  - Journalists should take responsibility for the accuracy of their work. Verify information before releasing it. Use original sources whenever possible.

  - Remember that neither speed nor format excuses inaccuracy.

  - Provide context. Take special care not to misrepresent or oversimplify in promoting, previewing, or summarizing a story.

  - Gather, update, and correct information through the life of a story.

- **Minimize Harm**

  - Avoid pandering to lurid curiosity, even if others do so.

  - Consider the long-term implications of the extended reach and permanence of publication. Provide updated and more complete information as appropriate.

- **Act Independently**
  - Distinguish news from advertising and shun hybrids that blur the lines between the two. Prominently label sponsored content.

- **Be Accountable and Transparent**
  - Explain ethical choices and processes to audiences. Encourage civil dialogue with the public about journalistic practices, coverage, and news content.
  - Acknowledge mistakes and correct them promptly and prominently. Explain corrections and clarifications carefully and clearly.

There's not a single mention of "social media" because the SPJ guidelines attempt to address current trends and themes in journalism without being technologically specific.

The Online News Association (ONA), on the other hand, has launched an initiative to address issues unique to social media and the nuanced situations journalists face today. ONA's Build Your Own Ethics Code (*ethics.journalists.org*) provides journalists and news organizations with the flexibility to create an ethics code that meets their needs. The online system allows them to visit specific modules that let them customize a code.

Using this do-it-yourself tool, journalists can review and select statements from a menu addressing more than 40 ethical issues, including user-generated content, verification, data journalism, social networks, privacy, gender and ethnicity, and hate speech. They then can tailor a code and export it for publication on their website as well as for internal use in the newsroom.

From the Newsroom

KAREN MAGNUSON (@KMAGNUSON)

Editor and Vice President of News, *Democrat & Chronicle*
Rochester, New York

TELLS US ABOUT THE *DEMOCRAT & CHRONICLE*'S SOCIAL MEDIA POLICY.

The policy was established by Gannett, our owner, and is used in all Gannett newsrooms, including *USA TODAY*. Journalists in our newsroom read and sign the policy every year. There are pages and pages of suggestions as well as red flags about online behavior that shouldn't be a surprise to journalists. As long as I have been with Gannett, since 1999, they've had a strict ethics policy. I serve on a committee, formed for the *USA TODAY* Network, that's revisiting the ethics policy to make sure it's as up-to-date as possible given the changes in technology. (The *USA TODAY* Network includes Gannett's national and local news outlets.)

WHAT ARE THE BIGGEST ISSUES YOU'VE SEEN RELATED TO JOURNALISTS' USE OF SOCIAL MEDIA?

Journalists who feel strongly about issues, such as one presidential candidate or another. Some have a difficult time refraining from what comes naturally as a human—sharing their thoughts. We've reminded people consistently that you're a representative of the *Democrat & Chronicle*, and you cannot share your opinion publically. When it comes to something that stirs emotion, journalists should know innately that they should not express how they feel. It's very obvious that it's a bad thing to do, but sometimes even the most veteran journalists can get sucked into something that they care deeply about.

On another note, one of the greatest challenges is that journalists are now easily accessible. I myself probably get about 500 e-mails a day. I'm also accessible via Twitter, LinkedIn, Instagram, and Facebook. So, I have people coming to me all the time with story ideas, news releases, and, yes, complaints. I can't respond to it all, even if I work nonstop. One of the expectations for all of our reporters and other staff members is audience engagement. So, time management and being able to adequately prioritize and try to respond to as many people as possible are critical.

DO YOU RECOMMEND SEPARATE ACCOUNTS FOR PROFESSIONAL AND PERSONAL USE?

We leave it up to the individual. Some feel strongly that they want professional pages so that their professional exchanges are off personal pages. In addition, a lot of times those are folks who have kids. They don't want the public to have access to that kind of information. For me, I don't have two separate accounts for any of my social media. Who I am is who I am. I can't see that anything I put out there is going to cause any problem. By the public seeing who I am personally, it lets them know I'm an individual who really cares about this community and has a life outside of work.

HOW DO YOU APPROACH VERIFICATION OF USER-GENERATED CONTENT?

We don't publish anything we can't verify. We get beat by TV on visuals quite a bit because we refuse to simply grab off Facebook or another platform without permission. We're very conservative when it comes to that. There's a lot of pressure to be competitive. But, we verify everything. In terms of submitted photos, our editors do the same thing. We want to make sure it's real and we have permission to use the visual.

NEWSROOM SOCIAL MEDIA POLICIES

News outlets have implemented social media policies that define and manage journalists' use of social media, indicating what is and is not permitted on these platforms. Most of these policies encourage the use of social media for journalistic purposes and provide recommendations for how to act appropriately. Newsroom social media policies are typically guided by the ethical principles outlined in the ethics codes of professional journalism organizations such as SPJ and ONA. In many newsrooms, journalists are asked to review and sign the policy upon being hired.

Newsroom policies convey to staff and the public that standards and accountability are important to a news organization. They provide a best-practices guide that can be consulted when issues arise, which promotes consistent standards within a news outlet.

As new platforms and practices emerge, so do new ethical dilemmas. As a result, social media policies must evolve as well. They'll need to be periodically reviewed and revised to address new challenges that arise.

Not every situation is going to fit neatly into a social media policy, no matter how well thought out the policy is. As with any ethical dilemma, social media related or otherwise, there's often no clear-cut answer. That's why it's important for newsroom staff to regularly discuss policies and ethical dilemmas.

"When you confront an ethical issue, you should bring multiple tools to the decision-making process. The ethics code is key, but so is the wisdom you've gained through your own experiences, the insights others can provide and a clear framework for working through ethical questions. The framework has to be flexible," ONA advises journalists on its Build Your Own Ethics Code website.[7]

ONA has created this framework to walk journalists through a process that is, ideally, conducted as a dialogue with others in their newsrooms.[8] These questions are intended to be used in conjunction with newsroom policies.

- What is the issue? What's creating the ethical concern?
- Who are the stakeholders we need to consider? In other words, who will likely be affected by the decision we make?
- What clauses from our code of ethics—or other guiding documents—can inform deliberation on the issue?
- What consequences (for stakeholders and beyond) can we predict might occur from different decisions we might make?
- Have we encountered cases like this in the past? What did we learn?
- What else, if anything, do we need to consider?
- Once we've made our decision, how will we justify it, particularly to those who disagree with us?

The rest of this chapter discusses best practices and standards for the seven key areas in which journalists are facing new ethical challenges.

You Can't Post That! Professional and Personal Activity

Journalistic ethics and values are being put to the test as reporters are active on social spaces for professional and personal purposes. Balancing personal and professional lives on social media can be the thorniest of issues for journalists. Journalists are people. They have emotions and opinions. But sharing those thoughts in public forums, such as social media, can call into question a journalist's ability to be fair and balanced in her or his reporting. It also damages the news outlet's reputation as an unbiased source of news.

Assume everything you post, even on a "private" account, is public. Journalists should avoid the following on social media:

- Sharing of personal opinion
- Sharing of political affiliation
- Sharing of religious beliefs
- Advocating on behalf of a particular issue or agenda
- Joining social network groups associated with a particular issue or agenda
- Sharing the most intimate details of their personal lives
- Sharing internal newsroom communications intended for staff members only

Even as a student, you must be cautious about what you're sharing. It can come back to haunt you in the job search process, as we discussed in Chapter 3. Start following these guidelines now.

When considering sharing personal thoughts on social media, your decision should be held to the same standards that have always been at the heart of journalism ethics. Conduct yourself online as you would in any circumstance as a journalist. For example, solid journalists avoid placing political bumper stickers on their cars or political signs in their front yards. Journalists should take the same approach on new media platforms.

Recognize that your actions can be misinterpreted, even if you have the best of intentions. Journalists frequently "like" or "follow" the pages of political parties or activist groups as a way to track story ideas from those sources. If you become the fan

---

Add Context to Your Retweets

When retweeting a post, add a comment to make sure your retweet isn't interpreted as an endorsement of someone's opinion or stance. In its social media guidelines, the Associated Press uses these examples to highlight the type of retweets that should be avoided:

- RT @jonescampaign: Smith's policies would destroy our schools.
- RT @dailyeuropean: At last, a euro plan that works.

If you want to retweet these posts, introductory text is needed to help clarify that you're simply reporting someone's view, just like you would quote a source. The AP recommends this approach:

- Jones campaign now denouncing Smith on education. RT @jonescampaign: Smith's policies would destroy our schools.
- Big European paper praises euro plan. RT @dailyeuropean: At last, a euro plan that works.

of one political candidate or party, you should do the same for the other. Become a "fan" of lots of groups, not just those that align with your views.

Contacting Sources on Social Media

Just as you would in person, be upfront and honest when contacting sources on social media. Contact sources through one of your professional accounts that states in the profile you're a reporter. You should also immediately tell the source that you're a journalist and explain why you're reaching out. Make your intentions clear. What's the story you're working on? How will the information you gather be used? Avoid communication with minors through social networking sites, unless you have permission from one of their parents or guardians.

When news breaks, information from sources on social media can enhance reporting. However, sources in these situations should be approached with respect for what they might be going through. The number one rule: Journalists should always consider the physical and emotional welfare of eyewitnesses when communicating with them during a news event, according to Eyewitness Media Hub, a nonprofit that helps newsrooms navigate challenges presented by social media sourcing.[9]

Sources may be involved in traumatic situations in which they're in danger or have suffered personal loss. Reaching out to victims or their families on social media has been compared to the old-school practice of a journalist knocking on a door in an effort to interview someone. But the experience of talking with someone face to face is quite different from a tweet that expresses sympathy and in the same "breath" requests an interview.

Conducting interviews online is not a substitute for face-to-face or phone conversations with sources, no matter the type of story. Talking directly with sources not only builds rapport but also is the best way to verify their identity and claims. After establishing contact with a source on social media, take the conversation offline. If you're contacting sources on Twitter, for example, ask them to direct message you a phone number or e-mail address if they'd like to talk about what they're going through. You could also give them your contact information.

The Associated Press recommends starting a message with "If it is safe to do so . . ." or "If you're in a safe place . . . ," instead of asking something along the lines of "Do you have any photos to use?" or "Can I talk to you?"[10] One ask is plenty.

Connecting with sources on social media also raises the question of whether it's appropriate to become "friends" with them on Facebook. This issue often comes up with public officials—the police department spokesman or chief of staff for the mayor, for instance.

Stuart Leavenworth (@sleavenworth), a correspondent with McClatchy, recalls facing this social media dilemma: to friend or not to friend. Leavenworth was a reporter for the *Sacramento Bee* when California's secretary of state sent him a Facebook friend request.[11] Leavenworth questioned whether the public could interpret such a relationship as a conflict of interest. He ignored the request.

"As a journalist in this town, I really wanted to keep a little bit of distance from public officials and other sources I deal with on a regular basis," said

Leavenworth. "But I also just felt strange about them having so much access to my personal information, since I like to have fun on Facebook."[12]

This is an ethical grey area, and many social media policies are ambiguous in terms of the proper approach. For example, Gannett, which owns news outlets in communities across the country, advises its hundreds of news employees to "exercise discretion when friending or liking other individuals or groups to avoid any actual or perceived conflicts."[13] The Associated Press policy states, "It is acceptable to extend and accept Facebook friend requests from sources, politicians and newsmakers if necessary for reporting purposes, and to follow them on Twitter."[14]

However, public officials and the places they work typically have public Facebook pages that allow journalists to track newsworthy activity. This would be the preferred approach rather than becoming "friends" on personal accounts.

Consider also that Facebook can be perceived as a more personal, private platform than others such as Twitter. Even if a newsroom policy allows you to become "friends" with a source, you may not feel comfortable sharing that more personal side of your life with sources with whom you want to maintain a strictly "professional" relationship.

If you decline a source's friend request, explain your reasoning to the source. Whatever you choose to do, be consistent with your friending activity. The *Roanoke Times* recommends either accepting no sources or people you cover as friends, or welcoming them all.[15]

> **Art!** @artayd2 5h
> Good friend of mine lives < 10 minutes from Sandy Hook Elementary and has a daughter in kindergarten. Trying to get a hold of him. #newtown
> Details
>
> **Nadine Shubailat** @NadineatABC 👤▾ 🐦 Follow
>
> @artayd2 can we talk to your friend who lives in Sandy Hook and whose daughter goes to kindergarten? I'm w ABC News nadine.shubailat@abc.com
> ↩ Reply ⟲ Retweet ★ Favorite
> 1:52 PM - 14 Dec 12 - Embed this Tweet
>
> **Art!** @artayd2 4h
> @NadineatABC eat a ▮▮▮
> Details

A producer reaches out to a potential source following the 2012 shooting at Sandy Hook Elementary in Newtown, Connecticut. Journalists must use caution and compassion when contacting people during traumatic situations.

Interacting with the Audience

The interactive nature of social media fosters informal engagement between journalists and the public. Social media is just that—social. As we've discussed from the beginning of this book, these two-way conversations can strengthen journalists' connections and trust with those they serve.

It also opens the door to criticism. Not responding can be viewed as ignoring the commenter. On the other hand, engaging someone who is out of line could easily escalate—and for all to see online.

Pick your battles. Stand up for your work, but don't be defensive when it comes to legitimate criticism about a story or your reporting. This type of dialogue can be healthy and build respect. After all, journalists are ultimately accountable to the public. Avoid getting into an extended back-and-forth with someone.

Your response will often be determined by the type and tone of the audience member's comment. It's best to consult with a manager when a comment is out of line or you aren't sure how to respond, as each newsroom policy varies. Some outlets have a policy in which the reply to disparaging remarks comes from someone other than the journalist who is the target, such as a digital media manager.

At the Associated Press, for instance, journalists are advised to send abusive, bigoted, obscene, and/or racist comments to the AP Nerve Center, which coordinates the outlet's worldwide coverage. Members of AP's social media team are based out of the Nerve Center.

Keep in mind that any response to an audience member, even through e-mail or direct messaging, should be considered public.

Verification of User-Generated Content

A photo of a shark swimming along a street flooded during a hurricane. A grainy image of Paul McCartney—yes, Sir Paul of Beatles fame—visiting a trucking company in a suburb of central New York. What's the real deal? Too good to be true? These images were shared over and over again on social media.

As a journalist, what would you do if you came across this type of content? How would you verify the information?

With all user-generated content—whether it contains a video, photo, or written claims, you should proceed with skepticism. A journalist's job is to report the truth. That can't be accomplished unless you take the appropriate actions to verify not only the content, but also the source.

This is where traditional reporting skills—a combination of offline and online sleuthing and fact-checking—are critical. The following steps can help you determine the credibility of content and sources.

- If it looks/sounds **too good to be true**, assume it is. Be skeptical.
- **Contact the source** of the post to ask questions, preferably on the phone or in person, in order to clarify the source's identity and claims. If the information was retweeted or reposted via another person, track down the *original* source—the person who initially posted the information.
- A review of the **original source's social media/online history** can reveal whether the person typically posts about the topic under scrutiny, the tone/type of previous posts, when the account was created, and the location the source normally tweets about, among other items.
- **Cross-check information**. Conduct online searches related to the story and people involved in order to corroborate or poke holes in the claims. In the

Mulcahy, 2012.[17]

Too good to be true? What steps would you take to verify this grainy photo posted to social media? The image supposedly shows Paul McCartney visiting a trucking company in the Syracuse, New York, area.

case of McCartney, if he tweeted from London five hours before he supposedly visited the trucking company, the story probably doesn't add up. If you were to check his official website and see that he had an event the night before in Europe, that would also raise a red flag.

- If the source has the geo-location feature enabled for the social media site on which you found the post in question, you can view **the location of the post** to see if it matches the location the source is talking about or supposedly shared a photo from.

- **Seek social corroboration** by asking social media users in the respective location if they can verify the information. Are they seeing or experiencing the same thing? You can use advance search methods and the lists feature (Chapter 4) to help in this process.

- **Seek official corroboration** of the social media information by contacting traditional sources, such as a police agency or company. For example, it should seem obvious that calling the trucking company that McCartney supposedly visited would be essential. (Yes, the photo with McCartney was real. His wife's family owns the trucking company.)

- **Use Google Images or TinEye.com** to help verify images. After you upload a photo to one of these sites, it will search for similar images to help determine if the photo was altered. In the case of the shark swimming in the flooded street, this could help you uncover the fact that the shark was actually from a *National Geographic* photo. It had been edited into a fake photo. Through these sites, you can also find if the image has appeared online before. It could be a "real" image but associated with a prior news story.

- **Inspect an image's metadata**, which contains when and where the photo was taken and on what type of device, among other details. To find this data, which is stored in a standard format call Exif (for Exchangeable image file format), right click on a photo and select "properties" or "find info" (depending on the type of operating system you use). This action should be completed in photo software, such as Apple's Photo app for Mac. Checking the metadata could help you determine if a photo was taken at a time or location other than the source claims. Unfortunately, most social media sites remove metadata from photos, so this will only work with originals.

- **Use Google Earth** to debunk rumors and fake images. Google Earth contains landmarks, such as buildings and bus stops, that can help confirm the location of a photo or video. You can zoom down to street level after entering a specific location. On its website, First Draft News shows how it used Google Earth to verify a photo.[18] In January 2016, shortly after an explosion at Sultanahmet Square in Istanbul, Turkey, eyewitness images surfaced on social media. One photograph appeared to show a building on fire in Sultanahmet Square. Exploring the area on Google Earth raised doubts. The landscape on the Google Earth image didn't match the landscape in the photo, and none of the features in the photograph could be found in the Google Earth search of that area. A Twitter keyword search of "fire" and "Istanbul" revealed similar photos from a blast in another location about 10 miles from the square. The photo of the building was real, but not associated with the Sultanahmet Square explosion.

Seeking Permission, Copyright, and Fair Use

Only after verifying user-generated content should you consider sharing the material on social media, broadcasting, or publishing it. If you want to post the content to social media, the best approach is to share a user's original post. Through reposting, you give credit to the source by "linking" directly to the source, and you are transparent about how the information was obtained. Provide background context when needed to clarify the news value of what you're sharing.

Before broadcasting on air or publishing online or in print, ask for permission to do so. It's not appropriate—ethically or legally—to snatch user-generated content and use it as you wish. As the Social Media Guidelines for AP Employees state, "To include photos, videos or other multimedia content from social networks in our news report, we must determine who controls the copyright to the material and get permission from that person or organization to use it."[19]

Can I Embed a Social Media Post without Permission?

Embedding a social media post in an online news story is common practice nowadays. Often, the embedded post contains a photo or video that is newsworthy. "That does not, generally, infringe any copyright because no copy of the embedded content has been made—the inline link is simply a piece of code that represents the content as it exists on the originating site," explains media attorney and journalism professor Jonathan Peters (@jonathanwpeters). "Moreover, most third-party platforms, like Twitter, include in their terms of service a provision that says the user permits others to embed his or her content."[20]

However, Peters said posting a screenshot of content should be avoided unless you have permission. "That's basically the electronic equivalent of making a copy of the work, putting it squarely in the crosshairs of copyright law."

All photos and videos are copyrighted, whether indicated on the visual or not. Copyright belongs to the creator of the content, and in most cases anyone who wants to broadcast or publish it must obtain permission from the copyright holder. Just because someone shared an image doesn't mean the sharer is the copyright holder. In seeking permission, it's important to establish that the person actually took the photo or video. Be direct: "Did you take the photo?" In addition, be clear about what you plan on doing with the content.

Journalists also have a responsibility to properly credit sources. Once permission is granted, ask how they would like to be named. In sensitive situations, where someone's safety is at risk, the person may not wish to be identified by his or her full name.

Attribution helps people determine the credibility of sources and ultimately your reporting. Make clear in your report that the information was gathered from a social networking site.

Media law is often part of journalism ethics discussions. However, there's an important distinction to be made between law and ethics. Just because a journalist's action in a certain situation may be legal doesn't necessarily mean it's ethically acceptable. For example, even if a journalist has the legal right to publish certain information, it would be unethical to do so if the content were not verified. "It was legal" is not a sufficient ethical justification.

While media law provides guidance in terms of legal boundaries, it can be ambiguous. Journalists often rely on protections they believe are afforded to them under the fair use doctrine. Fair use, part of US copyright law, allows for the excerpting of content for the purposes of commentary and critique without permission. How much can be used is open for interpretation. The fact that something is newsworthy doesn't automatically mean it's fair use, making it all the more important to secure permission.

"True, news reporting, is one of the categories protected by the fair use doctrine, but because news is a commercial use, and because photographs and video are typically used in full, there is a strong likelihood that republishing them for news purposes does not qualify as fair use," according to attorney and journalism professor Daxton Stewart (@MediaLawProf).[21]

Breaking the law can land newsrooms in legal hot water—and be costly. An editor at Agence France-Presse, an international news agency, turned to Twitter to find photos of an earthquake in Haiti.[22] The editor asked the uploader for permission to use the photos. There was a big problem though. A professional photographer captured the photos, not the Twitter user. The photographer sued for $1.2 million and

Once a journalist locates content he or she would like to publish, it's important to ask for permission and who should be credited, as happened in this exchange between journalists and a Twitter user.

won. Other outlets, including the *Washington Post*, CBS, ABC, and CNN, also settled claims with the photographer.

Smaller outlets have also come under fire for using photos and videos without securing permission.[23] The *Portland Press Herald*, for instance, had to pay a woman $400 after the outlet published a photograph from her account on Flickr, a photo management and sharing site. She hadn't given the outlet permission.

Another option when in need of a visual element for a story is to search for Creative Commons (CC) content. Material licensed under CC can be used as long as you properly credit the source. CC licenses offer content creators a way to maintain copyright while allowing their work to be used, for free, under certain conditions.[24] Many social media sites, including YouTube, allow users to choose whether they would like their content to be marked with a CC license. There are six different types of CC licenses. For example, the "CC BY-ND" license allows anyone to use the work, as long as it is credited and not altered. Each piece of Creative Commons content has instructions on how it should be attributed and which CC code applies to it. You can search for Creative Commons content at *search.creativecommons.org* or by using Google's advanced search option.

Ethical Considerations: Live Streaming and Graphic Video

Streaming video via Facebook Live, Periscope, or a similar tool can be captivating for an audience. Followers get a front-row seat to events unfolding at a news scene. The downfall is that journalists don't know what may happen next, particularly in a crisis situation. Live-streaming is unfiltered and could lead to broadcasting sensitive footage. Ethical judgment is critical. Could something tragic happen during the live stream? Are you prepared to broadcast the worst possible outcome? Will the live-streaming put witnesses or law enforcement in harm? How will you justify your decision?

During tragic situations, it's also become a habit for witnesses to grab their mobile devices, record, and share raw unedited footage that contains graphic content. During the deadly shooting rampage at an Orlando nightclub in 2016, some of those inside posted chilling video of what was unfolding. When Philando Castile was shot by a Minneapolis police officer in 2016, his girlfriend used Facebook Live to broadcast from the front seat of her car. The live stream showed Castile dying beside her. Millions of people have watched the archived video. Even if these videos are deemed newsworthy, journalists must determine if and how they'll share this type of content. In the case of Castile, many outlets that shared the footage on social media included a warning slide at the beginning of the video. Others chose to use only portions of the video (removing the most graphic elements) or blurred out graphic elements such as his bloody t-shirt.

@NBCNews. Twitter Post. July 7, 2016.

Correction Guidelines

Acknowledging mistakes and correcting them quickly is one tenet of ethical journalism. Most news outlets have policies for addressing errors. However, these guidelines are being tested by the speed at which information travels on social media. Once a social media post with misinformation is published, dozens or even hundreds of users could share it. Correction guidelines are evolving as social media presents new and unfamiliar challenges.

Here's a responsible approach to correcting errors in social media posts:

- Acknowledge the error and push out the correction in the same place where it was originally shared. This approach will get the correction in front of the audience that may have seen the original post.

- Don't just delete the post containing the incorrect information and leave it at that. As the ONA ethics code notes, "That method does not acknowledge the error and can leave misinformation uncorrected, allowing it to spread."[25] Some outlets, including NPR, advise staff never to delete the original post unless there's a legal or safety issue. Deleting a tweet can convey a lack of transparency to the public.

- Create a new post that indicates you made an error, and explain exactly what's being corrected. The AP guidelines use this example from Twitter:

  > Correction: U.S. Embassy in Nigeria says bombings could happen this week at luxury hotels in Abuja (previously we incorrectly said Lagos).

  Some outlets also attach a screenshot image of the post with the incorrect tweet and/or include a link to it. This provides context and a frame of reference for followers—they can see how the information was corrected.

- In addition to the new post, add a comment with the correct information to the original post. For example, on Twitter, include the correction in a reply to your original tweet. This reply will always be attached to the original tweet, including previous retweets of it.

In this tweet, the *Washington Post* clearly states that the information is a correction and it includes an image of the previous, incorrect tweet.

- Facebook, unlike Twitter, allows you to edit posts. If doing so for an error, be clear that you're updating the post with a correction. At the top of the post, write "Correction" and add the corrected information. Make sure you indicate what was inaccurate about the original version of the post.

- If a follower alerted you to the error, thank the follower, and direct him or her to the corrected post.

@washingtonpost. Twitter Post. February 4, 2016.

Ownership of Social Media Accounts

It's the policy of an increasing number of news outlets to retain ownership of the professional social media accounts of their reporters. A study of local TV stations' social media guidelines sheds light on this emerging policy.[26] Two-thirds of stations own the professional social media accounts of their journalists, according to the research.

In some cases, this means journalists are required to submit their passwords to newsroom management, and such a policy raises the question of whether an employee is allowed to keep the account and its associated followers when the employee leaves the newsroom.[27] Under this type of policy, typically when employment with the news outlet ends, the journalist no longer has access to the account—the process is similar to what happens with a company e-mail address.

The E.W. Scripps Company, which owns news outlets in more than two dozen markets across the United States, makes this clear in its social media policy.[28] "Your professional account is the company's property and the name and contents remain company property if you leave Scripps. Scripps reserves the right to edit, monitor, promote or cancel a professional account."[29]

What is defined as "professional" under this type policy? Any account on which you're sharing information as part of your position with the outlet or representing yourself as a staff member of the outlet. That means even if you created an account prior to working at the outlet, the outlet could retain ownership of that account if you use it for professional purposes. This may in fact be a reason for creating separate social media accounts for personal and professional purposes.

Rachel Barnhart learned this lesson firsthand when she worked as a reporter for WHAM-TV in Rochester, New York. Barnhart spent years building a robust social media following. She has tens of thousands of Facebook and Twitter followers combined.[30] Barnhart's "following" was very much tied to the brand she had built on social media.

When Sinclair Broadcasting bought WHAM-TV, Barnhart was faced with a choice: Create new accounts, or keep using the accounts she had created and risk losing them if she left the station. It's the policy of Sinclair to own the social media accounts of its on-air personalities. She decided to use new social media accounts for work purposes only. She explained her decision in a note to followers.

> At this juncture, I am retaining ownership of my existing Facebook and Twitter pages. Therefore, the company has started new social media accounts in my name for me to use during work hours when I am covering stories. The company has administrative control over these accounts.[31]

She added that her station remains supportive of her social media activity as "we are all trying to navigate the new frontier of social media and journalism."[32]

Checklist

✓ **Stay Informed.** The following sites are helpful resources for staying up to date with the latest industry discussions about journalism ethics and social media policies. They provide case studies of ethical challenges, training, and how-to guides. Consider adding their Twitter accounts to the Twitter list for mobile and social media journalism that you were asked to create earlier in the book (Chapter 4's checklist).

> First Draft News: @firstdraftnews and *firstdraftnews.com* (Check out the downloadable one-page guides to verifying user-generated content.)

> Eyewitness Media Hub: @emhub and *eyewitnessmediahub.com*

> Verification Handbook: *verificationhandbook.com*

✓ **Share Your Knowledge.** We can learn from each other. Remember to extend the conversation beyond this book and your classroom. If you come across an example of an ethical dilemma in the industry, please share it on the book's Facebook page (*fb.com/MobileandSocialMediaJournalism*) or tweet @MobileJourn. I'll be sure to reshare with followers.

✓ **Mobile and Social Media Strategy Analysis.** As we near the end of the book, you should be wrapping up the mobile and social media strategy analysis that was first introduced in Chapter 2's checklist. Use what you learned in this chapter to analyze the social media policies of the outlet you're monitoring. How does the policy address each of the seven categories above? If the policy isn't available online, interview someone from the newsroom's social media team to discuss the guidelines. In your presentation to the class, include what you learned about the policy.

✓ **What's the Real Deal?** How would go you about verifying the information in this scenario?

You see retweets about the Republican vice presidential candidate's plane making an emergency landing in Colorado. Many of these retweets include a photo of firefighters entering a small airplane on what appears to be the tarmac of an airport. Discuss with your class what steps you would take before sharing this information.

✓ **What Would You Do?** The *New Haven Independent* was covering the murder of Annie Le, a Yale University graduate student. The story became a national media sensation. The *Independent* learned the name of the murder suspect, Raymond Clark, through police reports and other sources. The police report led the *Independent* reporter covering the story to Clark's former girlfriend, Jessica Del Rocco. The reporter sent a Facebook friend request to Del Rocco. She accepted it. With access to the woman's Facebook wall, the reporter was able to read Del Rocco's reaction to the murder. The reporter then sent Del Rocco a message identifying herself as a journalist and asking for an interview. Del Rocco declined to be interviewed but kept the reporter as a "friend." Discuss the following as a class:

What ethical issues are raised in this case?

> Was it appropriate for the reporter to send Del Rocco a friend request?

> Would it be ethical to publish Del Rocco's posts in a story?

(Continued)

(Continued)

> The outlet decided to use the comments from her Facebook page without asking for permission from Del Rocco. It didn't publish Del Rocco's name in the story. At that point, she "defriended" the reporter. Do you agree with the *Independent*'s decision? Why or why not?

This scenario has been adapted from "The Facebook Conundrum: The *New Haven Independent* and the Annie Le Murder," a case study published by The Case Consortium at Columbia University. To read the full case study and explore other ethical issues raised, visit *casestudies .ccnmtl.columbia.edu.*

✓ **Reminders.** Time for a social media check-up. By now you should be carving out time every day to manage your social media accounts. I hope it's becoming second nature. In order to maintain consistent social media activity, aim for the following each week:

> 15–20 tweets and a combination of 10 retweets, replies, and likes

> 3–5 posts on your professional Facebook page

> A few posts to LinkedIn

> A few posts to Instagram

> Two tweets about class discussions and/or readings that you found interesting. Tell followers why and include your class hashtag.

> Follow a handful of people on each platform. On Twitter, make it a goal to follow at least five people every week.

And don't forget:

> Come up with a mobile and social media plan for each story you cover. Use the checklist (Sharing as You Go) in the last chapter as a guide. Explain your plan in every story pitch.

> Continue to blog (first mentioned in Chapter 3's checklist), and share those posts on social media. Make it a goal to blog twice during the weeks in which you aren't producing a story for your website.

> Use the analytics checklist (Making Sense of the Data) in the last chapter to analyze the effectiveness of your website and social media activity on a weekly basis.

Mobile and Social Media in Your Career

Shortly after Eddie Dowd (@DowdKNOP) graduated from journalism school in 2016, he landed an interview for a video journalist position at KNOP-TV in Nebraska. The station's assistant news director sent him a breaking news scenario and asked Dowd to write stories for television and web as well as craft posts for Facebook and Twitter.

"They wanted to see if I understood that each platform offers different ways to give news to people, but also comes with different audiences," said Dowd.

Fortunately, Dowd had learned how to take a story and distribute it across mobile and social media platforms. He landed the job.

"News directors were impressed that I not only understood this changing field, but that I also put that into practice."

QUALIFICATIONS NEEDED IN TODAY'S NEWSROOMS

Journalists just entering the field, such as Dowd, and those who are more seasoned must be able to assume a range of job responsibilities in order to thrive in today's newsrooms. This book has made that point abundantly clear, and all you have to do is look at job openings in newsrooms.

Mobile and social media skills are must-have qualifications listed in a broad range of journalism job postings. Journalism professors Debora Wenger (@dhwenger) and Lynn Owens (@lynncowens) analyzed more than 1,100 journalism job openings in the United States.[1]

In this chapter, you will

- Discover why mobile and social media savvy is important to the success of current and future journalists' careers.

- Unpack the data about the skills newsroom hiring managers are prioritizing.

- Explore the increasing number of newsroom positions dedicated solely to mobile and social media.

- Discuss the use of social media as a tool in the job hunt and how the topic is now a key part of the interview process.

Superpowers: Skills Newsrooms Need Now

Digital skills. Traditional reporting competence. Entrepreneurial mindset. Journalists who have a combination of all three of these qualities are a journalism employer's dream hire, according to a report by the Tow-Knight Center for Entrepreneurial Journalism.[2]

When it comes to digital skills, newsroom managers surveyed for the study said the following were among the top hiring priorities:

- Social media distribution
- Visual storytelling, particularly for social
- Social/engagement reporting
- User experience
- Audience development/user data and metrics
- Computer coding and development

The positions were posted in 2015. The results show a decided shift in requirements for journalism positions from years prior. You guessed it—the number of postings that mention "mobile" and "social" has increased dramatically.

Regardless of the type of newsroom, more jobs than ever before require journalists to produce content across multiple platforms and to understand how to monitor and increase audience engagement for their work, the study found.

For multiple platform jobs, 60 percent of the positions referenced the use of mobile devices in the journalism production process and/or the delivery of content via mobile channels. Seventy percent mentioned social networking skills. Social media was listed nearly as often as strong writing skills, which was mentioned in 71 percent of the job descriptions. As the audience becomes more mobile and social, the number of job descriptions with these mentions will only increase.

Wenger and Owens note that experimentation with mobile content and exploring issues such as video orientation (vertical versus horizontal), social graphic design, and story formats are important for journalism students. For instance, photography and videography skills are not new. But adapting photo and video techniques for an audience that increasingly consumes news on mobile devices and social media is critical to capturing their attention.

In another study, journalism professionals and educators were asked: "If you sent a journalism graduate to his or her first professional reporting assignment with just ONE reporting tool, which tool would you choose?"[3]

"Smartphone" was the most selected choice.

Being a solid journalist is about more than just technology. Writing, fact-checking, and critical thinking—those kinds of foundational journalistic skills still matter. In job descriptions for all sorts of positions in newsrooms large and small, you can see the demand for journalists who have digital and core journalism skills. The combination of both is what will give you the best chance of being hired and succeeding in the industry.

When the Cox Media Group was hiring an entry-level reporter to work out of its digital-first newsroom in Dayton, Ohio, the job description noted the need for "an All-Media Journalist whose enterprise and watchdog stories will reach customers through our wired and mobile digital sites, apps, newspaper, TV and radio stations." "Excellent reporting and writing skills" and "a demonstrated social media presence" were listed as priorities. An understanding of the economics of the business (addressed in Chapter 2) was also mentioned in the job listing. The person in this position would be expected to build the outlet's audience through the use of social media and ultimately "increase our digital revenues."

Likewise, the job description for a Government Watchdog Reporter at the *Jackson Sun* in Tennessee highlighted the importance of serving the audience across multiple platforms with "top-notch watchdog journalism." Here's a sampling of the job duties in the ad:

- Researches, writes, and reports compelling journalism that continuously grows a fan base by informing and engaging readers.
- Promotes personal brand, the brands of colleagues, and the institutional brand, especially through the use of social media.
- Connects with the community through storytelling and outreach (social media, on-camera, forums, community leadership, etc.). Should have a strong understanding of building and interacting with social media followers.
- Collaborates with content team to provide all appropriate elements for stories (i.e., photos, videos and graphics).
- Works with content strategist and audience analyst to evaluate what's working and what's not, and develops ongoing plans to better satisfy audience needs.

MOBILE AND SOCIAL MEDIA JOBS AND INTERNSHIPS

While mobile and social skills are now embedded in the job descriptions of reporters and other newsroom staff, there's an entire new world of journalism positions that have exploded in number: those dedicated to mobile and social media.

Social media producer at CNBC. Community engagement specialist at the Syracuse Media Group. Facebook Live producer at the *Washington Post*.

New Roles, New Opportunities

Who's behind the scenes, shaping a newsroom's mobile and social media strategy? Newsrooms have created new roles, such as these, to lead digital-first efforts:

- Social media producer
- Social media photo editor

- Social sourcing producer
- Facebook Live producer
- Snapchat producer
- Audience engagement editor
- Mobile editor

These positions reflect how newsrooms are adapting to the mobile audience. With the right mix of skills and willingness to experiment, you may find yourself in one of these positions in the not too distant future. They're ripe for the taking for journalists who are innovative and not afraid to test out new ways of doing journalism.

What do people in these positions do? While nearly everyone in a newsroom is expected to contribute to new media platforms, spearheading the newsroom strategy is the responsibility of staff in these roles. And, that's where the excitement comes in. In these positions, you can lead the charge in shaping the future of journalism.

It's about more than just tweeting and snapping. Duties include these:

- Developing a strategy and using analytics to monitor its effectiveness
- Advising staff members about the latest trends and training them on how to use mobile devices and social media for newsgathering, distribution, and engaging the audience
- Planning and executing crowdsourced projects
- Curating user-generated content and identifying misleading information
- Managing the outlet's social media accounts, including posting content, responding to comments, and engaging and growing an audience
- Ensuring users have a positive experience on all platforms on which the outlet is publishing content

JOB DESCRIPTION

THV11, the TEGNA-owned CBS property in Little Rock, Arkansas is seeking a highly motivated, dynamic Social Media Coordinator to join our team and help develop social strategy and create content for the No. 1 website in the market thv11.com and its social and mobile counterparts.

The ideal candidate will have a knack for understanding and talking about digital analytics and possess excellent, fast writing skills. They should be a self-motivator and be confident working solo and as a team member.

THV11's Social Media Coordinator should have a love for communication, a passion for news, and a sense of urgency.

Job responsibilities:

- Report news as it happens on digital and social media platforms
- Monitor, track, and analyze digital and social data and compile reports based on findings
- Monitor traditional and emerging technologies to receive, filter, and share content
- Scour the Internet for local and national viral/shareable stories
- Work closely with THV11 reporters and anchors to inspire and encourage the use of evolving/emerging social and digital media tools
- Contribute story ideas to the THV11 news department
- Research story tips and work as part of THV11's "Digital Desk"

Job Posting: Facebook Live Producers. Tumblr Post. July 25, 2016.

-------- 25TH JUL 2016 | 3 NOTES --------

JOB POSTING: FACEBOOK LIVE PRODUCERS

The Washington Post is seeking digital-savvy social video news producers for Facebook Live programming. The ideal candidates for these contract positions have demonstrated experience with developing and executing on social video programming for a national audience. Washington Post video producers are a critical part of the department's workflow, handling live video programming, pitching and creating video stories and breaking news production. Live video producers must be able to build relationships across the newsroom.

Washington Post video producers have at least one-year experience in a high-pressure newsroom environment, strong news judgment, familiarity with search and SEO best practices, strong writing skills, a record of excellence in new media, social media and emerging platforms and the ability to use Adobe Premiere, Photoshop and social video tools.

Washington Post video producers are proficient in managing social media efforts and online community development, especially Facebook and Twitter, participate in daily news and enterprise meetings, monitor analytics and perform other duties as assigned. Must be available to work all shifts.

If interested, please send cover letter, resume and links to recent work to T.J. Ortenzi (**tj.ortenzi@washpost.com**), Phoebe Connelly (**phoebe.connelly@washpost.com**), or Tracy Grant (**tracy.grant@washpost.com**) with the subject line: "Live Video Producer" by August 5.

THV11.

From major news outlets to newsrooms in smaller markets, there are an increasing number of positions focused on social media.

Not even a year after graduating from journalism school in 2014, Dylan Lyons (@dylanlyons91) began managing social media for the *CBS Evening News with Scott Pelley*. Yes, he taught even the most veteran journalists, such as Scott Pelley, how to use Periscope and the like.

"A huge part of my job was working to expand the *CBS Evening News* brand to reach as many different people as possible," said Lyons. "The only way to do this successfully was to post consistently and accurately across social media platforms. CBS News has a reputation of fair and accurate reporting to uphold, and I was careful to mirror those values on our social media platforms."

Lyons shared stories, videos, photos, and breaking news updates throughout the day on the *CBS Evening News's* social media accounts. He also monitored social media analytics to determine how much the *CBS Evening News* presence and engagement on social was growing. In editorial meetings, Lyons updated producers on the latest analytics and trends.

His job responsibilities were really a mixed bag. Some days he produced social videos and created infographics. Lyons was also responsible for gathering elements from social media and securing permission to use the content. During the evening broadcast, he was in the control room where he live tweeted each story as it aired.

"If journalism students want to get hired, it will be necessary for them to jump on the social bandwagon in journalistic ways starting in college," said Lyons.

That learning can happen during internships. When interning, pay close attention to how journalists and other staff members integrate mobile and social into their workday as well as to the responsibilities of those on the digital team.

Some outlets are looking for interns to focus solely on mobile and social platforms. Journalism major Ashley Lynne Nicole interned at WTAJ-TV in Altoona, Pennsylvania. Nicole was asked to manage social media for the station's *On the Road* segments, in which the outlet featured unique parts of the community.

"During our special *On the Road* shows, I was in charge of our social media pages. I was holding Facebook Live events, creating photo galleries, and updating our audience," said Nicole. "I was able to gain the most valuable experience from these days."

Using social media skillfully as an intern is one way to grab the attention of people in the newsroom. Andrew Gibson (@AndrewGibson27), app developer at the *Orlando Sentinel*, recommends interacting with newsroom staff not only in person, but also on social media.

"Just following them isn't enough. It's crucial to prove you understand why it's called social media. Talk to reporters about their stories, share links relevant to their beats and maybe even drop a few cheesy journalist jokes," said Gibson.[4]

The interactions and connections you make during internships are invaluable. They're one reason why internship experience leads to better hiring opportunities for journalism graduates.

In fact, before being hired by the *Sentinel*, Gibson was an interactive/online intern at the outlet. It's a similar story for Lyons. He already had a foot in the door at CBS News, having interned at the network's London bureau and with its investigative unit in New York City.

Start now to plan your career path. In college, explore the job listings and descriptions in the journalism field. Decide what your postcollege career goals are, and use the job descriptions as guides to the skills and qualifications you'll need.

Part of that plan should be at least one internship in a newsroom. The earlier you set foot in a newsroom, the better. Internships give you a taste of newsroom culture and the different journalism positions, as well as connections to industry professionals. Internship experiences can help you decide the type of newsroom where you'd ideally like to work and the position you can see yourself in.

Here are some of the key places to look for job and internship opportunities:

- **News outlets' websites.** Search the job postings section on the websites of news outlets.

- **Media company websites.** Make a list of media companies that own news outlets, and then check the career/employment section of their websites. Each media company's site typically has a listing of open positions for the company's news operations in different markets.

- **General Internet search.** Using a search engine is a good starting point. Look for job websites, such as Indeed.com, that aggregate search results from all over the web. Advanced search functionality will help to pinpoint what you're looking for.

- **Professional organizations.** The websites of professional journalism organizations have job boards. These groups include the Society of Professional Journalists, Online News Association, National Association of Black Journalists, National Association of Hispanic Journalists, and the National Lesbian and Gay Journalists Association. Access to some of these job boards is restricted to members only.

- **Social networking sites.** Follow the Twitter accounts of media companies. Many have separate Twitter accounts dedicated to job postings for their news outlets. For example, The E.W. Scripps Company uses @EWScrippsJobs to tweet out job and internship opportunities at its newsrooms across the country. In addition, there are Twitter accounts, such as @MEOjobs, that share openings from across the media industry. Consider creating a Twitter list for job and internship leads.

Journalism Fellowships

Most major news outlets have fellowship programs to recruit and train the very best journalists. Open to recent graduates, the fellowships are highly competitive and can lead to permanent employment with the company at the end of the program. The Hearst Journalism Fellowship (@HearstFellows), for example, consists of two 12-month rotations at Hearst's top metro papers and websites. The fellowship focuses on digital innovation, multiplatform storytelling, and creating experiences that let audiences get involved with reporting.

E.W. Scripps is one of many media companies that regularly tweets out job openings in its newsrooms across the country.

@EWScrippsco. Twitter Post. February 19, 2016.

Also, search for **LinkedIn** Company Pages of news outlets where you'd love to work and the companies that own them. Company Pages have a section for job and internship openings. Click Follow Company to get regular updates, including job postings, in your LinkedIn news feed. When on a company's LinkedIn page, you can see if you're connected to current or former employees there. Another great feature of LinkedIn is the Find Alumni section, which allows you to search for alumni of your school and narrow down the results by location, type of industry, and company where they work (see the image on page 172). You could, for instance, use this feature to find and make a connection with an alumnus who is employed at a news outlet where you'd like to work. Finally, don't forget about LinkedIn's robust Jobs section where you can search for employment opportunities.

- **Faculty.** Your journalism instructors are an important, yet sometimes overlooked, resource in job and internship hunts. Many faculty members have been working journalists and still maintain strong ties with the industry. Touch base with your faculty advisor and other professors as you map out your career plans. As mentors, they can provide guidance on everything from your resume to contacts in newsrooms where you'd like to intern or work.

- **Career centers.** Become familiar with the staff and services at your school's career center. Career center counselors provide guidance in your internship and job hunt and facilitate networking with alumni and prospective employers. Campus career centers maintain a database of internship and job opportunities, often provided to them by alumni interested in hiring someone from their alma mater. Once you graduate and progress through your career, don't forget about your school's career center. These offices also assist alumni with career development and job opportunities.

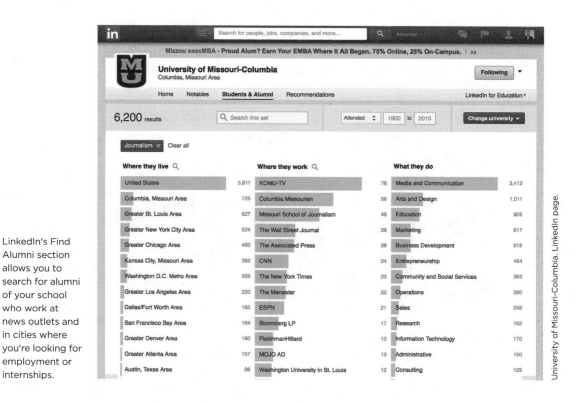

LinkedIn's Find Alumni section allows you to search for alumni of your school who work at news outlets and in cities where you're looking for employment or internships.

University of Missouri-Columbia. LinkedIn page.

- **Networking.** As you grow your network of contacts, those people should become an important part of your professional development. Maintain relationships with those whom you've met at internships and through other networking opportunities. As you look for career opportunities, reach out to them. But don't simply rely on them when you're in need of a job. Check in with them periodically to build and maintain a relationship. For example, ask them to review your portfolio of work once a year. Most journalists will be more than willing to lend a hand. They've been in your spot before and are happy to provide mentorship. Remember, despite all the technology at our fingertips, there's no replacement for one-on-one conversations. Schedule a phone chat or meet in person periodically.

BREAKING INTO THE BUSINESS: LEVERAGE YOUR DIGITAL KNOW-HOW

Social media has changed the way employers recruit and "interview" job candidates. It's no longer good enough to simply have a solid resume. How you present yourself online—your brand—is now part of the mix, as discussed in detail in Chapter 3.

From the Newsroom

**AMBER SMITH
(@AMBERSMITH1011)**

Assistant Director of News
Gray Television, Nebraska

Amber Smith is responsible for recruiting and hiring newsroom staff at Gray Television's four news outlets throughout Nebraska, including KNOP-TV. She also trains staff on new technology and oversees website and social media content.

WHAT ARE YOU LOOKING FOR IN NEW HIRES?

My ideal candidates have already established a professional presence—somebody who is using Facebook, Twitter, and Instagram for professional purposes and not just for personal use. Before they get here, they should have been experimenting on a professional level—even at the college media outlets. If you're not in the practice of using social media in a professional way, it's a different mindset. Also, I'm looking for someone who cares about how new tools can be used in journalism. I like to see that they're an early adopter of new platforms and social media features, not someone who is going to wait for me to say, "Okay, you have to start doing this." I also want to see that they understand how to differentiate content on each platform. Don't put the same thing on every platform. There needs to be a purpose for each one.

WHAT SKILLS DO YOU FIND CANDIDATES ARE LACKING?

I find while many millennials consume social media constantly, it still takes hard work and effort for them to know how to use those tools to engage an audience. Most candidates struggle with how to engage on social media. I see a lot of them simply pushing out content and thinking their job is done. You have to make sure you tag people, @mention them, and ask questions to maximize your reach.

WHAT'S THE BEST MIX OF PROFESSIONAL AND PERSONAL POSTS ON SOCIAL MEDIA? DO YOU LOOK FOR THE "PERSONAL SIDE" OF A CANDIDATE?

When I view candidates' online presence, I like when they have some personal content on social media. If I see a clever post, as long as it's within boundaries, that reflects positively on you. I want to see if it's someone who is going to get along with our staff. Somebody who can be a "personal professional," because as a reporter, you're not just here to regurgitate the news. Your job is to deliver it in an interesting and informative way, and part of that is making you relatable to people.

HOW CAN RECENT GRADUATES PUT THEIR BEST FOOT FORWARD ON SOCIAL MEDIA TO LAND A JOB?

Don't be dormant. Say you're done with college and not reporting for a class or student outlet anymore: Be your own boss. Think that you're the company. You're working for yourself. You're promoting yourself and your brand. Whether it be local or national news, share content. Live tweet news events as they happen. I want to see that you're following news and active.

Your activity on social media can make or break your chances of getting the interview. If the person reviewing intern or job candidates finds unprofessional posts, you're probably not going to get very far in the hiring process. Your digital footprint has to be clean and free of questionable activity. In addition, you need to demonstrate that you understand how to use mobile and social media in journalistic ways.

Having a professional presence online will also make you more discoverable to employers who are turning online in their recruiting efforts—as was the case with Eddie Dowd. He received an e-mail from a TV news manager who came across his online portfolio while conducting an Internet search for job candidates. She found Dowd's resume reel on YouTube and was able to locate his contact information on his website. That landed him an interview even though he hadn't ever actually applied for the job.

Online Portfolio and Brand

Now is an ideal time to review the key steps for building your brand (outlined in Chapter 3):

- **Conduct a social media audit** to ensure you have positive search results.
- **Create a website** that serves as a portfolio for your journalism work and includes your bio, resume, and contact information. Choose a website domain that is as close to your name as possible.
- **Use social media skillfully and consistently** to show you have the digital chops and journalistic abilities. Don't only promote your work. Share content you care about and engage with people on these platforms.
- Make sure your **profile photos and bios are up to date**. Include keywords that describe you professionally, such as those related to a beat you're interested in and your skills.

Resume

Keep your resume to one page. Don't oversell, get to the point, and make sure the layout is easy to follow. Your resume should be an accurate reflection of your education, experiences, and skills up to this point in your career. Proofread. It's unlikely you'll be taken seriously if your resume has spelling and grammatical errors. Remember, this is journalism after all. Get feedback from mentors and have your school's career service office review your resume.

You'll want to bring paper copies of your resume to job interviews. But, the electronic version is more important nowadays. Make your resume accessible online. The best way to do this is by embedding your resume on your website, rather than attaching a PDF or Word file to the webpage. Displaying it within a webpage is more visually appealing. To embed a document on most websites, you first must upload your resume to a site that allows you to host documents, such as Slideshare.net or Scribd.com. Then, copy the embed code to your website. The other option is to copy and paste the text from a word document directly into a page on your website. Keep in mind, sometimes this doesn't look the most appealing.

What should you include in a resume?

- **Heading** with name, address, phone number, e-mail address, link to your website, and Twitter handle. To avoid clutter, it's not recommended you include all social media profiles. For resumes posted publicly, remove your home address.

- **Relevant experience,** including paid positions, internships, and student media roles. Don't forget to include the dates of each position and several bullet points about your responsibilities. If you contributed to a journalism project, such as a multimedia website, as part of a course, list that as well. Explain in a bullet point which class it was part of.

- **Education** section with school name, title of major and minor degrees, years of attendance, and any honors received.

- **Skills** section should include knowledge you have of multimedia hardware (photo, audio, and video equipment) and software (editing programs such as Adobe Premiere). This is also where you want to highlight your savvy with mobile and social media. There's no need to list every social networking platform. Instead, list broader skills that employers are in need of—for example, social media optimization and social media analytics. Knowledge of foreign languages should also go in this section.

- Other sections to include, if applicable to you: **honors and awards, community service,** and memberships in **professional organizations**, such as your school's chapter of the Society of Professional Journalists.

- **Keywords** from a job description are important to include in a resume, because sometimes a staff member from an outlet's human resources department is the first to review resumes. Staff scan for keywords when choosing resumes that make it to the next round.

- **Do not include "references available upon request."** Of course, you'll need to pass along the names and contact information of references. Instead, list three references on a second page that includes the same heading you used for your resume. First, ask those people if it's alright to list them. As a courtesy, keep them updated when you actually land an interview. That way they know to expect a call or e-mail from a newsroom.

Cover Letter

Your cover letter is an opportunity to write a narrative about your interest in the position and your background, and how these align with the position you're applying for. The cover letter is not intended to repeat what's in your resume, but rather to expand on it. Keep the cover letter to one page. The cover letter also gives hiring managers a sense of your writing abilities and style.

- Do not start the letter with "To Whom It May Concern." Find out the name of the hiring manager, and address the letter to him or her.
- In the opening paragraph, explain where you are now and why you're applying for the position.
- If you have a connection with the outlet—for example, if you interned there or an alumnus who works there told you about the position—put that early in the letter.
- Tailor the letter. Hiring managers should get a sense of your passion for the industry and what excites you about the outlet and the position.
- Highlight your digital skills. Tell about how you used mobile devices and social media during the reporting process for one or two stories you've covered.
- Just as you would with a story you're writing, edit and proofread.

Applying and the Interview

Pay close attention to how a job posting indicates applicants should apply. In most cases, you'll need to apply through an online system to which you upload your cover letter, resume, and a link to your portfolio. Some outlets might prefer you e-mail the information to a specific person, which is often the case for internships at smaller outlets.

Before applying, give a heads-up to any contacts you have in the newsroom. They may share additional information about the position or be willing to drop a note about you to the hiring manager.

A few weeks have gone by and you haven't heard anything from the outlet you applied to. Should you contact the hiring manager? If the job description says "no calls or e-mails," there's the answer: Do not reach out. Otherwise, it's appropriate to follow up after a few weeks via e-mail if you haven't heard about your status as an applicant.

Do your homework. Become familiar with the outlet's news products and audience. Follow the outlet's social media platforms and several of its reporters, so you have a sense of how they use digital tools for reporting.

During the interview, you'll want to express your familiarity with the news outlet. The very best interviews feel like conversations. Here's some of what you can expect during the interview process:

- Writing test to determine your news judgment, writing skills, and ability to tailor your writing for different platforms.
- Current events/general knowledge quiz about the latest happening in the country and around the world. Some outlets also include questions about the region where they're located.
- Audit of your social media accounts (whether they tell you or not, expect this to already have happened by the time you're invited to interview for a position).

- Evidence that you're familiar with the outlet's reporting and audience.
- Passion for the industry and willingness to learn.

Finally, come prepared with your own questions and talking points. You should be curious about the culture of the newsroom, what will be expected of the person in the role, and the type of mentorship opportunities available to help you grow as a journalist, among other items. Engage in discussion about the outlet's mobile and social media strategy and how this role fits into that plan. A conversation about industry trends shows you have a broad understanding of both the business of journalism and the day-to-day skills needed to thrive. After all, you are the future leaders of this industry.

Breaking into the Business: The Journalism Job Hunt

Emily Masters (@emilysmasters), who graduated from journalism school in 2016, is a Hearst Journalism Fellow. During her first year in the fellowship, she worked as a multimedia breaking news reporter at the Times Union *in New York's capital region. Before accepting the Hearst Fellowship, Masters interviewed for a number of positions. Here's what she had to say about the job hunt process.*

In interviews for social media producer positions, I was asked to give a detailed critique of the newsrooms' current social media output and then lay out a specific plan for improvement, while defending my reasoning. In every interview for any journalism job, I was asked how I would handle certain ethical situations on social media and how I use social media for sourcing and story ideas.

During a lengthy interview process that included test taking, I was given a four-page hour-long exam on my "digital producer skills." For this exam, I had to take text headlines and rewrite them for web using search engine optimization (SEO) and social media optimization (SMO); pitch "online extra" multimedia components to supplement print/broadcast coverage; convert a traditional story to one told using interactive, multimedia components; and write a Tweet, a Facebook post, and a 125-word blog post to promote an online story.

During interviews for positions as a mobile multimedia reporter covering breaking news, I was asked to describe my reporting process in detail from my arrival on scene to the end of the day. I was also asked how I utilize the latest mobile hardware and software. What mobile devices can I shoot and edit on? What mobile devices can I file stories from? What social media platforms can I use from the field and how do I use them? What apps do I use in my work and why?

My brand and my experience impressed a lot of hiring managers, but a majority of my opportunities came from years of networking and maintaining contacts with industry leaders I had met at my college or at conferences, had reached out to personally, or had been introduced to via a mutual connection. My mentor relationships have been natural relationships formed through friendship and mutual interests. I always make sure I can offer something to someone I'm networking with. I have to make the relationship professionally valuable to them if I want it to last. Maybe I can offer a millennial's perspective on the industry, maybe we have a common interest in government reporting, maybe we both are involved in movements to support women in journalism. Then I stay in touch—buy them coffee when I'm in their city or send them an article that made me think of our past conversations. Finding common ground has fostered my networking relationships, and that translated to real job prospects senior year.

Checklist

✓ **Polish and Present Your Profile.** Perform an audit of your online brand, including your website and social media platforms. Have two of your classmates do the same and provide feedback. Now is a good time to update skills on your resume to include those related to mobile and social media. In a brief presentation to your class, reflect on your experience using mobile and social media in your reporting and to build your online brand. What worked? What didn't? In your discussion, include what you learned from monitoring your website and social media analytics. Finally, discuss how you plan to use mobile and social media in the future.

✓ **Infographic Resume.** Create an infographic resume to tell your story in a highly visual manner. It's not only a unique way to highlight your qualifications; it also demonstrates you understand data visualization and how to create infographics. Be selective about what you include on an infographic resume. It should highlight key points of your resume, not be overloaded with everything. Consider including a photo, a headline that describes who you are, and a timeline that shows when you acquired your experience, education, and skills. Infogr.am and Piktochart are web-based platforms where you can build infographics. Post the infographic on your website.

Journalism student Kelli Kyle created this infographic resume to highlight her background and skills in a highly-engaging way.

✓ **Review Job Descriptions.** Find three job descriptions for journalism positions at outlets you'd eventually like to work at. Analyze the qualifications, paying close attention to digital skills.

✓ **Beyond the Book.** This may be the end of the book, but let's keep the conversation going. Stay connected via the book's Facebook page (*fb.com/MobileandSocialMediaJournalism*) and Twitter account (@MobileJourn). And don't forget to check out the companion website (*MobileandSocialMediaJournalism.com*), where I provide additional resources, including video tutorials and industry related news.

Notes

CHAPTER 1

1. Jay Rosen, "The People Formerly Known as the Audience," The Huffington Post, May 25, 2011. http://www.huffingtonpost.com/jay-rosen/the-people-formerly-known_1_b_24113.html.
2. David Sarno, "Citizen Photo of Hudson River Plane Crash Shows Web's Reporting Power," Los Angeles Times, January 15, 2009. http://latimesb logs.latimes.com/technology/2009/01/citizen-photo-o.html.
3. Carl Quintanilla, "#TwitterRevolution" [documentary], CNBC Originals, air date August 17, 2013.
4. Pamela J. Shoemaker & Tim P. Vos, Gatekeeping Theory, Routledge, 2009.
5. Anthony C. Adornato, "Forces at the Gate: Social Media's Influence on Editorial and Production Decisions in Local Television Newsrooms," Electronic News 10, no. 2 (June 2016): 87–104, doi:0.1177/1931243116647768.
6. Anthony C. Adornato, "A Digital Juggling Act: New Media's Impact on the Responsibilities of Local Television Reporters." Electronic News 8, no. 1 (March 2014): 3–29. doi:10.1177/1931243114523963.
7. "U.S. Smartphone Use in 2015," Pew Research Center, April 1, 2015. http://www.pewinternet.org/2015/04/01/us-smartphone-use-in-2015/.
8. Mina Nacheva, "Putting the U in User-Generated Content," International Journalism Festival, May 3, 2014. http://magazine.journalism festival.com/putting-the-u-in-user-generated-content/.
9. Hillary Brenhouse, "Man Live-Tweets U.S. Raid on Osama bin Laden Without Knowing It," Time, May 2, 2011. http://newsfeed.time.com/2011/05/02/man-live-tweets-u-s-raid-on-osama-bin-laden-without-knowing-it/.
10. Adornato, "Forces at the Gate."
11. Mina Nacheva, "Putting the U in User-Generated Content."
12. "Digital News Report 2015," Reuters Institute for the Study of Journalism, n.d. Accessed February 3, 2017, at http://www.digitalnewsre port.org/survey/2015/executive-summary-and-key-findings-2015/.
13. "Mobile-First News: How People Use Smartphones to Access Information," Knight Foundation, May 11, 2016. http://www.knight foundation.org/publications/mobile-first-news-how-people-use-smartphones-acces.
14. "How Social Media is Reshaping News," Pew Research Center, September 24, 2014. http://www.pewresearch.org/fact-tank/2014/09/24/how-social-media-is-reshaping-news/.
15. "How Is Mobile Consumption Changing Journalism?" The Wall Street Journal, November 5, 2013. http://on.wsj.com/1upNwBl.
16. Mathew Ingram, "Facebook Has Taken Over From Google as a Traffic Source for News," Fortune, August 18, 2015. http://fortune.com/2015/08/18/facebook-google/.
17. "Digital News Report 2015."
18. "The 2016 Presidential Campaign—A News Event That's Hard to Miss," Pew Research Center, February 4, 2016. http://www.journal ism.org/2016/02/04/the-2016-presidential-campaign-a-news-event-thats-hard-to-miss/.
19. Amy Mitchell and Jesse Holcomb, "State of the News Media 2016," Pew Research Center, June 15, 2016. http://www.journalism.org/2016/06/15/state-of-the-news-media-2016.
20. "Rolling Out the Mobile-Friendly Update," Google Webmaster Central Blog, April 21, 2015. https://webmasters.googleblog.com/2015/04/rolling-out-mobile-friendly-update.html.
21. Adornato, "A Digital Juggling Act."
22. Quintanilla, "#TwitterRevolution."
23. Adornato, "A Digital Juggling Act."
24. Natalie Jomini Stroud, "Interaction on Twitter Enhances Journalists' Credibility," American Press Institute, December 4, 2015. https://www.americanpressinstitute.org/publications/research-review/twitter-credibility/.

CHAPTER 2

1. Robin Wauters, "You Need to See This Video (1981 TV Report on Birth of Internet News)," Tech Crunch, January 29, 2009. http://techcrunch.com/2009/01/29/you-need-to-see-this-video.
2. Michael Barthel, "Newspapers: Fact Sheet," Pew Research Center, April 29, 2015.

http://www.journalism.org/2015/04/29/news papers-fact-sheet.

3. Peter Drucker, *Managing in a Time of Great Change* (New York: Truman Talley Books/Plum, 1995).

4. George Sylvie, Jan LeBlanc Wicks, C. Ann Hollifield, Stephen Lacy, and Ardyth Broadrick Sohn, *Media Management: A Casebook Approach* (New York: Taylor & Francis, 2009).

5. Jim Bach, "Pew: Digital Ventures Bring Jobs and Money to Journalism," *American Journalism Review*, March 26, 2014. http://ajr .org/2014/03/26/pew-digital-ventures-bring-jobs-money-journalism.

6. Monica Anderson and Andrea Caumont, "How Social Media Is Reshaping News," Pew Research Center, September 24, 2014. http://www.pewre search.org/fact-tank/2014/09/24/how-social-media-is-reshaping-news.

7. Jessica Weiss, "How NPR Has Gone 'Mobile First,'" International Journalists Network, September 23, 2013. http://ijnet.org/en/blog/how-npr-has-gone-mobile-first.

8. Benjamin Mullin, "Dean Baquet: NYT Will Retire 'System of Pitching Stories for the Print Page 1,'" Poynter, February 19, 2015. http:// www.poynter.org/2015/dean-baquet-nyt-will-retire-system-of-pitching-stories-for-the-print-page-1/321637.

9. Joshua Benton, "The Leaked *New York Times* Innovation Report Is One of the Key Documents of This Media Age," Nieman Lab, May 15, 2015. http://www.niemanlab.org/2014/05/the-leaked-new-york-times-innovation-report-is-one-of-the-key-documents-of-this-media-age.

10. Lou Carlozo, "The Digital Push Is Smoother in Syracuse," NetNewsCheck, February 21, 2013. http://www.netnewscheck.com/article/24535/advance-digital-push-is-smoother-in-syracuse.

11. Michael Depp, "For CNN, Platform Publishing Now in DNA," NetNewsCheck, April 26, 2016. http://www.netnewscheck.com/article/50018/for-cnn-platform-publishing-now-in-dna?dg.

12. Mike Shields, "CNN to Pump $20 Million Into Digital Expansion," *Wall Street Journal*, March 16, 2016. http://www.wsj.com/articles/cnn-to-pump-20-million-into-digital-expansion-1458122401.

13. Tamar Charney, "8 NPR One Things I Wish I Had Known or Done When I Was at a Station," National Public Radio, April 20, 2016. http:// digitalservices.npr.org/post/8-npr-one-things-i-wish-i-had-known-or-done-when-i-was-station.

14. Shan Wang, "NPR One Is Getting Serious About the Promise of New Digital Audiences for Local Journalism," Nieman Lab, May 16, 2016. http://www.niemanlab.org/2016/05/npr-one-is-getting-serious-about-the-promise-of-new-digital-audiences-for-local-journalism.

15. Alex T. Williams, "Paying for Digital News: The Rapid Adoption and Current Landscape of Digital Subscriptions at US Newspapers," American Press Institute, February 29, 2016. https://www.americanpressinstitute.org/publica tions/reports/digital-subscriptions/single-page.

16. Amy Mitchell, "State of the News Media 2015," Pew Research Center, April 29, 2015. http:// www.journalism.org/2015/04/29/state-of-the-news-media-2015.

17. Amy Mitchell and Jesse Holcomb, "State of the News Media 2016," Pew Research Center, June 15, 2016. http://www.journalism .org/2016/06/15/state-of-the-news-media -2016.

18. "In Changing News Landscape, Even Television Is Vulnerable," Pew Research Center, September 27, 2012. http://www.people-press .org/2012/09/27/in-changing-news-landscape-even-television-is-vulnerable.

19. Anthony C. Adornato, "Forces at the Gate: Social Media's Influence on Editorial and Production Decisions in Local Television Newsrooms," *Electronic News* 10, no. 2 (June 2016): 87–104. doi:10.1177/1931243116647768.

20. Bob Papper, "RTDNA Research: The Business of TV News," Radio Television Digital News Association, May 16, 2016. http://rtdna.org/article/rtdna_research_the_business_of_tv_news#sthash.LOFZ5Rfl.dpuf.

21. Samir Husni, Debora Halpern Wenger, and Hank Price, *Managing Today's News Media: Audience First* (Thousand Oaks, CA: Sage, 2016).

22. Nancy Vogt, "Audio Fact Sheet," Pew Research Center, April 29, 2015. http://www.journalism .org/2015/04/29/audio-fact-sheet.

23. Bob Papper, "RTDNA Research: Newsrooms Grow Mobile and Social," Radio Television Digital News Association, April 18, 2016. http:// rtdna.org/article/rtdna_research_newsrooms_grow_mobile_and_social#sthash.aTRlOp6p .dpuf.

24. Michael Barthel, "5 Key Takeaways From State of the News Media 2015," Pew Research Center, April 29, 2015. http://www.pewresearch.org/fact-tank/2015/04/29/5-key-takeaways-from-state-of-the-news-media-2015.

25. Mark Jurkowitz, "The Growth in Digital Reporting," Pew Research Center, March 26, 2014. http://www.journalism.org/2014/03/26/the-growth-in-digital-reporting.

26. Deron Lee, "Will Readers Pay for Local News? A Digital Startup in Tulsa Bets That They Will," *Columbia Journalism Review,* April 26, 2016. http://www.cjr.org/united_states_project/the_frontier_for_profit_digital_startup_oklahoma.php.

27. Carolyn Maynard-Parisi and Mary Mann, "The Value of Local News: Why the Village Green Now Has a Limited Paywall," The Village Green, May 15, 2016. http://villagegreennj.com/salon/value-local-news-village-green-now-limited-paywall-2.

28. "A New Understanding: What Makes People Trust and Rely on News," American Press Institute, April 17, 2016. https://www.americanpressinstitute.org/publications/reports/survey-research/trust-news.

29. Shan Wang, "Out of Many, NPR One: The App That Wants to be the 'Netflix of Listening' Gets More Local," Nieman Lab, January 11, 2016. http://www.niemanlab.org/2016/01/out-of-many-npr-one-the-app-that-wants-to-be-the-netflix-of-listening-gets-more-local.

30. "A New Understanding."

31. "Subscriber Benefits," *Chicago Tribune.* http://membership.chicagotribune.com.

32. Adornato, "Forces at the Gate."

33. Josh Stearns, "How Journalists Build and Break Trust With Their Audience Online," First Draft News, May 27, 2016. https://firstdraftnews.com/how-journalists-build-and-break-trust-online.

34. Emily Bell, "The End of the News as We Know It: How Facebook Swallowed Journalism," Tow Center for Digital Journalism, March 7, 2016. https://medium.com/@TowCenter/the-end-of-the-news-as-we-know-it-how-facebook-swallowed-journalism-60344fa50962#.9qp019ovg.

35. "Demographic Profile of Social Networking Site Users," Pew Research Center, May 25, 2016. http://www.journalism.org/2016/05/26/news-use-across-social-media-platforms-2016/pj_2016-05-26_social-media-and-news_0-06.

36. Joy Mayer, "Earning Trust on Social: Engage Authentically," Reynolds Journalism Institute, April 21, 2016. https://www.rjionline.org/stories/earning-trust-on-social-engage-authentically.

37. Michael Barthel, Elisa Shearer, Jeffrey Gottfried, and Amy Mitchell, "News Habits on Facebook and Twitter," Pew Research Center, July 14, 2015. http://www.journalism.org/2015/07/14/news-habits-on-facebook-and-twitter.

38. "When and Where Do We Access the News?" Reuters Institute for the Study of Journalism, 2015. http://www.digitalnewsreport.org/survey/2015/when-and-where-do-we-access-the-news-2015.

CHAPTER 3

1. Mark Glaser, Personal Branding Becomes a Necessity in Digital Age, MediaShift, July 16, 2009. http://mediashift.org/2009/07/personal-branding-becomes-a-necessity-in-digital-age197.

2. Social Recruiting Survey, Jobvite, 2014. https://www.jobvite.com/wp-content/uploads/2014/10/Jobvite_SocialRecruiting_Survey2014.pdf.

3. Robinson, as quoted in Glaser, 2009.

4. Anthony C. Adornato and Suzanne Lysak, "A Survey of Social Media Policies in U.S. Television Newsrooms" (paper presented at the annual conference of the Association for Education in Journalism and Mass Communication, San Francisco, CA, August 2015).

5. Ibrahim Ahmed, "Why Your Profile Picture Is So Important," *The National,* February 26, 2015. http://www.thenational.ae/business/the-life/why-your-profile-picture-is-so-important.

6. Sree Sreenivasan, "Why Profile Photos Matter— Is Yours Appropriate?" DNAinfo, April 12, 2010. https://www.dnainfo.com/new-york/20100412/morningside-heights/why-profile-photos-matter-mdash-is-yours-appropriate.

7. Mallary Jean Tenore, "10 Ways Young Journalists Can Make Themselves More Marketable," Poynter, January 7, 2013. http://www.poynter.org/2013/10-ways-journalists-can-make-themselves-more-marketable/198780.

8. "Social Media Guidelines for Student Journalists," Walter Cronkite School of Journalism and Mass Communication, accessed January 22, 2017. https://cronkite.asu.edu/degree-programs/admissions/student-resources/social-media-guidelines.

9. Benjamin Mullin, "*New York Times* Editor: After Orlando Shooting, Don't Editorialize on Social Media," Poynter, June 13, 2016. http://www.poynter.org/2016/new-york-times-editor-after-orlando-shooting-dont-editorialize-on-social-media/416566.

10. Adornato and Lysak, 2015.

11. Scott Kleinberg, "The Rule of Thirds Will Change How You Share on Social Media,"

Chicago Tribune, August 6, 2014. http://www
.chicagotribune.com/lifestyles/ct-social-media-
rule-of-thirds-20140806-column.html.

12. Sue Burzynski Bullard, "Best Practices for Social
Media and Journalism," American Copy Editors
Society, July 8, 2014. http://www.copydesk.org/
blog/2014/07/08/best-practices-for-social-
media-and-journalism.

13. James Breiner, "How Journalist Built His
Brand From College Dorm Room," News
Entrepreneurs, January 27, 2013. http://newsent
repreneurs.blogspot.com/2013/01/how-journal
ist-built-his-brand-from.html.

CHAPTER 4

1. Rachel Barron and Alexa Lardieri, "Newspapers
Hunt for New Readers on Instagram," *American
Journalism Review,* April 7, 2015. http://ajr
.org/2015/04/07/newspapers-hunt-for-new-
readers-on-instagram.

2. Michael Roston, "If a Tweet Worked Once,
Send It Again—and Other Lessons From the
New York Times' Social Media Desk," Nieman
Lab, January 6, 2014. http://www.niemanlab
.org/2014/01/if-a-tweet-worked-once-send-it-
again-and-other-lessons-from-the-new-york-
times-social-media-desk.

3. Henk van Ess, "How to Use Private Twitter
Lists to Deepen Coverage of Companies,"
MediaShift, January 2015. http://mediashift
.org/2015/06/how-to-use-private-twitter-lists-
to-deepen-coverage-of-companies.

4. van Ess, "How to Use Private Twitter Lists,"
2015.

5. NPR Ethics Handbook, n.d. Accessed February
4, 2017, at http://ethics.npr.org/tag/social-media.

6. Meena Thiruvengadam, "Instagram for
Newsrooms: A Community Tool, a Reporting
Tool, a Source of Web Content," Poynter, May 27,
2103. http://www.poynter.org/2013/instagram-
for-newsrooms-a-community-tool-a-reporting-
tool-a-source-of-web-content/214435.

7. Thiruvengadam, "Instagram for Newsrooms," 2103.

8. Daniel Victor, "The One Word Journalists Should
Add to Twitter Searches That You Probably Haven't
Considered," April 27, 2015. https://medium
.com/@bydanielvictor/the-one-word-reporters-
should-add-to-twitter-searches-that-you-probably-
haven-t-considered-fadab1bc34e8#.3p8egd8jq.

9. Victor, "The One Word Journalists Should Add,"
2015.

10. Blair Hickman, "How We Used Facebook to
Power Our Investigation Into Patient Harm,"
ProPublica, December 19, 2012. https://www
.propublica.org/article/how-we-used-facebook-
to-power-our-investigation-into-patient-harm.

11. Joseph Lichterman, "What Are the Best Practices
for Crowdsourcing the Reporting Process?"
Nieman Lab, November 20, 2015. http://www
.niemanlab.org/2015/11/what-are-the-best-prac
tices-for-crowdsourcing-the-reporting-process.

12. Serri Graslie, "6 Ways to Use Social Callouts,"
NPR Social Media Desk, April 29, 2015. http://
socialmediadesk.tumblr.com/post/117706055331/
6-ways-to-use-social-callouts.

13. "Guide to Crowdsourcing," Tow Center for
Digital Journalism, November 20, 2015. http://
towcenter.org/research/guide-to-crowdsourcing.

14. Hickman, "How We Used Facebook," 2012.

15. Reuben Stern, "Infographics," American Society
of News Editors Youth Journalism Initiative, n.d.
Accessed February 5, 2017, at http://schooljour
nalism.org/wp-content/uploads/adobe_captivate_
uploads/Infographics_ASNE-rev/multiscreen.html

CHAPTER 5

1. Paul Greeley, "WFAA Reporter Works Alone
With His iPhone," TVNewsCheck, January 29,
2016. http://www.tvnewscheck.com/market-
share/2016/01/29/wfaa-reporter-works-alone-
using-his-iphone.

2. Neal Augenstein, "How to Edit a Reporter
Wrap With Ferrite App," #iphonereporting,
December 3, 2015. https://iphonereporting
.com/2015/12/03/how-to-edit-a-reporter-
wrap-with-ferrite-app.

3. Jessica Weiss, "7 Tips for Budding Mobile
Journalists," MediaShift, December 7, 2014.
http://mediashift.org/2014/12/7-tips-for-
budding-mobile-journalists.

4. Caroline Scott, "Ditching the DSLR: Why a BBC
Journalist Filmed Only on a Mobile Phone for a
Month," journalism.co.uk, August 1, 2016. https://
www.journalism.co.uk/news/ditching-the-dslr-
how-a-bbc-journalist-swopped-his-professional-
camera-for-a-mobile-phone-for-a-month/s2/
a660935.

5. Catalina Albeanu, "Why the *Washington Post*
Is Integrating Vertical Video Into Its Strategy,"
journalism.co.uk, July 7, 2016. https://www
.journalism.co.uk/news/washington-post-vertical-
video/s2/a653586.

6. Lino Lotveit, "How to Mojo: Using Mobile Phones for Reporting," Global Investigative Journalism Conference, October 15, 2015. http://gijc2015.org/2015/10/15/how-to-mojo-using-mobile-phones-for-reporting.

7. Robert Channick, "*Chicago Sun-Times* Lays Off Its Photo Staff," *Chicago Tribune,* May 30, 2013. http://articles.chicagotribune.com/2013-05-30/business/chi-chicago-sun-times-photo-20130530_1_chicago-sun-times-photo-staff-video.

8. Emil Pakarklis, "9 iPhone Camera Features Every Photographer Should Use," iPhone Photography School, July 20, 2016. http://iphonephotographyschool.com/iphone-camera.

CHAPTER 6

1. Katie Yaeger, "Finding a Voice on Social Media: Insights for Local Newsrooms," American Press Institute, December 16, 2016. http://www.americanpressinstitute.org/publications/reports/strategy-studies/social-media-voice.

2. Amy Mitchell, "State of the News Media 2015," Pew Research Center, April 29, 2015. http://www.journalism.org/2015/04/29/state-of-the-news-media-2015/.

3. Liliana Honorato, "Practitioners Panel Discusses the Increasing Impact of Social Media on Journalism on the Second Day of ISOJ," The Knight Center for Journalism, April 21, 2012. https://knightcenter.utexas.edu/blog/00-9831-practitioners-panel-discusses-increasing-impact-social-media-journalism-second-day-isoj.

4. Simon Rogers, "What Fuels a Tweet's Engagement," Twitter, March 10, 2014. https://blog.twitter.com/2014/what-fuels-a-tweets-engagement.

5. Yaeger, "Finding a Voice on Social Media."

6. Rogers, "What Fuels a Tweet's Engagement."

7. "The Personal News Cycle: How Americans Choose to Get Their News," American Press Institute, March 17, 2014, https://www.americanpressinstitute.org/publications/reports/survey-research/personal-news-cycle/.

8. Mallory Jean Tenore, "What Twitter Teaches Us About Writing Short & Well," Poynter, August 30, 2012. http://www.poynter.org/2012/what-twitter-teaches-us-about-writing-short-well/186371/.

9. Michael Roston, "If a Tweet Worked Once, Send It Again—and Other Lessons From the New York Times' Social Media Desk," Nieman Lab, January 6, 2014. http://www.niemanlab.org/2014/01/if-a-tweet-worked-once-send-it-again-and-other-lessons-from-the-new-york-times-social-media-desk/.

10. "Writing for Mobile: Bite-Size Basics," BBC Academy, n.d. Accessed January 27, 2017, at http://www.bbc.co.uk/academy/journalism/article/art20141202144618106.

11. Jakob Nielsen, "Website Reading: It (Sometimes) Does Happen," Nielsen Norman Group, June 24, 2013. https://www.nngroup.com/articles/website-reading/.

12. Sue Burzynski Bullard, "Best Practices for Social Media and Journalism," American Copy Editors Association, July 8, 2014. http://www.copydesk.org/blog/2014/07/08/best-practices-for-social-media-and-journalism/.

13. Natalie Jomini Stroud, "Interaction on Twitter Enhances Journalists' Credibility," American Press Institute, December 4, 2015. https://www.americanpressinstitute.org/publications/research-review/twitter-credibility/.

14. Steve Buttry, "10 Ways Twitter Is Valuable to Journalists," The Buttry Diary, August 27, 2012. https://stevebuttry.wordpress.com/2012/08/27/10-ways-twitter-is-valuable-to-journalists/.

15. Rachel Bartlett, "How Newsrooms Can Use Social Analytics to Guide Editorial Strategy," Journalism.co.uk, June 19, 2013. https://www.journalism.co.uk/news/how-newsrooms-can-use-social-analytics-to-guide-editorial-strategy/s2/a553295.

16. JP Mangalindan, "Why Facebook Now Sends More Traffic to News Websites than Google," Mashable, August 19, 2015. http://mashable.com/2015/08/19/facebook-traffic-news-sites-google/#WzLzoRe2GOqr.

17. Amy Mitchell, "State of the News Media 2015," Pew Research Center, April 29, 2015. http://www.journalism.org/2015/04/29/state-of-the-news-media-2015/.

18. Ravi Somaiya, "How Facebook Is Changing the Way Its Users Consume Journalism," *New York Times,* October 26, 2014. http://www.nytimes.com/2014/10/27/business/media/how-facebook-is-changing-the-way-its-users-consume-journalism.html?_r=0.

19. Michael Jenner, "Newsrooms Using Web Metrics to Evaluate Staff, Guide Editorial Decisions," Reynolds Journalism Institute, November 14,

2013. https://www.rjionline.org/stories/news-rooms-using-web-metrics-to-evaluate-staff-guide-editorial-decisions.

20. Anthony C. Adornato, "Forces at the Gate: Social Media's Influence on Editorial and Production Decisions in Television Newsrooms," *Electronic News* 10, no. 2 (June 2016): 87–104. doi:0.1177/1931243116647768.

21. Yaeger, "Finding a Voice on Social Media.

22. David Carr, "Risks Abound as Reporters Play in Traffic," *New York Times,* March 23, 2014. http://www.nytimes.com/2014/03/24/business/media/risks-abound-as-reporters-play-in-traffic.html.

23. Katie Yaeger, "Implementing a Voice," American Press Institute, December 16, 2015. https://www.americanpressinstitute.org/publications/reports/strategy-studies/implementing-a-voice/.

24. Ibid.

25. Rachel Wise and Reuben Stern, "Q&A with Parse.ly CEO Sachin Kamdar: Choosing the Right Metrics," Reynolds Journalism Institute, December 16, 2015. https://www.rjionline.org/stories/futures-lab-interview-parsely-ceo-sachin-kamdar-choosing-the-right-metrics.

CHAPTER 7

1. Samantha Goldberg, "The Age of iPhone Reporting: Q & A with Neal Augenstein," *American Journalism Review,* December 23, 2013. http://ajr.org/2013/12/23/age-iphone-reporting.

2. Julie Moos, "TV Station Says It Fired Meteorologist for Replying to Viewer on Facebook," Poynter, December 12, 2012. http://www.poynter.org/2012/tv-station-says-it-fired-meteorologist-for-replying-to-viewer-on-facebook/197877.

3. Joey Morona, "'Good Morning Cleveland' anchors Jackie Fernandez, Somara Theodore let go after social media posts," Cleveland.com, October 31, 2016. http://www.cleveland.com/entertainment/index.ssf/2016/10/good_morning_cleveland_anchors.html

4. "Journalism Personal Statement by Scott Pelley," United Worldwide Web, May 27, 2013. https://www.youtube.com/watch?v=guIvUPjeNzI.

5. Steve Buttry, "Journalists Code of Ethics: Time for an Update," The Buttry Diary, November 7, 2010. https://stevebuttry.wordpress.com/2010/11/07/journalists-code-of-ethics-time-for-an-update.

6. Anthony C. Adornato and Suzanne Lysak, "A Survey of Social Media Policies in US Television Newsrooms" (paper presented at the annual convention of the Association for Education in Journalism and Mass Communication, San Francisco, CA, August 2015).

7. "Building and Using Your Customized Ethics Code," Online News Association Build Your Own Ethics Code, n.d. Accessed January 27, 2017, at http://ethics.journalists.org/instructions.

8. Ibid.

9. "Eyewitness Media Hub Launch Guiding Principles for Journalists," Eyewitness Media Hub, September 9, 2015. https://medium.com/@emhub/eyewitness-media-hub-launch-guiding-principles-for-journalists-54aaf-c786eeb#.icml5c8qt.

10. "Social Newsgathering in Sensitive Circumstances," Associated Press, n.d. Accessed January 30, 2017, at https://web.archive.org/web/20150913235517/http://www.ap.org/Images/Social-Newsgathering_tcm28-12860.pdf.

11. Steven Mendoza, "To Friend or Not to Friend?" *American Journalism Review*, October/November 2008, http://ajrarchive.org/Article.asp?id=4628.

12. Ibid.

13. Jim Romenesko, "Gannett Releases Its Social Media Policy," jimromenesko.com, September 10, 2013. http://jimromenesko.com/2013/09/10/read-gannetts-social-media-policy-memo.

14. "Social Media Guidelines for AP Employees," Associated Press, May 2013. http://www.ap.org/Images/Social-Media-Guidelines_tcm28-9832.pdf.

15. "10 Best Practices for Social Media: Helpful Guidelines for News Organizations," American Society of News Editors, May 2011. http://asne.org/Files/pdf/10_Best_Practices_for_Social_Media.pdf.

16. Anthony C. Adornato, "Forces at the Gate: Social Media's Influence on Editorial and Production Decisions in Local Television Newsrooms," *Electronic News* 10, no. 2 (June 2016): 87–104. doi:0.1177/1931243116647768.

17. Matt Mulcahy, "Maybe I'm Amazed Paul McCartney lunched with East Syracuse workers: Matt's Memo," CNYCentral.com, September 5, 2012. http://cnycentral.com/news/matts-memo/maybe-im-amazed-paul-mccartney-lunched-with-east-syracuse-workers-matts-memo

18. Jenni Sargent, "How to Verify Images Like a Pro With Google Earth," First Draft News, January 19, 2016. https://firstdraftnews.com/resource/how-to-verify-images-like-a-pro-with-google-earth.

19. "Social Media Guidelines for AP Employees," Associated Press, May 2013. http://www.ap.org/Images/Social-Media-Guidelines_tcm28-9832.pdf.

20. Jonathan Peters, "Can I Use That? A Legal Primer for Journalists," *Columbia Journalism Review*, October 1, 2015. http://www.cjr.org/united_states_project/journalist_legal_questions.php.

21. Daxton Stewart, ed., *Social Media and the Law: A Guidebook for Communication Students and Professionals* (New York: Routledge, 2013), 208.

22. Alastair Reid, "5 Points to Remember About Copyright and Breaking News," First Draft News, April 21, 2016. https://firstdraftnews.com/5-points-to-remember-about-copyright-and-breaking-news.

23. Steve Myers, "*Portland Press Herald* to Pay Woman for Using Photograph Without Permission," Poynter, August 14, 2012. http://www.poynter.org/2012/portland-press-herald-to-pay-woman-for-using-photograph-flickr/184871.

24. David Trilling, "Copyright-Free Images: Tips on How to Find Free Photos and Graphics," Harvard University Shorenstein Center, August 15, 2016. http://journalistsresource.org/tip-sheets/find-copyright-free-images-photos.

25. "Corrections," Online News Association Build Your Own Ethics Code, n.d. Accessed January 27, 2017, at http://ethics.journalists.org/topics/corrections.

26. Adornato and Lysak, "A Survey of Social Media Policies."

27. Jasmine McNealy, "Who Owns Your Friends?: *Phonedog v. Kravitz* and Business Claims of Trade Secret in Social Media Information," *Rutgers University Computer & Technology Law Journal* 39 (2013), 30–55.

28. Jim Romenesko, "E.W. Scripps Co. Issues Social Media Policy," Poynter, June 30, 2011. http://www.poynter.org/2011/e-w-scripps-announces-social-media-policy-to-staff/137564.

29. Ibid.

30. Diane Marszalek, "Who Owns, Controls Social Media Activity?" TVNewsCheck, January 29, 2013. http://www.tvnewscheck.com/article/65102/who-owns-controls-social-media-activity.

31. Rachel Barnhart, "An Important Note to My Twitter and Facebook Friends," Barnhart's Google Plus page, January 15, 2013. https://plus.google.com/u/0/+RachelBarnhart/posts/GnJodo5zBig.

32. Ibid.

CHAPTER 8

1. Debora Wenger and Lynn Owens, "Help Wanted: Expanding Social Media, Mobile and Analytics Skills in Journalism Education" (paper presented at annual conference of the Association for Education in Journalism and Mass Communication, Minneapolis, Minnesota, August 5, 2016).

2. Mark Stencel and Kim Perry, "Superpowers: The Digital Skills Media Leaders Say Newsrooms Need Going Forward," Tow-Knight Center for Entrepreneurial Journalism, April 2016. http://towknight.org/research/superpowers.

3. Bernard McCoy, "2014 Journalism Graduate Skills for the Professional Workplace: Expectations From Journalism Professionals and Educators Journal of Media Education," April 2015. http://en.calameo.com/read/000091789c8c66aef92f0.

4. Andrew Gibson, "How to Stand Out on Social Media During Your Internship," Online News Association, August 8, 2013. http://journalists.org/2013/08/08/how-to-stand-out-on-social-media-during-your-internship.

5. Matt Thompson, "10 Ways to Make Your Journalism Job Application Better Than Everyone Else's," Poynter, September 27, 2012. http://www.poynter.org/2012/10-ways-to-make-your-journalism-job-application-better-than-everyone-elses/189491.

Index

Active audience role, 2
  audience engagement and, 19–21
  citizen journalism and, 5–6, 7
  content production and, 7–9
  gatekeeper process, impact on, 6–7, 17
  mobile majority and, 10, 12, 13
  mobile/social media journalism and, 1, 2, 4, 5–6
  news consumption habits and, 10–13, 12 (table)
  news websites, access to, 11
  one-way communication, traditional mass
      communication and, 3–4
  trending stories and, 7
  two-way conversation, social media era and, 4–5, 40
  user-generated content and, 7–9, 16
  See also Crowdsourcing; Mobile-first newsroom;
      Mobile journalism; Social media
      engagement/audience analytics;
      Social media journalism
Adobe Photoshop Express app, 109
Adobe Spark Post app, 125
Advance Publications, 27, 31
Advertising revenue, 23–24, 31, 32–33, 39
American Press Institute, 30, 126
Analytics tools, 134, 138
  Facebook Insights, 138–140
  tutorials for, 138
  Twitter Analytics, 140–141
  website analytics tools and, 65, 141–143
  See also Social media engagement/
      audience analytics
Apps. *See* Audio-editing apps; Graphics apps;
    Mobile journalist practices; Photo apps; Social
    media platforms; Storage/file management
    apps; Technology; Video apps
Associated Press (AP), 9, 18, 125, 154, 156
Associated Press Nerve Center, 156
Associated Press Stylebook, 129
Athar, S., 8
Atlantic, 101
Auciello, J., 52–53, 64
Audiences. *See* Active audience role; Crowdsourcing;
    Mobile-first newsroom; Mobile journalism;
    Social media engagement/audience analytics;
    Social media journalism
Audio-editing apps, 109–110
  Ferrite Recording Studio, 110
  Hokusai Audio Editor, 110

live scrubbing and, 110
SoundCloud, 110
Voddio, 110
See also Mobile journalist practices
Augenstein, N., 101–103, 110, 147

Banjo app, 84, 111
Baquet, D., 26
Barnhart, R., 162
Barry, S., 27
BBC Academy, 77
BBC News, 13, 129
Bell, E., 11
Bell, F., 9
Bell, W., 148
Bezos, J., 34
bin Laden raid, 8
Blogging, 63, 64–65, 100–101
Bluetooth keyboards, 106
Boston Marathon bombings, 5–6, 17, 82, 147
Boyer, B., 25, 26
Branding process. *See* Social media branding
Breaking news, 10, 17, 18, 119–120
British Broadcasting Corporation (BBC),
    13, 38, 77, 112, 129
Build Your Own Ethics Code, 150, 152
Business Insider, 34
The Buttry Diary, 132
Buttry, S., 132
BuzzFeed, 11, 34, 138

Cable News Network (CNN), 7, 27–28, 42, 51, 63
Call Recorder app, 111
Camera + app, 109
Canva app, 125
Career development, 165
  all-media expertise, demand for, 166–167
  application process and, 176
  career center resources and, 171–172
  cover letters and, 175–176
  evolving job responsibilities and, 167–169
  faculty resources and, 171
  fellowship opportunities and, 170
  foundational journalistic skills and, 166
  hiring practices and, 172–174
  internship opportunities and, 170–172
  interview process and, 48, 49, 176–177

About the Author

Anthony Adornato (@AnthonyAdornato) is an assistant professor of journalism at Ithaca College's Roy H. Park School of Communications. Adornato's teaching and research focus on the role of social media and mobile technology in journalism. He has been interviewed about this topic by news outlets including the Associated Press, BBC News, and Germany's Deutsche Welle News. Prior to working in academia, Adornato was an anchor, reporter, and producer at television stations in New York. Adornato received a bachelor's degree in broadcast journalism from Syracuse University's S. I. Newhouse School of Public Communications and a master's degree in journalism from the University of Missouri's School of Journalism.